Establishing Law and Order After Conflict

T0302967

Seth G. Jones, Jeremy M. Wilson, Andrew Rathmell,
K. Jack Riley

RAND INFRASTRUCTURE, SAFETY, AND ENVIRONMENT

The research described in this report results from the RAND Corporation's continuing program of self-initiated research. Support for such research is provided, in part, by donors and by the independent research and development provisions of RAND's contracts for the operation of its U.S. Department of Defense federally funded research and development centers.

Library of Congress Cataloging-in-Publication Data

Establishing law and order after conflict / Seth G. Jones ... [et al.].
p. cm.
"MG-374."
Includes bibliographical references.
ISBN 0-8330-3814-1 (pbk. : alk. paper)
1. Law enforcement. 2. Criminal justice, Administration of. I. Jones, Seth G., 1972– II. Rand Infrastructure, Safety, and Environment (Organization)

HV7921.E88 2005
355.4'9—dc22

2005014939

Cover photo courtesy Reuters/Landov. Andrees Latif, photographer.

The RAND Corporation is a nonprofit research organization providing objective analysis and effective solutions that address the challenges facing the public and private sectors around the world. RAND's publications do not necessarily reflect the opinions of its research clients and sponsors.

Published 2005 by the RAND Corporation
1776 Main Street, P.O. Box 2138, Santa Monica, CA 90407-2138
1200 South Hayes Street, Arlington, VA 22202-5050
201 North Craig Street, Suite 202, Pittsburgh, PA 15213-1516
RAND URL: http://www.rand.org/
To order RAND documents or to obtain additional information, contact
Distribution Services: Telephone: (310) 451-7002;
Fax: (310) 451-6915; Email: order@rand.org

Preface

This study contains the results of research on reconstructing internal security institutions during nation-building missions. It analyzes the activities of the United States and other countries in building viable police, internal security forces, and justice structures. This study examines in detail the reconstruction efforts in Iraq, Afghanistan, and Kosovo, three of the most important instances in the post–Cold War era in which the United States and its allies have attempted to reconstruct security institutions. It then compares these cases with six others in the post–Cold War era: Panama, El Salvador, Somalia, Haiti, Bosnia, and East Timor. Finally, the study draws conclusions from the case studies and analysis, and derives recommendations to help the United States and other international actors improve their performance in the delivery of post-conflict security. The results should be of interest to a broad audience of policymakers and academics concerned with the successes and shortcomings of past security efforts. Although the study is not intended to be a detailed analysis of U.S. or allied military doctrine regarding stability operations, we believe it provides a useful set of guidelines and recommendations for a wide range of military, civilian, and other practitioners.

This research was conducted within RAND Infrastructure, Safety, and Environment (ISE), a unit of the RAND Corporation. The mission of ISE is to improve the development, operation, use, and protection of society's essential built and natural assets, and to enhance the related social assets of safety and security of individuals in transit and in their workplaces and communities. The ISE research portfolio encompasses research and analysis on a broad range of policy areas including homeland security, criminal justice, public safety, occupational safety, the environment, energy, natural resources, climate, agriculture, economic development, transportation, information and telecommunications technologies, space exploration, and other aspects of science and technology policy.

This study results from the RAND Corporation's continuing program of self-initiated research. Support for such research is provided, in part, by donors and by the independent research and development provisions of RAND's contracts for the operation of its U.S. Department of Defense federally funded research and development centers.

Inquiries regarding RAND Infrastructure, Safety, and Environment may be directed to:

Debra Knopman, Director
1200 S. Hayes Street
Arlington, VA 22202-5050
Tel: 703.413.1100, extension 5667
Email: ise@rand.org
http://www.rand.org/ise

Contents

Figures

Tables

Summary

Providing security and reconstructing internal security institutions is a key component of nation-building operations. As the U.S. military's *Field Manual 3-07.31 Peace Ops* notes, these tasks are vital to establish "a secure environment" in order to "create the conditions for other political, economic, and humanitarian peace building activities."[1] They are also vital to lay the foundations for a strong and legitimate state. Consequently, this study asks two major questions: How successful have U.S. and allied efforts been in reconstructing internal security institutions? What are the most important lessons for current and future operations? To help answer these questions, we examine data from efforts to reconstruct internal security in Kosovo, Afghanistan, and Iraq. We then compare the results with data from six other cases in which the United States has helped reconstruct security institutions during nation-building missions: Panama, El Salvador, Somalia, Haiti, Bosnia, and East Timor.

Success in Reconstructing Internal Security

This study makes three main arguments. First, establishing security during the "golden hour"[2] should be the most immediate concern of

---

[1] U.S. Army, Marine Corps, Navy, and Air Force, *Peace Ops: Multi-Service Tactics, Techniques, and Procedures for Conducting Peace Operations*, FM 3-07.31, October 2003, p. III-1.

[2] The golden hour refers to the critical hour following a life trauma when intervention—or lack thereof—determines the fate of the victim.

policymakers after the conclusion of major combat operations. This golden hour is a time frame of several weeks to several months, during which external intervention may enjoy some popular support and international legitimacy, and when potential spoilers may have insufficient time to organize. Key tasks include rapidly deploying international military and police forces, vetting and deploying indigenous police and other security forces, and establishing at least a temporary rule of law. Establishing security is critical in the short run to avert chaos and prevent criminal and insurgent organizations from securing a foothold in society, as well as to facilitate reconstruction in other areas such as health, basic infrastructure, and the economy. It is also important over the long run, since a state's prospects for stability depend on viable police, security forces, and justice structures that can establish order. This means dealing with the most significant internal threats. Examples include defeating and deterring insurgent groups, organized criminal enterprises such as those that facilitate drug trafficking, and local militia and warlords.

Second, past cases demonstrate that reconstructing and reforming the police and security forces are not enough to create a secure environment and protect civil liberties. Effective police and internal security forces require a functioning justice system. Arbitrary or politicized sentencing, an incompetent or corrupt judiciary, and inhumane prison conditions quickly undermine the benefits that come from better policing. A weak justice system also increases the prevalence of organized crime and can lead to a spiral of political assassinations, extrajudicial killings, and petty crime.[3] The inability to establish a viable justice system has plagued most efforts to reconstruct foreign police and security forces.

Third, our research indicates some very rough guidelines for successfully reconstructing security after major combat. They suggest that U.S.-led efforts in Iraq and Afghanistan have not met most of these minimum resource levels. Although the following levels will not

---

[3] This point was made forcefully in the U.S. domestic context as far back as 1967. President's Commission on Law Enforcement and Administration of Justice, *Task Force Report: The Police*, Washington, D.C., 1967.

guarantee success in establishing security, we believe that anything less would make it more difficult for outside powers to improve the security environment and rapidly reconstruct internal security institutions.

- **International troops and police.** International troop levels should be at least 1,000 soldiers per 100,000 inhabitants and international police levels should be at least 150 police officers per 100,000 inhabitants, especially when there is the potential for severe instability. These numbers are important for policing streets, defeating and deterring insurgents, patrolling borders, securing roads, and combating organized crime.
- **Domestic police.** After five years, the level of domestic police should be at least 200 police per 100,000 inhabitants. Police are important for conducting general law enforcement functions such as dealing with petty crime, as well as more specialized functions such as conducting counter-drug operations.
- **Assistance.** Total annual financial assistance should be at least $250 per capita for the first two years of reconstruction. This amount is critical to pay the high costs of such objectives as deploying military and police forces, training indigenous police and other personnel, providing equipment, and building infrastructure.
- **Duration.** Security assistance should last for at least five years. Time is critical because it can take several years to train, equip, and mentor police and other security forces, as well as to build and refurbish infrastructure. Justice systems can be extremely difficult and time consuming to build, especially in countries that have little formal rule of law when reconstruction begins.

According to our analysis, U.S. and allied efforts were most successful in Kosovo and East Timor in decreasing the level of violence and improving the rule of law. Afghanistan experienced increasing levels of violence and a slightly deteriorating rule of law. It is still too early to assess Iraq, but current data show increasing levels of violence and little change in the rule of law. The rest of the cases are either mixed or not successful. It is worth noting that Kosovo and East Timor had the highest level of civilian police forces, which were armed and given arrest authority. While it is important to ensure that military authorities are ready to assume public security responsibilities after major combat, it is also necessary to recognize the successful use of international civilian police and the growing reliance of UN missions on a strong police component. In Kosovo, for example, carabinieri and gendarmerie forces were put under civilian, not military, authority. This contrasts with recent U.S. practices in Iraq and Afghanistan.

All societies in transition experience a rise in crime and an increase in violence as old security institutions are dismantled and new ones are built. Thus, an increase in violence and crime, especially in the initial period after reconstruction begins, does not by itself demonstrate that the mission is failing. In addition, the overall objectives of a nation-building mission—such as the creation of a peaceful, democratic, and market-oriented government—can be achieved against the backdrop of some increase in criminality and violence. However, rising levels of crime and political violence after several years do provide an important indication of the competence of police and other internal security forces. The issue, therefore, is one of degree and duration (summarized in Figure S.1). The x-axis indicates the level of violence; the y-axis denotes the rule of law. The locations of countries are rough estimates. We plotted them according to the percentage increase or decrease in homicide or terrorist rates over the first five years of reconstruction, as well as the percentage improvement or deterioration in the rule of law.

Future Implications

What are the implications for the U.S. government that should inform its approaches to reconstructing internal security? Afghanistan and Iraq have reinforced well-worn lessons, even if they have pro-

Figure S.1
Outcome Measures

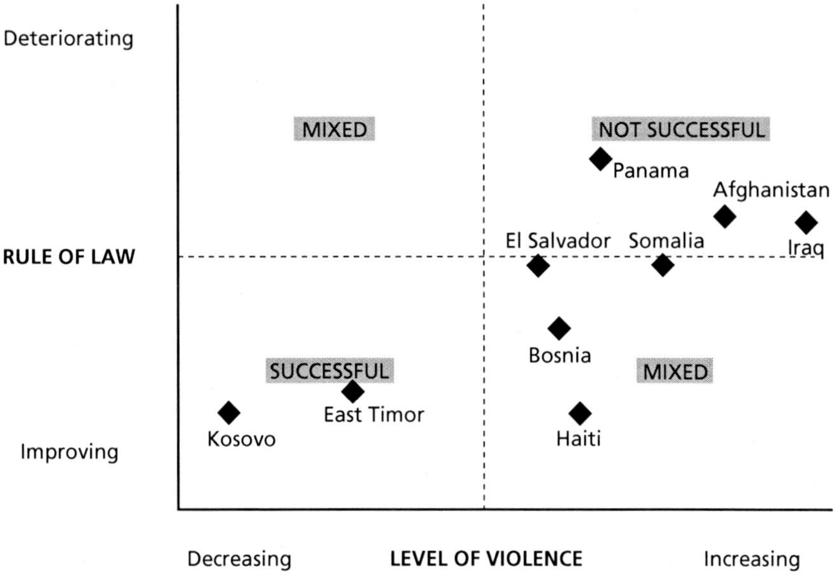

RAND *MG374-S.1*

vided new models for the management and implementation of post-conflict internal security programs. Although the international community learned a great deal about post-conflict policing during the 1990s, the United States and its allies applied few of the lessons in Afghanistan or Iraq. As summarized in Table S.1, we believe it important to highlight six policy implications for U.S. policy on post-conflict internal security.

Give as Much Attention to Planning Post-Conflict Policing as to Planning Combat Operations

There are three key factors that would improve performance here. First, policing and internal security reconstruction missions need to be provided with intelligence as good as, if different in kind, to that

Table S.1
Summary of Policy Recommendations

Recommendation	Detail
Give as much attention to planning post-conflict internal security as to planning combat operations	• Gather systematic, actionable intelligence on internal security systems prior to an intervention • Improve institutional planning mechanisms within the U.S. government • Ensure pre-intervention mobilization of post-conflict police and justice resources
Negotiate a peace treaty or formal surrender	• In cases of civil war, devote sufficient resources to negotiating a peace treaty among warring parties • In cases of interstate war, secure a formal surrender from defeated parties where possible
Fill the security gap quickly with U.S. (and allied) military and constabulary forces	• Amend U.S. joint doctrine, training, and posture • Develop shared (combined) international military doctrine and practices on post-conflict policing • Boost U.S. and international deployable constabulary forces
Develop comprehensive doctrine for post-conflict internal security reconstruction	• Develop shared international doctrine informed by best practices • Lay out options to ensure unity of command and effort via a new U.S. presidential directive on stability operations • Codify holistic approaches to rule-of-law sector • Integrate internal security reconstruction and reform programs with the wider conflict management agenda
Build mechanisms to ensure faster mobilization of personnel, funds, and equipment	• Improve U.S. government capabilities to rapidly mobilize, deliver, and manage police and justice resources • Encourage the development of international initiatives such as the UN civilian police system and the European Union's policing and justice programs
Focus on outcome measures to shape programs	• Develop and use outcome-based metrics to define program success and managerial performance

which is standard in military operations. In many of the cases studied here, the international police mission was hampered by a remarkably limited knowledge base about the host country's internal security system. This limitation stems from the failure both to collect and disseminate the right information and to involve knowledgeable individuals from the host nation. Even the famed State Department "Future of Iraq" project that many have touted as an example of unused prewar planning did not seriously address internal security institutions.

Second, institutional mechanisms for planning must be improved. Unlike the combat phase of most interventions, the post-conflict phase usually receives little attention. This is in part a result of the weakness of the institutions in the United States and other governments charged with policing reform; they simply do not have the corporate capacity to undertake detailed pre-intervention planning. It is also a failure of political will at the national and international levels, since it is the task of the political leadership to make the public case for the lengthy preparation, extensive resourcing, and long-term commitment that is required for post-conflict policing missions. The establishment of such organizations as the U.S. State Department's Office of the Coordinator for Reconstruction and Stabilization and the United Kingdom's Post-Conflict Reconstruction Unit may lead to some improvements in this area—especially if coupled with efforts in the U.S. Department of Defense and allied ministries of defense.

Third, the early mobilization of policing resources must be ensured to take advantage of the golden hour. By having in place plans, staffs, funds, personnel, and equipment before any intervention, the international community will be much better placed to avoid the debilitating deployment lag that has affected all previous operations. The philosophy needs to be one of policing "shock and awe" rather than that of "too little, too late."

Negotiate a Peace Treaty or Formal Surrender

Peace treaties and formal surrenders are highly correlated with peaceful security environments. Peace treaties are usually indicators of relatively low levels of hostility; at the moment of signing, they represent the parties' will to end the violent phase of their conflict. They also facilitate international involvement in providing loans and foreign aid. Formal surrenders can also increase the likelihood of stability. The destructive defeat of a regime undermines its credibility and demonstrates that it can no longer deliver vital needs to the population, and this is codified in a surrender. This lesson was ignored in

Iraq and Afghanistan, where the United States and its allies did not secure either a peace treaty or formal surrender. In the future, the broader lesson is to direct sufficient diplomatic and military resources toward negotiating peace treaties among warring parties in cases of civil war, and formal surrenders from defeated powers in cases of interstate war.

Fill the Security Gap Quickly with U.S. (and Allied) Military and Constabulary Forces

The U.S. military has sought to avoid being tasked with filling the security gap that invariably emerges after an intervention. The painful experience of Iraq may have forced a change in attitudes, but more far-reaching changes are required than simply the creation of extra military police units. The key will be to ensure that U.S. joint doctrine, training, and force structures incorporate the post-conflict policing and security sector reform roles. More broadly, it will be important that all allied forces engaged in an intervention operate according to a common policing and security sector reform doctrine. However, filling the security gap with international military forces will always be a second-best solution in the absence of sufficient, deployable international policing assets. Constabulary forces, such as the Italian carabinieri, are a more appropriate instrument, and their use needs to be encouraged. The United States also needs to consider how it can develop its own constabulary force.

Develop Comprehensive Doctrine for Post-Conflict Internal Security Reconstruction

To ensure that civil-military planning and implementation for post-conflict policing proceeds more smoothly, the United States needs to develop, adopt, and share with its allies a common doctrinal approach to reconstruction of the internal security sector in post-conflict environments. Although the concept of doctrine may seem overly militaristic, police forces use doctrine in all but name. It should not be too difficult for civilian agencies such as the U.S. Departments of State and Justice to distil lessons learned and good practices into a shared doctrine. The benefit of a shared interagency and international doctrine is that it would provide a common frame of reference for planners and managers of post-conflict policing operations. In developing this doctrine, the United States and its allies need to be realistic regarding the limits of their knowledge about how to successfully transfer strong state institutions to developing countries. Many reconstruction and reform programs, often implemented by Western policing, justice, and intelligence professionals, are overly positivist and technocratic in their approach. To ensure that reconstruction and reform programs are of lasting value, it is important that internal security specialists and development specialists work together with regional experts to structure programs that are adapted to the context.

This doctrine should lay out command and control responsibilities of nation-building missions. Ideally, it should flow from a new iteration of the Clinton administration's Presidential Decision Directive 56 (PDD-56) on "Managing Complex Contingency Operations." After coming into office, the Bush administration developed National Security Policy Directive "XX" (NSPD-XX). It was broader in scope than PDD-56 and provided guidance on warning, advanced planning, prevention, and response options for what it called "complex contingency operations." Unfortunately, NSPD-XX was never signed by the President. This created confusion about agency roles and responsibilities, which complicated efforts to respond to the crises in Afghanistan and Iraq.

At least two documents would be helpful to rectify these challenges. One is a presidential directive on the civilian component of nation-building operations. Critical questions include: What is the lead civilian agency for nation-building operations? What are the primary objectives? What are the key tasks, how should they be prioritized, and which agencies are in charge of which tasks? The doctrine also needs to take a holistic approach to the internal security sector. It should treat the internal security sector as a whole and as part of the broader security sector. It should therefore include the criminal justice and intelligence institutions. This will help avoid the often repeated mistakes in developing these institutions—or not developing them—independently of the police.

The second document is a U.S. Defense Department directive on the military component of nation-building operations, what the department refers to as "stability operations." The directive should set policy for the Defense Department, be signed by the Secretary of Defense, and assign roles and responsibilities for the military component of stability operations. It should assign the U.S. Army as the lead agency for stability operations, since this branch of the military plays the most significant military role in rebuilding countries after major combat.

Furthermore, these documents should be informed by the broader agenda of conflict mitigation and management. Development actors such as the U.S. Agency for International Development have developed conflict assessment methodologies that seek to understand the roots, motives, means, opportunities, and triggers for internal conflict. The UK Department for International Development (DFID) has adopted similar approaches to understanding how external assistance can be used to prevent or manage conflicts. These methodologies are implicitly mirrored by some of the military campaign plans drawn up by intervening international forces, which often address the symptoms, the means, and the motives for conflict.

This broader perspective on conflict prevention and management needs to inform the design and implementation of internal security reform. The focus of such reform programs is often on tangible, institutional results. However, building quality enforcement institutions is only one element of an approach to conflict prevention and management. Broader conflict prevention and management programs need to address the political or economic roots of conflicts as well as the organizational and logistical means by which discontent can be translated into organized violence. Although initiatives in some of these areas may seem outside the remit of an internal security sector reform program, they need to be treated as integral rather than as "nice to have" add-ons.

Build Mechanisms to Ensure Faster Mobilization of Personnel, Funds, and Equipment

Preplanning, common doctrine, and joint exercises will all help to accelerate the usually slow deployment of personnel, funds, and equipment for post-conflict police and justice operations. In addition, the U.S. government needs to build mechanisms that enable it to deploy such resources much faster. Initiatives such as the State Department's Coordinator for Stabilization and Reconstruction provide vehicles through which to drive such enhanced capabilities. Funding and equipment are relatively easy to stockpile and preposition. But the United States needs to do much better at identifying and mobilizing internal security professionals to post-conflict situations. Internationally, the United States should encourage similar initiatives. The UN civilian police system requires strengthening potential contributors to international policing missions in order to prepare, train, and make available personnel. Significant multilateral proposals such as that for a European gendarmerie and for a European Human Security Force need to be examined and evaluated.

Focus on Outcome Measures to Shape Programs

Policing assistance programs have fallen into the trap of many domestic governmental reform programs: "[P]rogram evaluations that emphasize outputs rather than outcomes as a measure of success inhibit organizational creativity."[4] The tools we have to assess internal security outcomes remain limited. However, by building such assessments into current and future assistance programs and encouraging host nations to undertake such assessments, we will be better placed to optimize assistance programs. A further advantage of using outcome-based measures to evaluate performance will be that they should encourage experimentation by local managers, whether international or local, rather than an adherence to largely meaningless output targets. In addition to the outcome measures outlined here—such as homicide rates, levels of political violence, and public

---

[4] David H. Bayley, *Democratizing the Police Abroad: What to Do and How to Do It*, National Institute of Justice, June 2001, p. 24.

opinion polls of security and the justice system—more tactical outcome measures may also be appropriate. In Somalia, for example, the U.S. military collected such indicators as the death rate per day due to starvation, new patients with gunshot wounds in hospitals, and the street price of an AK-47.[5] All outcome measures, however, should be tied to the overall mission objectives. In the case of internal security, the two primary objectives are establishing stability and a rule of law. Table S.2 summarizes critical internal security objectives, actors, and metrics.

[5] Headquarters, United States Marine Corps, *Small Wars*, 2005.

Table S.2
Internal Security Performance Matrix

	Police	Military/Other	Justice
Key Objectives	• Establish basic law and order • Protect population • Control border, ports of entry • Protect vital infrastructure • Ensure freedom of movement	• Establish security against major threats to the state • Demobilize, disrupt, and deter militia and other paramilitary organizations	• Establish rule of law • Eliminate corruption • Provide oversight and accountability for police and other security forces
External Actors (U.S.)	*Lead actor:* • State Department (especially International Narcotics and Law Enforcement, INL) *Supporting actors:* • Justice Department • Defense Department (Combined Joint Task Force, CJTF) • USAID • Foreign governments • Nongovernmental organizations (NGOs) and international organizations • Private contractors	*Lead actor:* • Defense Department (CJTF) *Supporting actors:* • Central Intelligence Agency • State Department • Foreign governments • NGOs and international organizations • Private contractors	*Lead actors:* • State Department • Justice Department *Supporting actors:* • USAID • Defense Department (CJTF) • Foreign governments • NGOs and international organizations • Private contractors
Indigenous Actors	• Ministry of interior • Local police	• Ministry of defense • Indigenous intelligence agency • Local militias and factions	• Ministry of justice • Local and national judges, courts • Office of attorney general
Input Metrics	• Police assistance and expenditures • International civilian and military police and advisors • Lethal and nonlethal equipment	• Military assistance and expenditures • International troops and advisors • Lethal and nonlethal equipment • Intelligence assistance and expenditures • Intelligence advisors	• Justice assistance and expenditures • International justice advisors • Equipment, such as computers and law books

Table S.2—Continued

	Police	Military/Other	Justice
Output Metrics	• Number and quality of police trained • Number and quality of police facilities built or refurbished • Institutional development and reform of ministry of interior	• Number and quality of troops trained; military facilities built or refurbished; institutional development • Development of reliable local intelligence • Number of ex-combatants who have completed disarmament, demobilization, and reintegration (DDR) • Number and quality of intelligence officials trained, facilities built, and institutional development	• Number and quality of judges, prosecutors, and corrections officers trained • Number and quality of judicial facilities built or refurbished • Institutional development of justice bodies: ministry of justice, local and national courts
Outcome Metrics	• Crime rates, especially violent crimes • Other crime indicators, such as illegal drug trade • International civilian police casualties • Public perception of security and performance of police	• Level of political violence and insurgency • Public perception of security • International military casualties	• Public perception of justice system's effectiveness • Public perception of corruption in justice system • Duration of pretrial detention • Duration that cases move through court system • Right to legal advice

Acknowledgments

This report would not have been possible without the help of numerous individuals. At RAND, Cheryl Benard, David Brannan, James Dobbins, Russell Glenn, Victoria Greenfield, Olga Oliker, William Rosenau, and Tom Sullivan commented on various chapters. James Quinlivan and Robert Perito offered frank and insightful reviews, which greatly improved the final manuscript. Anga Timilsina, Karen Stewart, and Ely Ratner provided key research support and collected data for many of the charts and graphs.

A number of U.S. government officials took time from their busy schedules to provide us with information and comments about Afghanistan. They include Ambassador Zalmay Khalilzad, Major General Craig P. Weston, Ambassador William Taylor, Marin Strmecki, Ken Thomas, Jack Bell, Martin Hoffman, Tom Berner, Colonel Gary Medvigy, Lieutenant Colonel Robert Polk, Lieutenant Colonel William R. Balkovetz, Lieutenant Colonel Michael Stollenwerk, Michael C. Martin, Robert Chamberlain, and Tod Wilson. We are also grateful to the assistance of officials from Afghanistan, Germany, Italy, the United Kingdom, and the United Nations who agreed to discuss reconstruction with us. A special thanks to Afghan Interior Minister Ali A. Jalali; Afghan Deputy Minister of Justice Dr. Mohammad Qasim Hashimzai; German Ambassador Rainald Steck; German Political Counselor Ursula Müller; Italian Deputy Chief of Mission Carlo Batori; United Nations Assistance Mission in Afghanistan (UNAMA) Chief of Staff Larry Sampler; Special Assistant to

President Karzai, Daoud Yaqub; and UN officials Paul George, Alexandre Schmidt, and Carla Ciavarella for their insights.

U.S. and British officials and military officers with whom one of the authors of this report worked with in Iraq were generous in providing their time once they had returned from the country to reflect on the challenges they had faced. Special thanks go to Douglas Brand, Bruce Fein, Ralph Sabatino, and Matt Sherman. In addition, the authors wish to thank all the Iraqi security forces personnel and officials who provided insights into the challenges of reconstruction in the midst of an ongoing conflict.

Abbreviations

ANA	Afghan National Army
CERP	Commander's Emergency Response Program
CFC-A	Combined Forces Command–Afghanistan
CIVPOL	International Civilian Police
CJTF-7	Combined Joint Task Force 7
CMATT	Coalition Military Assistance Training Team
CPA	Coalition Provisional Authority
CPATT	Civilian Police Advisory Training Team
DBE	Department of Border Enforcement
DDR	disarmament, demobilization, and reintegration
DFI	Development Fund for Iraq
DFID	UK Department for International Development
FPS	Facilities Protection Service
FY	fiscal year
IAF	Iraqi Armed Forces
ICDC	Iraqi Civil Defense Corps
ICITAP	International Criminal Investigation Training Assistance Program
ICS	Iraqi Correctional Service
IIG	Iraqi Interim Government
ILAC	International Legal Assistance Consortium

ING	Iraqi National Guard
INIS	Iraqi National Intelligence Service
IPA	international police advisors
IPCC	Iraq Property Claims Commission
IPS	Iraqi Police Service
IPT	international police trainer
ISAF	International Security Assistance Force
ISF	Iraqi security forces
IST	Iraq Special Tribunal
IT	information technology
KFOR	Kosovo Force
KLA	Kosovo Liberation Army
KPC	Kosovo Protection Corps
KPS	Kosovo Police Service
MCNS	Ministerial Committee on National Security
MNF-I	Multi-National Force–Iraq
MNSTC-I	Multi-National Security Transition Command–Iraq
MoD	Iraqi Ministry of Defense
MoI	Iraqi Ministry of Interior
MoJ	Iraqi Ministry of Justice
MP	military police
MSC	major subordinate command
NATO	North Atlantic Treaty Organization
NIA	New Iraqi Army
NGO	nongovernmental organization
ORHA	Office for Reconstruction and Humanitarian Assistance
ORI	Oxford Research International
OSCE	Organisation for Security and Co-operation in Europe

SCAP	Supreme Commander of Allied Powers
SIGACTS	Significant Activities
TAL	Transitional Administrative Law
TR	transition and reintegration
UNDP	United Nations Development Programme
UNMIK	United Nations Interim Administration Mission in Kosovo
UNSC	United Nations Security Council
USAID	U.S. Agency for International Development
WIA	wounded in action

CHAPTER ONE

Introduction

This study examines United States and allied efforts to provide security and rebuild internal security institutions in post-conflict environments. Establishing order during the "golden hour"[1] should be the most immediate concern of policymakers to avert chaos and prevent criminal and insurgent groups from securing a foothold in society. In addition, a state's long-term prospects for governance and stability depend on viable police, security forces, and justice structures to deal with the most significant internal threats from insurgent groups, criminal organizations, and local militia and warlords. Consequently, this study asks two major questions: How successful have U.S. and allied efforts been in reconstructing internal security institutions? What are the most important lessons for current and future operations?

Assessing U.S. and international efforts to build indigenous internal security structures is important for several reasons. First, nation-building operations have become more frequent in the post–Cold War era, and there is little reason to believe that this trend will decline. An examination of past successes and failures is therefore crucial to inform future efforts. Second, strengthening internal security and rule-of-law institutions is a critical U.S. interest. It enables foreign governments to cooperate in achieving such objectives as

[1] The golden hour refers to the critical hour following a life trauma when intervention—or lack thereof—determines the fate of the victim.

countering terrorist groups, improves governance institutions, and ultimately increases the prospects for development. Third, the United States and other countries have a poor track record of reconstructing war-torn societies in general and a troubled history in the construction of internal security structures in particular.[2] Past efforts have not always been successful. The United States plays a particularly important role as the world's only superpower. It is one of the largest contributors to international police missions and has played the leading role in using military force to encourage political transitions. It is therefore vital that U.S. policymakers understand past lessons to improve current and future performance.

Definitions

This study examines success in reconstructing internal security institutions. *Success* is defined as the establishment of stability and a rule of law. Definitions of stability may vary from case to case, but a stable environment is one in which violence-prone groups such as insurgents or criminals are subordinated to legitimate governmental authority, reintegrated into society, or defeated. A stable environment is one in which the population is free from major threats to their safety and where national and international actors are able to rebuild political, economic, and other key governance institutions. Indicators of stability include such elements as crime rates, level of political violence, and perception of security. The rule of law includes courts, legislatures, legal statutes and codes, executive agencies, and independent nongovernmental organizations (NGOs) such as bar associations and civic associations. It serves to protect people against anarchy, allows people to plan their affairs with confidence because they

---

[2] James Dobbins, John G. McGinn, Keith Crane, Seth G. Jones, Rollie Lal, Andrew Rathmell, Rachel Swanger, and Anga Timilsina, *America's Role in Nation-Building: From Germany to Iraq*, Santa Monica, Calif.: RAND Corporation, MR-1753-RC, 2003; Francis Fukuyama, *State-Building: Governance and World Order in the 21st Century*, Ithaca, N.Y.: Cornell University Press, 2004; Kimberly Marten Zisk, *Enforcing the Peace: Learning from the Imperial Past*, New York: Columbia University Press, 2004; Roland Paris, *At War's End: Building Peace After Civil Conflict*, New York: Cambridge University Press, 2004.

know the legal consequences of their action, and protects people from the arbitrary exercise of power by public officials. *Internal security institutions* encompass three broad areas:

- *Police*: ministry of interior, local police, border patrol, and counter-drug forces
- *Military and other security bodies*: ministry of defense (when it plays an internal security role), intelligence agencies, and paramilitary forces such as counterterrorist forces
- *Justice system*: ministry of justice, federal and local courts, corrections facilities, law schools, and the rule of law.

Although these institutions are the main focus of our attention, it is important to put them into the broader context of security sector reform and governance reform. Attention must therefore also be paid to national governance mechanisms (such as national security councils and legislative oversight bodies) and local governance mechanisms (such as citizen's police oversight committees).[3]

These internal security components are interdependent. Past reconstruction cases demonstrate that reconstructing and reforming the police and security forces is not enough to create a secure environment and to protect civil liberties. Effective police and internal security forces require a functioning justice system. Arbitrary or politicized sentencing, an incompetent or corrupt judiciary, and inhumane prison conditions quickly undermine the benefits that come from better policing. A weak justice system also increases the prevalence of organized crime and can lead to a spiral of political assassinations, extrajudicial killings, and petty crime.[4] The inability to establish a viable justice system has plagued most efforts to reconstruct foreign police and security forces. In Haiti, for example, the lack of a competent judiciary meant that improvements in the effectiveness of

---

[3] OECD, Development Assistance Committee, Network on Conflict, Peace and Development Co-operation, *Security System Reform: Policy and Good Practice*, October 1, 2003.

[4] This point was made forcefully in the U.S. domestic context as far back as 1967. President's Commission on Law Enforcement and Administration of Justice, *Task Force Report: The Police*, Washington, D.C., 1967.

law enforcement created an untenable situation in which there were more accused criminals than the courts could try or the prisons could hold. A weak justice system led to the emergence of powerful organized criminal organizations in Bosnia. In El Salvador, the deplorable state of the justice system resulted in a situation in which few prisoners were tried, and many in prison were never formally charged.

The reconstruction and reform of security sector institutions in post-conflict environments have become a priority topic for the international community over the past decade. Security sector reform has been recognized as a vital precursor to the achievement of good governance and sustainable development.[5] The security-sector reform agenda has broadened in recent years to encompass police and internal security agencies.[6] Security sector reconstruction within the narrower phase of post-conflict reconstruction has also begun to attract increasing attention.[7] Although security sector reconstruction must lay the groundwork for long-term reform, it must also build immediate capacity for the security sector to bring about order and stability. Our analysis focuses specifically on the reconstruction of the internal security sector as an element in broader security sector reform. More narrowly, this study focuses primarily on the formal internal security sector institutions rather than the broader set of societal mechanisms that surround these institutions.

Security sector reconstruction is an element in all post-conflict operations—whether these activities are known as post-conflict

---

[5] UK Department for International Development, *Understanding and Supporting Security Sector Reform*, London, undated; David C. Gompert, Olga Oliker, and Anga Timilsina, *Clean, Lean and Able: A Strategy for Defense Development*, Santa Monica, Calif.: RAND Corporation, OP-101-RC, 2004. However, there is a lively debate over the extent to which reformed policing institutions can actually contribute to democratic development. David H. Bayley, "The Contemporary Practices of Policing: A Comparative View," in James Burack, William Lewis, and Edward Marks, eds., *Civilian Police and Multinational Peacekeeping—A Workshop Series: A Role for Democratic Policing*, National Institute of Justice, Washington, D.C., October 6, 1997 (published in January 1999).

[6] Chris Ferguson, "Police Reform, Peacekeeping and SSR: The Need for Closer Synthesis," *Journal of Security Sector Management*, Vol. 2, No. 3, September 2004.

[7] Alan Bryden and Heiner Hänggi, eds., *Reform and Reconstruction of the Security Sector*, Münster, Germany: Lit Verlag, 2004.

reconstruction interventions, stabilization operations, peace support operations, or peace-building endeavors. We limit our scope to a class of interventions we define as *nation-building* operations. These are efforts after major combat to underpin a transition to peace and democracy. Nation-building involves the deployment of international military forces and includes comprehensive efforts to rebuild the security, political, and economic sectors. In some cases, nation-building occurs in a benign security environment with little or no resistance. In others, such as Somalia, Afghanistan, and Iraq, there is significant violence and insurgent activity.

The United States and other countries have, of course, provided internal security assistance to numerous countries in Africa, Latin America, Asia, the Middle East, and Europe. Those that are part of nation-building operations, however, tend to be much better funded and broader in scope because they are part of larger efforts to build political, health, economic, and other structures. Consequently, we believe that it is especially important to assess U.S. and allied efforts to reconstruct internal security during nation-building operations. Moreover, by focusing on internal security institutions, we are deliberately limiting our scope. We are not focusing on broader nation-building objectives of establishing democratic institutions and economic growth, although these are important objectives.

Methodology

This study uses two methodologies. First, it adopts a comparative case study approach. It focuses on three cases in which the United States and other nations and international organizations attempted to reconstruct security during nation-building operations: Kosovo, Afghanistan, and Iraq. We chose these cases because they are some of the most important instances in the post–Cold War era in which U.S. and other military forces have been used to reconstruct security and other sectors after major combat. In addition, they include a wide variation in input, output, and outcome variables. Furthermore, we compare these cases with others in the post–Cold War era in which the United States and allied governments have attempted to reconstruct security during nation-building missions, including Panama, El Salvador, Somalia, Haiti, Bosnia, and East Timor.

Second, this study compares and contrasts the cases using several quantitative and qualitative input, output, and outcome metrics, as well as initial conditions. Input metrics include the number of troops, amount of assistance, and duration of assistance. Output metrics include amount and quality of training, number and quality of infrastructure built or refurbished, and quality of institutional development of internal security ministries. Outcome metrics include crime rates, especially homicides and violent crime; other crime indicators such as the drug trade; level of political violence and insurgency; number of international police, military, and civilian casualties; and perception of security, rule of law, and corruption.

Outline

Chapter Two offers a theory for reconstructing internal security. Chapters Three, Four, and Five examine U.S. and allied efforts to reconstruct internal structures in Kosovo, Afghanistan, and Iraq respectively. These chapters ask several questions: How successful have U.S. and international efforts been in reconstructing internal security? How effective are the country's police, internal security forces, and justice system in dealing with the most pressing internal threats to state stability? What are the most important lessons learned? These chapters combine extensive qualitative descriptions of the context, course, and impact of internal security programs with quantitative performance metrics. The intention is to capture the qualitative variables and factors that have influenced the outcomes we observe. For Afghanistan and Iraq, these qualitative descriptions have the added benefit of providing a wealth of previously unpublished information based on primary sources and in-country research. Chapter Six summarizes major insights from the three cases in the context of other efforts to reconstruct internal security since the end of the Cold War. Chapter Seven offers recommendations for current and future efforts.

CHAPTER TWO

A Theory of Rebuilding Internal Security

This chapter identifies key factors that affect success in reconstructing internal security. Success is defined as the establishment of stability and a functioning rule of law. There are three major arguments. First, establishing internal security after major combat should be the most immediate and important concern of policymakers. This objective is critical to avert chaos and prevent criminal and insurgent organizations from securing a foothold in society, as well as to facilitate reconstruction in other areas such as health, basic infrastructure, and the economy. Establishing security is also important over the long run, since a state's prospects for stability depend on viable police, security forces, and justice structures that can establish order.

Second, past cases demonstrate that reconstructing and reforming the police and security forces are not enough to create a secure environment and protect civil liberties. Effective police and internal security forces require a functioning justice system.

Third, success in achieving stability and a rule of law is a function of inputs, outputs, and initial conditions. Inputs include the amount of financial assistance, the number of troops and police, the duration of assistance, and the extent of prewar planning. Outputs include training, infrastructure, and institutional development. Initial conditions include those conditions that exist at the beginning of reconstruction, such as the status of security organizations or the existence of a functioning central government. Figure 2.1 briefly summarizes the model.

Figure 2.1
Model of Reconstructing Internal Security

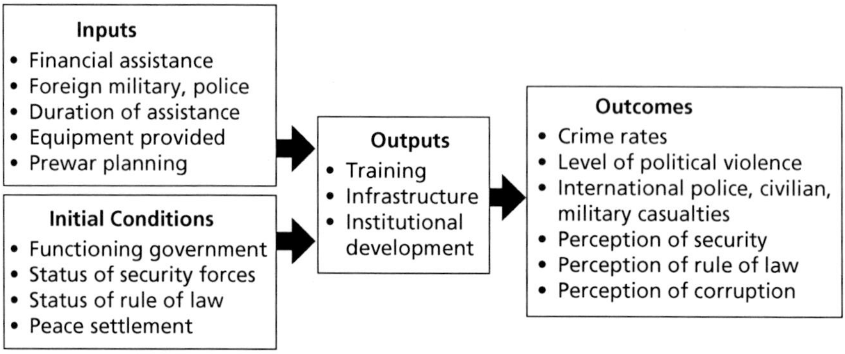

RAND *MG374-2.1*

This chapter begins by arguing that the establishment of internal security is a vital task after major combat and can have a significant impact on progress in reconstructing such sectors as health, governance, economics, and basic infrastructure. It then outlines key factors that affect success and identifies performance metrics.

The Primacy of Security

Establishing internal security after major combat should be the most immediate and important concern of policymakers. George Tanham, associate director for counterinsurgency for the U.S. Agency for International Development (USAID) in South Vietnam and special assistant for counterinsurgency to the U.S. ambassador in Thailand, argued in the 1960s: "Strange as it may seem, the military victory is the easiest part of the struggle. After this has been attained, the real challenge begins: the reestablishment of a secure environment opens a new opportunity for nation building."[1] Tanham's observation was

[1] George K. Tanham, *War Without Guns: American Civilians in Rural Vietnam*, New York: Praeger, 1966, p. 138.

just as appropriate then as it is today. Security is a critical component of reconstruction. War and regime change can increase the likelihood of criminality and political violence. In Panama, for example, the destruction of the Panamanian Defense Force during the 1989 U.S. invasion sparked disorder and looting. In East Timor, the August 1999 referendum for independence triggered substantial violence. Rampaging militiamen killed more than 1,000 people and destroyed nearly 70 percent of the public infrastructure and private housing. In Iraq, there was widespread disorder after the fall of Saddam Hussein's Ba'athist regime in April 2003. Most of the security sector institutions evaporated overnight; mobs and criminal gangs looted government and commercial property and launched a crime wave.

Over the long run, stability and a rule of law depend on viable police, security forces, and justice structures. This means dealing with the most significant internal threats. Examples include defeating and deterring insurgent groups, organized criminal enterprises such as drug traffickers, and local militia and warlords. The cost of failing to deal with major internal security threats is high. It can undermine the stability and strength of the central government; undercut efforts to reconstruct the political, social, and economic framework necessary for future stability; and ultimately undermine U.S. security. Indeed, failing to curb major threats may trigger the same problems that led to outside intervention in the first place. As the Afghan National Security Council's *National Threat Assessment* argues about the drug trade:

> Continued growth of the heroin and opium-producing poppy remains a major threat to the security of Afghanistan. The corruption and crime associated with the drug trade will proliferate in and around Afghanistan, discouraging international investment and assistance in rebuilding Afghanistan. Revenue from opium growth/production will continue to make Afghanistan an attractive haven for international terrorist groups, organized

crime and other extremists while also funding the continued, destabilizing presence of non-statutory armed forces.[2]

In practice, establishing stability and a rule of law has not always been the most important objectives of external powers. During the Cold War, for example, the United States frequently subordinated the goal of building effective internal security institutions to countering Soviet influence, and it supported allies that were repressive and incapable of maintaining order. The U.S. Department of Defense, Central Intelligence Agency, Department of State, and USAID provided assistance to police and internal security forces in such countries as Vietnam, Korea, and El Salvador. Successive U.S. administrations were influenced by "modernization theory" in offering internal security assistance and argued that weak state institutions would create ideal conditions for communist exploitation.[3] We believe this approach can have significant costs. By diverting attention and resources from building indigenous structures that ensure stability and a rule of law, this approach often fails to reform highly repressive governments. Building a viable justice system often gets short shrift, which can contribute to extrajudicial killings, corruption, and arbitrary or politicized sentencing. In addition, this approach often sidesteps fixing the underlying conditions that caused conflict and instability in the first place.

Reconstructing internal security structures is only one of several key aspects of nation-building. As Table 2.1 highlights, other important areas include health, governance, democratization, economics, and basic infrastructure. The functions within these areas may vary

---

[2] Afghan Presidential Office of National Security, *Afghanistan National Threat Assessment*, Kabul, 2004, p. 3.

[3] John Lewis Gaddis, *Strategies of Containment: A Critical Reappraisal of Postwar American National Security Policy*, New York: Oxford University Press, 1982; H. W. Brands, *The Devil We Know: Americans and the Cold War*, New York: Oxford University Press, 1993; William Rosenau, "The Eisenhower Administration, U.S. Foreign Internal Security Assistance, and the Struggle for the Developing World, 1954–1961," *Low Intensity Conflict and Law Enforcement*, Vol. 10, No. 3, Autumn 2001, pp. 1–32; William Rosenau, "The Kennedy Administration, U.S. Foreign Internal Security Assistance and the Challenge of 'Subterranean War,' 1961–63," *Small Wars and Insurgencies*, Vol. 14, No. 3, Autumn 2003, pp. 65–99.

from country to country. In health, critical functions may include providing emergency humanitarian relief and reconstructing public health and health care delivery systems. In governance, they include supplying national and local administrations with technical advice and resources to provide public services to their populations. In the area of democratization, key functions include encouraging the establishment of political parties, civil society, and a free press; writing a constitution; and holding elections. In the economic sector, they include establishing a stable currency, providing a regulatory framework, and offering agricultural assistance. Finally, basic infrastructure

Table 2.1
Key Areas of Nation-Building

Area	Function
Security	• Conduct peacekeeping and law enforcement • Rebuild internal security institutions, such as police and military • Engage in justice sector reform • Demilitarize, demobilize, and reintegrate ex-combatants
Health/education	• Provide emergency humanitarian relief • Return and repatriate refugees • Reconstruct public health and health care delivery systems • Reconstruct education system and infrastructure
Governance	• Supply national and local administration with immediate resources and advice necessary to provide basic public services • Encourage long-term sustainability
Democratization	• Build political parties, a free press, civil society, and a legal and constitutional framework for elections
Economics	• Establish a stable currency • Provide a regulatory framework in which local and international commerce can resume • Offer agricultural assistance
Basic infrastructure	• Build or rehabilitate infrastructure in key areas: –Transportation and distribution: highways, railways, ports, airports, waterways, mass transit, and trucking companies –Water and sanitation –Energy: electric power, oil, gas –Communications: television, radio, telephone, newspapers, magazines

can include building or rehabilitating electricity, transportation, water, oil, and gas systems.

Security has a significant impact on progress in other areas. As the U.S. Army's Field Manual 3-07, *Stability Operations and Support Operations*, argues, the deployment of military forces is important "to provide a secure environment for civil authorities as they work to achieve reconciliation, rebuild lost infrastructure, and resume vital services."[4] The absence of security makes it difficult to construct basic infrastructure such as water, oil, transportation, or electricity systems. In the health sector, a lack of security can impede progress in the construction of hospitals and health clinics, slow immunization campaigns, and affect the labor force if health care providers are intimidated or threatened with kidnapping. Patients can also be deterred from seeking health care because of security concerns. Since security conditions can vary within cities, provinces, and regions, reconstruction will be much more difficult in those areas where crime rates are high, insurgent attacks are frequent, and the public's perception of security is low.

Furthermore, there may be a negative feedback loop between security and other sectors. Slow progress in reconstructing health, infrastructure, and other sectors may fuel anger and ultimately worsen the security environment if individuals resort to violence. The inability to ensure sufficient levels of electricity, clean water, housing, and sanitation conditions can generate a large amount of frustration among the population, further increasing the level of insecurity.

Success of Internal Security

Success in reconstructing internal security is a function of initial conditions, inputs, and outputs. Initial conditions are the conditions that exist at the beginning of reconstruction. Inputs and outputs are elements such as financial assistance, international police and military

---

[4] Headquarters, Department of the Army, *Stability Operations and Support Operations*, FM 3-07, February 2003, p. 1-3.

forces, and duration of assistance that are provided by outside providers. Outside powers have some influence over the latter, but little influence over the former. However, initial conditions can have a significant impact on reconstruction. After World War II, for example, U.S., British, and French efforts to reconstruct western Germany were facilitated because Germany was a developed country with high levels of human capital and abundant resources. These conditions existed despite the physical damage caused by the allied air and ground campaigns. In the post–Cold War era, however, the absence of a strong, competent central government and an effective rule of law in Somalia and Afghanistan, for example, plagued reconstruction efforts.

Initial Conditions

The conditions that exist within a country at the beginning of reconstruction can significantly affect success. All countries are not alike; they may start from very different baselines at the beginning of reconstruction. External powers can run into serious challenges if they have a limited understanding of local conditions. There are at least four factors that can affect efforts to reconstruct internal security:

- Existence of a functioning central government
- Status and viability of security bodies
- Effectiveness of justice system
- Peace agreement or formal surrender.

The existence of a functioning central government that has a "monopoly of the legitimate use of physical forces within a given territory" can affect efforts to reconstruct internal security.[5] The need for management "buy-in" to reform programs has been amply demonstrated in studies of change management in the private and public sectors. A considerable body of literature and practice has emerged in the past decade on the importance of good governance institutions to

---

[5] Max Weber, "Politics as a Vocation," in H. H. Gerth and C. Wright Mills, eds., *From Max Weber: Essays in Sociology*, New York: Oxford University Press, 1958, p. 78.

promote economic development and transitions to pluralist, democratic, and effective political institutions.[6] Even after major combat or a regime change, countries can still have a functioning central government. For example, after World War II, U.S. policymakers working under the Supreme Commander of the Allied Powers (SCAP) encountered a Japanese bureaucracy that was intact and competent. Consequently, SCAP authorities relied on the existing bureaucracy to conduct government business.

Critical questions include: Was there a viable central government? Did it have a monopoly of force in the country before the war? If the answer is no, foreign powers will inevitably encounter a host of challenges. They may have to deal with powerful regional militias or criminal organizations that have usurped state functions and control territory; they may also have to devote valuable resources to building the central government's capacity just so that it can function and implement policies. U.S. and allied governments encountered no functioning central government in Somalia in 1992, East Timor in 1999, and Afghanistan in 2001. In Somalia and Afghanistan, there was no recent history of a viable central government. In East Timor, there was an exodus of more than 8,000 civil servants after the referendum for independence, leaving the nation with virtually no senior civil servants or police personnel.[7]

The effectiveness of the justice system and security forces at the beginning of reconstruction can also affect success. Was there a functioning rule of law? Was there a formal or informal justice system? How much training did police and security forces have? Were they used to repress the population? The status of the rule of law is particularly important. International assistance can build strong institutions in certain areas, such as central banking, which are isolated from

---

[6] Jessica Einhorn, "The World Bank's Mission Creep," *Foreign Affairs*, Vol. 80, No. 5, 2001, pp. 22–35; World Bank, *Reforming Public Institutions and Strengthening Governance*, Washington, D.C., 2000.

[7] Jonathan Steele, "Nation Building in East Timor," *World Policy Journal*, Vol. 19, No. 2, Summer 2002; UNDP, *The Way Ahead: East Timor Development Report, 2002*, Dili, East Timor, 2002; letter dated 4 October 1999 from the Secretary-General addressed to the President of the Security Council, S/1999/1025, October 4, 1999.

society and responsive to the application of external technocratic expertise. But rule-of-law institutions are much less easily strengthened by the application of external assistance. These institutions have high "transaction volumes," are much more deeply embedded in the societal fabric, form important elements of the state's basis of legitimation, and are heavily influenced by the cultural norms and values that shape institutions in any society.[8] Consequently, the absence of a viable rule of law at the beginning of reconstruction creates enormous challenges and may take a long time to improve.

The existence of a peace agreement or formal surrender is a key component of stability. A peace agreement, especially one with credible and enforceable guarantees, can significantly increase the likelihood of stability by convincing the combatants to shed their forces and surrender conquered territory. Peace agreements do not ipso facto lead to peace. There are numerous instances in which combatants have resumed fighting despite reaching a peace settlement. This often occurs because the process of demobilization and demilitarization creates a security dilemma in reverse: the more that groups disarm, the more vulnerable they feel, the more sensitive they become to possible violations, and the less likely they are to fulfill their side of the bargain. Consequently, outside powers can play a critical role in enforcing peace agreements by providing a security guarantee, such as the deployment of military forces or advisors to monitor cease-fires. Formal surrenders can also increase the likelihood of stability, especially in the aftermath of a destructive military defeat, because they undermine the former government's credibility and demonstrate that it can no longer deliver vital needs to the population. It also creates an impetus to reconstruct; without external support, the defeated country may face severe difficulties in reconstructing.

Inputs and Outputs

"Inputs" refer to the amount of resources used in reconstructing internal security, such as the amount of financial assistance and inter-

---

[8] Fukuyama (2004).

national personnel deployed. "Outputs" are the first-order results of the assistance program and include such examples as trained police officers and soldiers, functional courthouses, and refurbished prisons. Donor states and indigenous actors provide most of the inputs and outputs, although international organizations and NGOs also provide assistance. Several governments, such as the United States and United Kingdom, have developed offices to help plan and implement reconstruction. The U.S. State Department has established an Office of the Coordinator for Reconstruction and Stabilization, and the British government has created a Post Conflict Reconstruction Unit. Finally, private firms such as DynCorp and MPRI have played an increasingly significant role in training indigenous police and military personnel, as well as reforming security institutions such as the ministries of interior and defense.[9]

Table 2.2 summarizes critical internal security tasks, actors, and metrics. In the absence of a clear U.S. presidential directive on lead actors, the table includes plausible lead actors for reconstructing the police, military, and justice sectors. The most recent presidential decision directives on stability operations are Presidential Decision Directive 56 (Managing Complex Contingency Operations) and Presidential Decision Directive 71 (Strengthening Criminal Justice Systems in Support of Peace Operations and Other Complex Contingencies).[10] However, since President George W. Bush did not establish a comparable presidential directive on the organization and implementation of stability operations, our interviews with personnel from the State Department, Defense Department, National Security Council, and other agencies demonstrated significant disagreement about the tasks and roles of U.S. government agencies.

---

[9] P. W. Singer, *Corporate Warriors: The Rise of the Privatized Military Industry*, Ithaca, N.Y.: Cornell University Press, 2003.

[10] The White House, "Managing Complex Contingency Operations," PDD-56, 1997; The White House, "Strengthening Criminal Justice Systems in Support of Peace Operations and Other Complex Contingencies," PDD-71, 2000.

Table 2.2
Internal Security Performance Matrix

	Police	Military/Other	Justice
Key Objectives	• Establish basic law and order • Protect population • Control border, ports of entry • Protect vital infrastructure • Ensure freedom of movement	• Establish security against major threats to the state • Demobilize, disrupt, and deter militia and other paramilitary organizations	• Establish rule of law • Eliminate corruption • Provide oversight and accountability for police and other security forces
External Actors (U.S.)	*Lead actor:* • State Department (especially International Narcotics and Law Enforcement, INL) *Supporting actors:* • Justice Department • Defense Department (Combined Joint Task Force, CJTF) • USAID • Foreign governments • Nongovernmental organizations (NGOs) and international organizations • Private contractors	*Lead actor:* • Defense Department (CJTF) *Supporting actors:* • Central Intelligence Agency • State Department • Foreign governments • NGOs and international organizations • Private contractors	*Lead actors:* • State Department • Justice Department *Supporting actors:* • USAID • Defense Department (CJTF) • Foreign governments • NGOs and international organizations • Private contractors
Indigenous Actors	• Ministry of interior • Local police	• Ministry of defense • Indigenous intelligence agency • Local militias and factions	• Ministry of justice • Local and national judges, courts • Office of attorney general
Input Metrics	• Police assistance and expenditures • International civilian and military police and advisors • Lethal and nonlethal equipment	• Military assistance and expenditures • International troops and advisors • Lethal and nonlethal equipment • Intelligence assistance and expenditures • Intelligence advisors	• Justice assistance and expenditures • International justice advisors • Equipment, such as computers and law books

Table 2.2—Continued

	Police	Military/Other	Justice
Output Metrics	• Number and quality of police trained • Number and quality of police facilities built or refurbished • Institutional development and reform of ministry of interior	• Number and quality of troops trained; military facilities built or refurbished; institutional development • Development of reliable local intelligence • Number of ex-combatants who have completed disarmament, demobilization, and reintegration (DDR) • Number and quality of intelligence officials trained, facilities built, and institutional development	• Number and quality of judges, prosecutors, and corrections officers trained • Number and quality of judicial facilities built or refurbished • Institutional development of justice bodies: ministry of justice, local and national courts
Outcome Metrics	• Crime rates, especially violent crimes • Other crime indicators, such as illegal drug trade • International civilian police casualties • Public perception of security and performance of police	• Level of political violence and insurgency • Public perception of security • International military casualties	• Public perception of justice system's effectiveness • Public perception of corruption in justice system • Duration of pretrial detention • Duration that cases move through court system • Right to legal advice

Inputs. Critical internal security inputs include troops, police, and other personnel; financial assistance; and duration. First, the number, duration, and type of troops are important to accomplish key internal security tasks. Large numbers of troops are particularly critical for defeating and deterring insurgents; patrolling borders; securing roads; combating organized crime; and conducting general law enforcement functions such as policing streets. There are no simple answers to the question of how many police and troops are necessary to stabilize a population. Existing analysis suggests that force ratios of 1,000 troops or more per 100,000 inhabitants may be necessary during conditions where there is the potential for severe instability.[11] There were more than 10,000 U.S. troops per 100,000 inhabitants in the American sector of Germany after World War II, 1,900 troops in Bosnia, 3,400 in Eastern Slavonia, 2,000 in Kosovo, and 1,100 in East Timor in the first years of reconstruction. There are also no simple answers to the question of how many civilian police with executive authority are necessary. Some literature suggests that police ratios of 150 or more per 100,000 inhabitants are necessary in unstable conditions.[12] These levels of troops and police may not always be necessary. In cases in which all sides of a war may be exhausted by fighting and have agreed to a peace settlement or formal surrender, lower ratios may be possible. Ratios of less than 500 troops per 100,000 inhabitants were sufficient to successfully stabilize Japan after World War II, Namibia in 1989, El Salvador in 1991, and Mozambique in 1993.

Timing is also critical. The immediate aftermath of major combat is sometimes called the "golden hour." It includes a time frame of several weeks to several months during which external intervention may enjoy some popular support and international legitimacy, and

---

[11] James T. Quinlivan, "Force Requirements in Stability Operations," *Parameters*, Vol. 25, No. 4, Winter 1995–96, pp. 59–69; Dobbins et al. (2003); James Dobbins, Seth G. Jones, Keith Crane, Andrew Rathmell, Brett Steele, Richard Teltschik, and Anga Timilsina, *The UN's Role in Nation-Building: From the Congo to Iraq*, Santa Monica, Calif.: RAND Corporation, 2005.

[12] Dobbins et al. (2003); Dobbins et al. (2005).

when potential spoilers may have insufficient time to organize. During this period, efforts by outsiders can prevent—or trigger—a spiral of conflict that becomes an insurgency. Intervening early with overwhelming force is easier than trying to retrieve a deteriorating security situation when consent is declining and spoilers are on the offensive. This approach is akin to what is often referred to as the "Weinberger Doctrine" or the "Powell Doctrine": military force, when used, should be overwhelming and disproportionate to the force used by the enemy.[13] However, large numbers of foreign troops may trigger violence—and perhaps even an insurgency—if deployed for too long.[14] Despite repeated pledges to withdraw, for example, the United Kingdom did not fully leave Egypt until its independence in 1954, seventy-two years after British forces landed in the country. By staying, however, Britain fueled significant anti-imperialist nationalism and violence. The United States' experience during the Cold War in such countries as Vietnam also suggests that lengthy occupations can trigger violence or civil unrest. In short, timing is a critical factor. Large numbers of forces are important in the immediate aftermath of conflict but may trigger unrest if deployed for too long.

A major power should also be the lead military actor in cases where forced entry is required. This is true even in nation-building missions led by the United Nations or regional organizations. The logic is that only major powers have the military capabilities to win with overwhelming force. In East Timor, for example, the Australian-led International Force in East Timor (INTERFET) initially secured the territory and then quickly turned the operation over to UN management. Remaining combatants were disarmed, new security forces

---

[13] Colin L. Powell, "U.S. Forces: Challenges Ahead," *Foreign Affairs*, Vol. 72, No. 5, Winter 1992/93; Caspar W. Weinberger, *Fighting for Peace: Seven Critical Years in the Pentagon*, New York: Warner Books, 1990; Thomas R. Dubois, "The Weinberger Doctrine and the Liberation of Kuwait," *Parameters*, Vol. 21, No. 4, Winter 1991–1992, pp. 24–38. The Weinberger Doctrine and Powell Doctrine are named after Caspar Weinberger, Ronald Reagan's Secretary of Defense, and Colin Powell, most recently George W. Bush's first Secretary of State.

[14] David M. Edelstein, "Occupational Hazards: Why Military Occupations Succeed or Fail," *International Security*, Vol. 29, No. 1, Summer 2004, pp. 49–91.

established, a local administration recreated, elections held, and a democratically elected government inaugurated after three years. In Sierra Leone, British forces were critical in stabilizing a deteriorating security situation and preventing UN nation-building efforts from collapsing. In 2000, the UK government dispatched a task force of seven warships and an airborne battalion to stabilize the country and neutralize the forces of the Revolutionary United Front of Sierra Leone. In general, though, a major power may not be necessary in cases where entry is permissive, such as the UN nation-building operations in Namibia or El Salvador.

Second, financial assistance is a key input. States emerging from interstate or civil war have generally suffered significant damage. Some research suggests that annual per capita assistance should be approximately $250 per year.[15] These levels of funding are necessary to train indigenous police, army, and justice personnel; provide equipment; run ministries and courts; and build infrastructure. Assistance generally comes from an amalgam of donor states and international organizations such as the International Monetary Fund, the World Bank, and the European Union. In East Timor, for example, pro-Indonesian militias, with some support from the Indonesian military, initiated a wave of destruction and violence in September 1999, referred to as "Operation Clean Sweep."[16] The militias destroyed 70 percent of public infrastructure and private housing. Consequently, East Timor received annual assistance of $257 per capita to reconstruct the country.

---

[15] Dobbins et al. (2003); Dobbins et al. (2005).

[16] Authors' interview with Peter Galbraith, director for political, constitutional, and electoral affairs for the UN Transitional Administration in East Timor (UNTAET), January 9, 2004. In addition, Australian intelligence and UN documents leaked to the press indicate that the Indonesian army was involved in the violence. Shawn Donnan, "Evidence Grows Over Jakarta Hand in Violence," *Financial Times*, November 25, 1999, p. 6; Desmond Ball, "Silent Witness: Australian Intelligence and East Timor," *Pacific Review*, Vol. 14, No. 1, 2001, pp. 35–62; Craig Skehan, Hamish McDonald, Lindsay Murdoch, and Mark Dodd, "Jakarta's Bloody Hands: Military Backs Violence," *Sydney Morning Herald*, September 6, 1999, p. 1; Report of the Security Council Mission to Jakarta and Dili, S/1999/976, September 14, 1999.

But financial assistance has some limitations, and more is not always better. In developing countries, governments do not always have the capacity to spend large amounts of money. Furthermore, corruption may affect the viability of financial assistance. Corruption can be as much a problem for the United States, its allies, and international organizations as it is for indigenous governments. The United States' experience in Iraq and the role of contractors, as well as the United Nation's oil-for-food program in Iraq, demonstrate that reconstruction missions can be a tempting opportunity for corruption. Countries with poorly functioning justice systems are also likely candidates for corruption. Steps need to be taken to increase transparency in awarding contracts, to monitor financial transactions, and to hold accountable those who are guilty. Accountability could include a range of measures, from prosecuting U.S. individuals or companies guilty of corruption, to withholding assistance from corrupt foreign governments or agencies.

Third, duration is an important input. While staying for a long time does not guarantee success, leaving early usually assures failure. Time is critical because it can take years to train, equip, and mentor police and other security forces, as well as build and refurbish infrastructure. Justice systems can be extremely difficult and time consuming to build, especially in countries with little formal rule of law when reconstruction begins. Time is also necessary for other areas of nation-building, such as building public health and health care delivery systems, basic infrastructure, a functioning economic system, governance institutions, and democratic structures. Some research suggests that no successful effort at nation-building has taken hold in less than five years.[17] As noted earlier, there appears to be an inverse relationship with the size of outside forces and duration: the longer that foreign troops and police remain in host nations, the more likely they may trigger resistance and insurgency.

Fourth, prewar planning is a key input. This should involve an analysis of standard best practices with a knowledge of local cultures

[17] Dobbins et al. (2003); Dobbins et al. (2005).

and requirements. It should include answering such questions as: What are the strategic objectives of the operation, including key security and justice goals? Who is in charge? What are the key tasks, and how should they be prioritized? How should the programmatic elements be assembled, and how many personnel, how much money, and how much time will be required? How should progress be measured? Adequate prior planning should make it easier to close the "security gap" by ensuring that appropriate levels of funds, equipment, personnel, and trained and configured military and police forces are at hand. There will always be political sensitivities that restrict the amount of planning and preparation that can precede reconstruction efforts. In some cases, such as Afghanistan, there may not be sufficient time to plan for the reconstruction phase. Less than three months transpired between the September 11, 2001, terrorist attacks in New York and Washington and the December 5, 2001, Bonn Agreement that jump-started reconstruction. However, the price for undertaking inadequate prior planning, as in the case of Iraq, can be catastrophic. Once an operation begins, there is rarely enough time for policymakers to reflect on the strategic priorities or to adjust their standard templates to the peculiarities of the circumstance.

Outputs. Outputs are the first-order results of the assistance program. They include such examples as (1) number and quality of trained troops, police, judges, prosecutors, and corrections officers; (2) number and quality of infrastructure built or refurbished, such as police stations, courts, and prisons; (3) number of ex-combatants who have completed a demobilization, demilitarization, and reintegration program; and (4) institutional development and reform of security ministries. Since foreign assistance programs tend to focus on outputs as their end results, this assessment is perhaps of most immediate relevance to governments engaged in developing and managing such assistance programs. Outputs also include softer elements that are much more difficult to quantify, such as institutional development. Institutional development includes improving the institutional capacity of the recipient organization, whether a ministry or a security force, to perform its internal security mission. It may also include establishing democratic security institutions that give operational priority to serving individual citizens and private groups rather than the state, are accountable to the law rather than the government, protect human rights, and are transparent in their activities.[18]

Outcomes and Performance Metrics

We define success in reconstructing internal security as the ability to ensure stability and the rule of law. We refer to these as "outcomes."[19] They are conditions that directly affect the public. Outcomes are not what governments and international institutions do but rather represent the consequences of their efforts. Without the ability to measure performance (using such metrics as the following), policymakers lack an objective method for judging success and failure in ongoing crises, making midcourse corrections more difficult:[20]

- Crime rates, especially homicides and violent crime
- Other crime indicators, such as the drug trade
- Level of political violence and insurgency
- Number of international police, military, and civilian casualties
- Perception of security, rule of law, corruption.

Where possible, we have drawn on existing methodologies that provide cross-country and time-series assessments of internal security and rule-of-law indicators. These methodologies fall into at least three categories. The first category includes governance indicators. The World Bank has the most comprehensive methodology and the richest data set to address the quality of governance. Its Governance Indicators data set measures the quality of governments around the world

---

[18] David H. Bayley, *Democratizing the Police Abroad: What to Do and How to Do It*, Washington, D.C.: National Institute of Justice, June 2001, Chapter 2.

[19] On outcomes, see Harry P. Hatry, *Performance Measurement: Getting Results*, Washington, D.C.: Urban Institute Press, 1999, and William T. Gormley and David L. Weimer, *Organizational Report Cards*, Cambridge, Mass.: Harvard University Press, 1999.

[20] On performance measurement in this area generally, see Vera Institute of Justice, *Measuring Progress Toward Safety and Justice: A Global Guide to the Design of Performance Indicators Across the Justice Sector*, New York, November 2003.

in such areas as rule of law, political stability, and control of corruption.

The second category covers issue-specific indicators relevant to internal security. Freedom House measures political rights and civil liberties, both of which need to be underpinned by rule-of-law protections. More qualitative assessments of the state of human rights and quality of the police and judicial system are produced by human rights monitors. Examples include the Office of the United Nations High Commissioner for Human Rights, the U.S. State Department, and NGOs such as Amnesty International and Human Rights Watch. Several data sets also have useful indicators, such as the RAND-MIPT [National Memorial Institute for the Prevention of Terrorism] Terrorism Incident Database.

The third category includes country-specific indicators, including those developed by ministries of defense, foreign affairs, and other government bodies. For example, the U.S. government collects quantitative and qualitative data on reconstruction efforts in Afghanistan and Iraq. In addition, several research organizations have collected country-specific data. Examples include the Brookings Institution's Iraq Index and Afghanistan Index.

There are at least two methodological hurdles. One is that reliable data are often unavailable, especially across countries, because there is not a functioning central government that collects data. For example, in the absence of a viable central government in Afghanistan and Somalia, we could find no reliable crime statistics. Measuring the effectiveness of security and justice programs, even in a stable, democratic society, is fraught with difficulty. To overcome these challenges, we found useful proxies. Although there were no crime data available for Afghanistan, for example, we were able to gather data on terrorist attacks and data from public opinion polls. The second methodological hurdle is finding causal relationships. There is little hard evidence of causal linkages between inputs, outputs, initial conditions, and outcomes.[21] For example, a review of 27 studies that

---

[21] David H. Bayley, *Patterns of Policing: A Comparative International Analysis*, New Brunswick, N.J.: Rutgers University Press, 1985.

investigated the impact of police strength on violent crime in the United States summarized that "after nearly three decades of research on the relationship between police strength and violent crime, there is not a consistent body of evidence supporting the assertion that hiring more police is an effective method for reducing crime."[22] However, since the 1960s, there has been a wealth of experience in the West with designing and implementing police reform programs. Reviewing work in this area, David Bayley draws 17 core lessons about how to successfully change police operating practices in developed democracies. Some of these lessons are equally applicable in post-conflict and transitional environments.[23] Even though it is often not feasible to find clear relationships between inputs and outcomes, we identify potential links where possible.

Conclusions

In sum, establishing security after major combat should be the most immediate concern of policymakers. Failure can undermine the strength of the central government, undercut efforts to reconstruct other sectors such as infrastructure, and ultimately threaten U.S. security. Critical inputs that can affect the success of reconstruction include the amount of financial assistance; number, timing, and type of police and military forces; and duration of aid. Key initial conditions that may affect success include the existence of a functioning central government, status and viability of security bodies, effectiveness of justice system, and a peace agreement. Finally, establishing a set of performance metrics is vital so that policymakers can objectively assess success and failure during nation-building missions and make midcourse corrections if necessary. While these rules of thumb will not guarantee success in reconstructing internal security, we believe they will significantly increase the likelihood of success.

---

[22] John E. Eck and Edward R. Maguire, "Have Changes in Policing Reduced Violent Crime? An Assessment of the Evidence," in Alfred Blumstein and Joel Wallman, eds., *The Crime Drop in America*, New York: Cambridge University Press, 2000, p. 214.

[23] Bayley (2001).

CHAPTER THREE

Kosovo

On June 9, 1999, following 77 days of NATO air strikes, NATO and the Federal Republic of Yugoslavia signed a military technical agreement that led to the immediate withdrawal of Yugoslav army and police forces from Kosovo.[1] The United Nations Security Council subsequently authorized a 50,000-strong NATO-led Kosovo Force (KFOR) and established the United Nations Interim Administration Mission in Kosovo (UNMIK) to oversee the civilian administration of the territory.[2]

UNMIK divided the provision of public security in Kosovo into three elements: UNMIK international civilian police (CIVPOL), an indigenous Kosovo Police Service (KPS), and KFOR.[3] From the beginning, civil authority was principally responsible for law and order. CIVPOL maintained day-to-day security and was tasked with developing and deploying the KPS. KFOR's role was—and continues to be—to provide for law and order when and where CIVPOL lacked the capacity to ensure security. The full transfer of policing responsibilities from CIVPOL to the KPS is anticipated to occur by the end of 2005.[4]

---

[1] NATO, "NATO's Role in Relation to the Conflict in Kosovo," July 15, 1999.

[2] KFOR now stands at 17,500, temporarily increased to 20,000 after the upsurge of violence in March 2004. Jane's Information Group, Jane's Sentinel Security Assessments, Serbia and Montenegro, Kosovo Special Profile, April 21, 2004a.

[3] UNMIK, "Civilian Police—Mandate & Tasks," 2001a.

[4] UNMIK, "Pillar 1: Police and Justice, Presentation Paper," July 2003.

Security in Kosovo rests on overcoming three fundamental challenges: organized crime, corruption, and ethnic bias. Kosovo faces a multifaceted organized crime problem, which manifests itself in a number of areas pertaining to trafficking. First, the security infrastructure in Kosovo must deal with the difficult problem of trafficking in persons. Kosovo serves as both a destination and point of transfer for women being trafficked.[5] Specifically, it is necessary that security institutions focus on the salience of forced prostitution of women and children. Second, as in other countries experiencing transition, drug trafficking poses a significant challenge. Roughly 80 percent of heroin consumed in Western Europe travels through the Former Yugoslav Republic of Macedonia and Kosovo.[6] Finally, those seeking security in Kosovo must grapple with weapons smuggling. Often in support of domestic political and nationalistic ideals, this element of organized crime largely began with the Kosovo Liberation Army (KLA), an armed insurgence seeking to facilitate Kosovo's independence, and now includes members of the Kosovo Protection Corps (KPC).[7]

Kosovo's next fundamental security challenge pertains to the corruption of public officials. Throughout the post-conflict era, many high-ranking public administrators have engaged in unethical behavior such as taking bribes and racial discrimination. Organized crime and corruption are frequently linked in Kosovo. For example, organized crime has been linked to former KLA members and existing political parties, which in turn has led to bribes and intimidation of judges and prosecutors.[8] Such practices seriously call into question the public confidence in Kosovo's infrastructure, which could lead to a breakdown in social order.

The third fundamental security challenge rests with integrating the Serb and ethnic Albanian populations in Kosovo. To be sure,

---

[5] UNMIK (2003).

[6] UNMIK (2003).

[7] UNMIK (2003).

[8] USAID, USOP, and OSCE, *Judicial Assessment Mission II*, December 21, 2001.

ethnic discrimination and tension underlie Kosovo's history and function as a primary impetus for violence in this region. Progress rests with integrating both groups into the institutional and social fabric in an attempt to reduce tension among them.

The remainder of this chapter provides some background on Kosovo's history and illustrates the substance of the security environment established after the conflict. It describes the initial security conditions present when reconstruction began and the critical internal security components developed in Kosovo, including the police, justice system, and defense sector. It then discusses the effectiveness of the reconstruction efforts to improve security and offers some lessons derived from this analysis. Throughout the chapter, we draw specific attention to the ways in which reconstruction efforts addressed Kosovo's three fundamental security challenges.

Initial Conditions

The conflict in Kosovo is rooted in then–Yugoslav President Slobodan Milosevic's suspension of Kosovo's autonomous status and oppression of ethnic Albanians.[9] Kosovo had enjoyed semi-independence as an autonomous province of Serbia, which was granted under Josip Broz Tito's communist Yugoslavia in 1968 and reaffirmed in the 1974 constitution. Significant turmoil emerged in Kosovo after Tito died in 1980; Serb nationalists began an uprising, and demonstrations against Yugoslav authorities occurred. In 1989, Milosevic implemented direct rule from Belgrade and sought to re-Serbanize Kosovo.[10]

Ethnic Albanians in Kosovo responded by forming a parallel society, comprising its own public infrastructure and ideology of

---

[9] Ivo H. Daalder and Michael E. O'Hanlon, *Winning Ugly: NATO's War to Save Kosovo*, Washington, D.C.: Brookings Institution Press, 2001.

[10] William H. Hagen, "The Balkans' Lethal Nationalisms," *Foreign Affairs*, Vol. 78, No. 4, July/August 1999, pp. 52–64.

nonviolent nationalist separatism.[11] Prior to 1989, Kosovo had a civil law–based judicial system. But after 1989, Serbian officials prohibited the majority of ethnic Albanians from working in the system, except as private attorneys, and from attending law school. This eliminated ethnic Albanian representation as judges, prosecutors, and legal educators, which led the Albanians to create a parallel university. Hampering these efforts was the Serbian authority's failure to recognize degrees from this university or practice law in Kosovo. Given the complete exclusion from the legal system, ethnic Albanians returned to using traditional alternative dispute resolution mechanisms and Reconciliation Councils. These were essentially a form of arbitration overseen by village elders. These councils are credited with solving approximately 1,000 blood feuds throughout the 1990s.[12]

Ibrahim Rugova and his Democratic League of Kosovo spearheaded the movement toward nationalist separatism.[13] Support among Yugoslavia's Albanians for Kosovo's independence grew as Yugoslavia collapsed, and with this came the emergence of the KLA. The presence of the KLA, in turn, provided justification for Milosevic's ethnic cleansing of Kosovo in the form of displacing several hundred thousand Kosovar Albanians and murdering many others.[14]

As conditions worsened in Kosovo, the UN Security Council adopted Resolution 1199 on September 23, 1998. This resolution demanded an immediate end to hostilities, a withdrawal of security units used for civilian repression, and an international monitoring team. In October 1998, Milosevic agreed to cease civilian attacks and extract security forces from Kosovo. The Organisation for Security

[11] Hagen (1999), p. 58.

[12] This practice originated when Albanians sought to circumvent the Ottomans from intervening in their personal affairs. Common law known as Kanun of Leke Dukagjini formed over time by the council of elders or a well-known elder called *pleqnare* provided the legal basis by which Albanians conformed and resolved disputes. USAID, USOP, and OSCE (2001).

[13] Daalder and O'Hanlon (2001).

[14] Hagen (1999), p. 58.

and Co-operation in Europe (OSCE) deployed the Kosovo Verification Mission, which comprised 2,000 unarmed monitors, 500 of whom were police officers, to verify implementation of the agreement.[15] It became clear that the situation was not improving, and in February 1999 NATO brought the Serbs and the KLA together for negotiations at Rambouillet, France. Although an agreement was developed and signed by the Kosovar Albanians on March 18, Milosevic, who had been deploying Serbian forces to the Kosovo area during the talks, refused.[16] On March 24, 1999, NATO initiated Operation Allied Force and began a bombing campaign over Kosovo and Yugoslavia.[17] Milosevic yielded to NATO's demands on June 9, 1999, after 11 weeks of intensifying battle. This paved the way for UNMIK.

Inputs and Outputs

UNMIK's administration has been organized around four "pillars." Originally, CIVPOL (responsible for providing interim public security and developing the KPS) and the Department of Justice (responsible for rebuilding the judiciary and penal systems) were part of Pillar II, Civil Administration. However, the police and justice institutions lacked overall coordination.[18] As Pillar I, Humanitarian Assistance, was phased out, UNMIK reorganized in May 2001 and created the "Police and Justice Pillar." This new structure brought UNMIK CIVPOL and the Department of Judicial Affairs together to

---

[15] Robert M. Perito, *Where Is the Lone Ranger When We Need Him? America's Search for a Postconflict Stability Force*, Washington, D.C.: U.S. Institute of Peace, 2004.

[16] Javier Solana, "NATO's Success in Kosovo," *Foreign Affairs*, Vol. 78, No. 6, November/December 1999.

[17] For a review of the combat operation, see Bruce R. Nardulli, Walter L. Perry, Bruce Pirnie, John Gordon IV, and John G. McGinn, *Disjointed War: Military Operations in Kosovo, 1999*, Santa Monica, Calif.: RAND Corporation, MR-1406-A, 2002.

[18] UNMIK (2003).

comprise a new Pillar I.[19] The intent was to facilitate the establishment of a rule of law by linking under a distinct pillar the administration of law enforcement, judicial, and penal agencies. The UNMIK police organization is responsible for law enforcement, whereas the Department of Justice oversees all aspects pertaining to justice and corrections.

UNMIK was also charged with creating an unbiased, independent, and multiethnic judiciary. Established in July 1999, the Department of Justice (originally named the Department of Judicial Affairs) has four sections: the Judicial Development Division, the Penal Management Division, the International Judicial Support Section, and the Office of Missing Persons and Forensics.[20] An independent Kosovo Judicial and Prosecutorial Council comprised of both international and Kosovar members is responsible for recommending to UNMIK judicial candidates for appointment.

UNMIK and KFOR constructed the KPC, the final component of Kosovo's internal security system. This organization was designed as a "civil defense" organization, tasked with civilian reconstruction, search and rescue missions, disaster response, humanitarian relief, and infrastructure repair.[21]

The Interior Ministry and Police

Like other attempts to reconstruct police in nation-building efforts, international police assisted indigenous police in the provision of police service in Kosovo. As of March 2004, 46 countries were contributing to UNMIK CIVPOL, with the United States providing about 11 percent of the total amount.[22] As described above, two fundamental goals of UNMIK CIVPOL were (1) to help establish law

---

[19] The other pillars remaining included civil administration, democratization and institution building, and reconstruction and economic development. See UNMIK, "UNMIK at a Glance," 2001b.

[20] UNMIK (2003).

[21] Solana (1999).

[22] UNSC, *Report of the Secretary-General on the United Nations Interim Administration Mission in Kosovo*, S/2004/348, April 30, 2004.

and order, and (2) to develop, implement, and ultimately transfer these responsibilities to a professional KPS. To understand what form and level of civilian-based security has been provided in Kosovo, it is necessary to examine the substance of CIVPOL and the progress it has made in deploying KPS officers.[23]

Upon withdrawal of Yugoslav forces, UNMIK began deploying CIVPOL almost immediately, but it took several months to establish a viable police presence. Within the first few weeks after the conflict, many CIVPOL were transferred to Kosovo from Bosnia. These officers were unarmed, but they nonetheless created an immediate civil police presence. KFOR provided security when and where the civilian authorities could not. The difficulty of establishing the international police was threefold. First, it took time for the international police officers to arrive in Kosovo.[24] Second, international police officers had to undergo testing and training at UNMIK's Induction Training Center.[25] This process took additional time. Finally, once on site, CIVPOL officers lacked basic supplies and equipment such as vehicles, radios, and desks.[26]

UNMIK CIVPOL initially numbered about 1,800 in 1999, which represents a rate of 95 officers per 100,000 Kosovo residents.[27] By 2000, they grew to about 4,450 CIVPOL, or about 237 officers

---

[23] It is important to note that some Serbian enclaves developed parallel security and judicial structures after the Kosovo operation. However, a November 2002 agreement between Special Representative of the UN Secretary General Michael Steiner and the late Serbian Prime Minister Zoran Djindjic placed all of Kosovo under de facto UNMIK authority. As a result, Mitrovica and other Serbian centers now have Serbian-staffed KPS patrols. See Jane's Information Group (2004a).

[24] Dobbins et al. (2003).

[25] Once officers pass tests in driving, weapons handling/shooting, and the English language, they are trained in general mission information, sexual harassment, map reading, radio operation, mine awareness, HIV/AIDS awareness, officer survival, cultural awareness, human rights, UNMIK police code of conduct, use of force, local laws, and legal procedures. UNMIK, *Annual Report*, Police Commissioners Office, 2000.

[26] ICG, *Kosovo Report Card*, Washington, D.C., August 28, 2000.

[27] Robert M. Perito, *The American Experience with Police in Peace Operations*, The Academic Series, Clementsport, Nova Scotia, Canada: The Canadian Peace Keeping Press, Pearson Peacekeeping Centre, 2002a.

per 100,000 residents.[28] The number of CIVPOL officers is about the same today and therefore remained fairly steady from 2000 to 2004, which is more than double the rate of international officers on the street during the latter months of 1999.

UNMIK allocated its CIVPOL officers among three basic functions.[29] The first function encompasses traditional CIVPOL activities pertaining to law enforcement and basic policing. Second, UNMIK has created special police units, which are paramilitary forces capable of responding to high-risk circumstances. One specific special police unit is a canine unit composed of 35 men and 25 dogs. In 2003, about one in four CIVPOL personnel were assigned to such a unit.[30] Finally, UNMIK has assigned personnel as border police to enforce border laws and immigration regulations. These officers made up about 9 percent of the total CIVPOL force in 2003.[31]

As for the indigenous police force, the U.S. Department of Justice's International Criminal Investigative Training Assistance Program (ICITAP) began very detailed planning prior to reconstruction in Kosovo. Preparation began about one year prior to NATO's intervention when the Kosovo Verification Mission began its work. Many of the international police monitors working on the mission helped to establish security in Bosnia, Haiti, Eastern Slavonia, and other areas. ICITAP drew upon and benefited from the considerable experience of these officers. Together, they developed extensive plans for a first-responder system. This system incorporated elements of a police function but was much broader in scope. The idea was to create a general response system so that a trained professional could be dispatched to a host of urgent situations. Plans called for these individuals to be trained in a number of areas including first aid, human rights, and conflict resolution.

---

[28] Jane's Information Group (2004a).

[29] Other international efforts include the U.S.-led Kosovo Organized Crime Bureau and the UK-led Criminal Investigation Unit, which attempt to combat serious organized crime. See Jane's Information Group (2004a).

[30] UNMIK (2003).

[31] UNMIK (2003).

When the Kosovo Verification Mission withdrew prior to combat, ICITAP, working in Vienna with OSCE, stepped up its planning efforts. It began developing in considerable detail what a new police force would look like and how it would be trained. In addition to such elements as the number of officers to recruit from each area and the training curriculum, the comprehensive plans even outlined such items as application forms, psychological tests, newspaper announcements, and the number of desks required. It was originally thought that OSCE would have primary responsibility for constructing and operating this new police force, but overall responsibility was given to UNMIK at the last minute. Although this gave UNMIK little time to construct plans of its own, it was able to utilize the plans developed by ICITAP and OSCE. Under this scenario, UNMIK was charged with recruiting officers, while OSCE retained responsibility for training them.

Soon after KFOR entered Kosovo in June 1999, UNMIK began recruiting KPS officers. In September, OSCE, under the auspices of UNMIK, established the Kosovo Police Service School in Vushtrii.[32] Two hundred international police instructors from 22 OSCE member states staffed the school by the time it became fully operational in March 2000.[33] In addition to writing the curriculum for both basic training and instructor courses, ICITAP personnel comprised a quarter of the training staff, including the director of the school.[34] The purpose of the school is to recruit and train professional KPS officers who act according to democratic police principles as instilled through ICITAP's training program. The total amount of training offered to KPS recruits has more than doubled since the school was established. KPS training in 2000 comprised an eight-week basic training course

---

[32] UNMIK (2003), p. 7. In addition to the KSP, a separate Kosovo Security Services Division has been trained to provide security at government buildings.

[33] Perito (2004), p. 190.

[34] Perito (2004), p. 190. At its peak of operations, ICITAP had 45 personnel in country. U.S. Department of Justice, "Project Overviews: Kosovo," ICITAP, April 4, 2004b.

followed by 19 weeks of field training.[35] During the field training component, KPS recruits work with a mentor to focus on practical application of course work and to further develop police skills, while completing an additional 80 hours of classroom training in traffic accidents, criminal investigation, community policing, and domestic violence. Basic training was increased to 12 weeks and field training was reduced to 15 weeks in September 2001.[36] The basic training course was again increased to 20 weeks in May 2004.[37]

The Kosovo Police Service School graduated its first class with 176 recruits in October 1999.[38] The school produced a critical mass of trained officers by the end of 2000, at which point an additional 2,672 recruits had completed basic training.[39] Approaching the goal of 6,500 by end of 2004, more than 5,600 KPS officers were trained and deployed by the end of 2003.[40] As of May 2004, the number of trained KPS officers reached 6,586.[41] The steady increase of trained recruits coincides with a steady increase in the number of KPS officers deployed. In 2000, there were 2,516 KPS officers on the job in Kosovo.[42] This number continues to rise and reached 5,704 in 2004.[43] On a per-capita basis, KPS strength has more than doubled

---

[35] UNMIK (2000). Basic training includes patrol duties, use of firearms, use of force, criminal investigation, forensic evidence collection, traffic control, defensive tactics, first aid, legal training, and interviewing techniques. The Kosovo Police Service School also conducts a number of specialized courses, including first line supervision, mid-level and senior-level management, criminal investigations, and emergency response driving.

[36] OSCE, "Kosovo Police Service School," in *Mission in Kosovo Factsheets, Police Education*, Pristina, February 3, 2003.

[37] OSCE, "New Class of Cadets to Graduate from OSCE Kosovo Police School," May 28, 2004b.

[38] OSCE (2003).

[39] OSCE (2003).

[40] OSCE (2003).

[41] OSCE (2004b).

[42] UNSC, *Report of the Secretary-General on the United Nations Interim Administration Mission in Kosovo*, S/2000/1196, December 15, 2000.

[43] UNSC, *Report of the Secretary-General on the United Nations Interim Administration Mission in Kosovo*, S/2004/71, January 26, 2004.

from 2000 (132 officers per 100,000 residents) to 2004 (300 officers per 100,000 residents).

Figure 3.1 shows how the total police strength and its components have changed since reconstruction began in 1999. The objective of UNMIK's CIVPOL mission is to maintain law and order while developing and handing police authority over to an indigenous police force. The figure shows that, once established in 2000, the level of CIVPOL presence has remained constant. By contrast, KPS officers have grown from representing just over half the strength of CIVPOL to surpassing it. Meanwhile, the total international and national police strength in Kosovo rose from about 95 to 537 per 100,000 residents throughout this period. The growth of KPS suggests UNMIK is making progress toward its final objective, which is to transfer police authority to a professionally trained indigenous police force.

Figure 3.1
Police Strength in Kosovo, 1999–2004

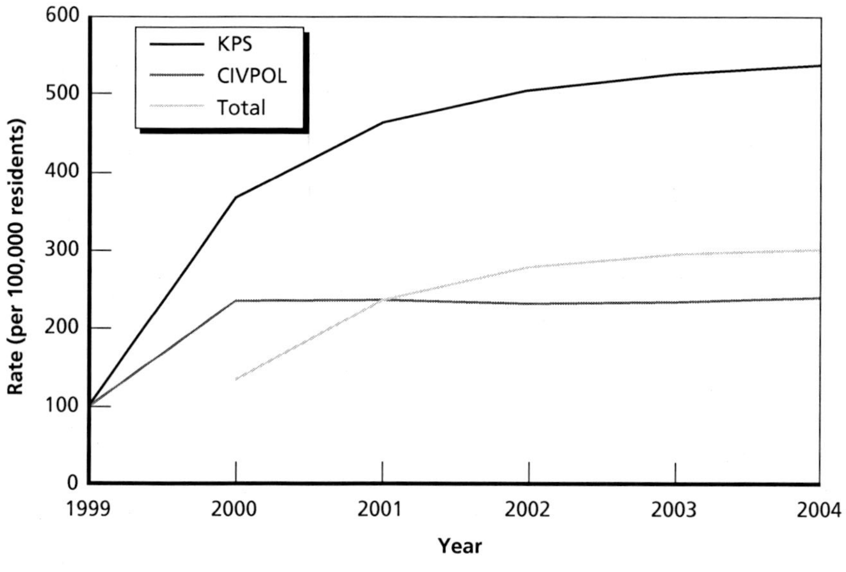

RAND *MG374-3.1*

UNMIK has taken direct action to tackle Kosovo's three primary security threats in its police sector. As identified earlier, organized crime problems include drug trafficking (particularly heroin), weapons smuggling, and trafficking in persons. UNMIK has attempted to act against organized crime through the use of several initiatives.[44] First, it implemented several organizational units throughout the Police and Justice Pillar that are focused on these issues. They include the following:

- Central Intelligence Unit, which is composed of 40 intelligence specialists who gather intelligence about those involved in organized crime and terrorism
- Kosovo Organized Crime Bureau, which translates the Central Intelligence Unit's intelligence into evidence for criminal proceedings
- Sensitive Information and Operations Unit, which provides guidance on prosecution evidence to KFOR and UNMIK CIVPOL and processes sensitive information for use in court
- Trafficking and Prostitution Investigation Unit, which specializes in anti-trafficking operations and employs investigators trained in victim sensitivity
- Victim Advocacy and Assistance Unit, which works to establish and ensure rights and interests of victims within the justice system
- Interim Secure Facility, where victims of trafficking in persons receive short-term accommodations and assistance.

Second, UNMIK has implemented various forms of legislation centered on organized crime and criminal procedure.[45] Of particular

[44] See UNMIK (2003) for a thorough discussion of these initiatives.

[45] Specifically, these included trafficking in persons, possession of weapons, unauthorized border and boundary crossing, terrorism, protection of injured parties and witnesses, witness cooperation, organized crime, covert and technical measures of surveillance and investigation, use of written records in criminal proceedings, criminal code, and criminal procedure code.

importance is the new Provisional Criminal Code enforced as of April 6, 2004, which incorporates principles consistent with international human rights and proscribes crimes such as terrorism, trafficking in persons, and organized crime.[46] Finally, UNMIK has established cross-border police information sharing through cooperative agreements with Serbia, Albania, and the former Yugoslav Republic of Macedonia.

Like organized crime, corruption of public officials is a serious threat to Kosovo's security. Throughout 2002–2003, police made several high-profile arrests of those involved in corruption. For example, in September 2002, UNMIK CIVPOL arrested the director of the property registration office for the Pristina municipality. According to CIVPOL:

> He was accused of registering illegal property transfers, such as fraudulent sales of public land or illegitimate purchases of property belonging to ethnic minorities, and of demanding bribes, to register legitimate property transfers. It is estimated that 12,000 of the 15,000 property transfers recorded in the office since 2000 are of questionable legality.[47]

Other high-profile arrests included those of the director of the public housing authority in Pristina and the director of the vehicle registration office for Pec.[48]

To further enhance the effectiveness of combating the corruption of public officials, UNMIK created the Financial Inspection Unit within the Police and Justice Pillar in January 2003. Ten financial inspectors, from the Italian Guardia di Finanza, comprise this unit. Their primary purpose is to conduct random audits of any entity that receives public funds. The new provisional criminal code

---

[46] UNMIK, "SRSG's Remarks on the Entry into Force of the Provisional Criminal Code and the Provisional Criminal Procedure Code," press release, UNMIK/PR/1163, April 6, 2004.

[47] UNMIK, *Police Report for 2002, A Year of Transition*, Pristina: Commissioner's Press Office, 2002, p. 5.

[48] UNMIK (2002), p. 3.

also encompasses international conventions with regard to corruption.[49]

Kosovo's third primary threat to security pertains to interethnic conflict. A key way UNMIK addressed this issue was to create a multiethnic KPS so that it reflects the various ethnicities represented in the population. The data suggest that UNMIK has been successful in this endeavor. As of 2000, the ethnic distribution of Kosovo was 88 percent Albanian, 7 percent Serbian, and other ethnic groups comprised the remaining 5 percent.[50] By 2003, the composition of KPS was 9 percent Serbian and 7 percent from other minorities.[51] This will not necessarily prevent ethnic hostility among Kosovo's population or even bias on the part of KPS toward the population. But it is a step toward ethnic integration and has symbolic importance, thereby enhancing its legitimacy as an institution.

Justice System

When UNMIK began its mission in Kosovo, no formal court system existed. Now there exists a tiered court structure to process criminal and other cases. There are 24 municipal courts in place throughout Kosovo. These courts adjudicate criminal cases carrying no more than a five-year penalty. District courts provide second-instance review of cases initiated in the municipal courts. There are five districts courts, located in Pristina, Gnjilane, Pec, Prizren, and Mitrovica. The Kosovo Supreme Court, which is the court of last resort, enjoys jurisdiction over the entire Kosovo territory.[52]

Within two weeks of their arrival, UNMIK staff created the Joint Advisory Council on Judicial Appointments (later replaced by the Advisory Judicial Commission), and the council began recommending judges and prosecutors. On June 30, 1999, UNMIK had

---

[49] UNMIK (2004).

[50] Statistical Office of Kosovo, *Living Standard Measurement Survey, 2000*, September 2003.

[51] UNMIK (2003).

[52] OSCE, "Kosovo: Review of the Criminal Justice System: The Administration of Justice in the Municipal Courts," *OSCE Mission in Kosovo, Department of Human Rights and Rule of Law, Legal System Monitoring Section,* Pristina, March 2004a.

appointed nine judges and prosecutors who served as a mobile judicial unit with jurisdiction consisting of the entire Kosovo region.[53] By the middle of September, UNMIK had appointed 48 judges and prosecutors to work on pretrial criminal matters, and by December 29, it had put in place another 301.[54] The number of judges and prosecutors continued to grow. UNMIK appointed an additional 140 in 2000, 48 in 2002, and 8 in 2003, so that as of July 2003, Kosovo had in place 317 judges and 45 prosecutors.[55] As of May 2004, the Special Representative of the UN Secretary General had appointed more than 320 judges.[56] Establishing and staffing the court system was a positive step for responding to Kosovo's security challenges. With the system in place, those arrested for organized crime, corruption, and violence could be brought to justice.

Yet it is not enough to have a structure and personnel in place to properly adjudicate criminal cases. To ensure justice and fairness, it is necessary to have a rule of law and professional, unbiased justice personnel to comprise the fundamental components of the court system. UNMIK faced significant challenges in both regards, and the justice system has evolved in response to them.

One of UNMIK's first tasks was to determine an appropriate rule of law to govern Kosovo. UNMIK initially established Kosovo law to be the Yugoslavia and Serbia law that was in place immediately prior to NATO's March 1999 bombing.[57] Albanian Kosovars vehemently opposed this legal doctrine as a basis for law. It was grounded in Milosevic's elimination of Kosovo's autonomy within Serbia and

---

[53] HansJorg Strohmeyer, "Collapse and Reconstruction of a Judicial System: The United Nations Missions in Kosovo and East Timor," *American Journal of International Law,* Vol. 95, No. 46, January 2001.

[54] UNMIK (2003).

[55] UNMIK (2003).

[56] UNMIK, "PDSRSG Swears in Two Court Presidents and Six Other Kosovo Judges," press release, UNMIK/PR/1182, May 11, 2004.

[57] Michael E. Hartmann, *International Judges and Prosecutors in Kosovo: A New Model for Post-Conflict Peacekeeping,* Special Report 112, Washington, D.C.: U.S. Institute of Peace, 2003.

was applied in a discriminatory fashion against the Albanians over the previous decade. Upon refusal to apply the law by Kosovar judiciary and from Albanian Kosovar opposition, UNMIK ultimately revoked this law and placed in its stead the 1989 law in effect during Kosovo's autonomy within Serbia.

A subsequent challenge that UNMIK confronted was in the application of law. The Kosovar judiciary primarily comprised ethnic Albanians because Serbs refused to accept appointments as judges and prosecutors out of fear or general resentment.[58] Unlike with KPS, UNMIK had a greater challenge developing a multiethnic judiciary. As of 2003, the ethnic composition of judges and prosecutors was 4 percent Serb and 5 percent other minorities.[59] This leaves Serbians underrepresented as judges and prosecutors and hampers efforts to reduce interethnic conflict—one of Kosovo's primary threats to establishing stability. The primarily Albanian judiciary failed to apply the law equally between the ethnic Albanians and Serbs. Through Regulation 2000/6 on February 15, 2000, the Special Representative of the UN Secretary-General attempted to improve the current judicial system by permitting internationals to serve on the judiciary.[60] The first appointments were an international judge and prosecutor to the district court in Mitrovica, but Regulation 2000/34 on May 27, 2000 expanded the use of internationals to encompass all five judicial districts. By July 2003, 16 international judges and 10 international prosecutors partially staffed Kosovo's court system.[61]

Despite the presence of international judges and prosecutors, miscarriages of justice occurred because Kosovar judges could still "outvote" the international judges who sat on a panel with them. This led to the creation of "64" panels via Regulation 2000/64, established on December 15, 2000. This statute permits the Special

---

[58] Hartmann (2003), p. 50.

[59] UNMIK (2003).

[60] UNMIK originally decided not to integrate international judges and prosecutors into the Kosovar legal system, but this decision was reversed following civil unrest in Mitrovica in February 2000. See UNMIK (2003), pp. 11–12.

[61] UNMIK (2003), p. 13.

Representative of the UN Secretary-General to assign specific cases to a panel of three professional judges where at least two are international, as opposed to the standard five-judge panel composed of two professional and three lay judges. UNMIK chooses the international judges and prosecutors in these instances.

A recent review of the municipal courts in Kosovo by OSCE identified several shortcomings in the administration of cases and protection of individual rights.[62] One major challenge to the justice system is the growing backlog of cases. In 2003, for example, 61,713 civil and criminal cases were carried over from previous years. While this created a total caseload of 249,695, only 167,795 were completed, thereby increasing the carryover into 2004 to 81,900 cases. As 33,538 cases were carried over into 2002, the backlog increased 144 percent from 2002 to 2004. Possible causes of this problem include a lack of judges (37 posts were vacant in 2003) and the distribution of cases to judges (seven courts received more than 300 complex cases per judge, while seven others received less than 150 per judge).[63] Additional problems identified by OSCE include noncompliance with established time frames and failure of necessary parties to attend proceedings.

The OSCE review pointed out numerous rights violations.[64] The organization anticipates some, but not all, of these issues to improve with the new Provisional Criminal Procedural Code of Kosovo, implemented as of April 6, 2004. This code helps to improve efficiency and the protection of those being processed through the criminal justice system.[65]

---

[62] OSCE (2004a).

[63] Complex cases, according to the review, encompassed investigation, criminal cases, juvenile cases, civil cases, inheritance, and non-contentious cases.

[64] Examples included the right to be tried by a tribunal established by law (e.g., two-judge panels were used instead of three-judge panels for some cases), right to an impartial tribunal (e.g., judges assume role of prosecutors when they do not attend; retrials heard before the same panel of judges as in the first instance), right to a public trial (e.g., date and place of hearings are not consistently available), and the right to cross-examine witnesses (e.g., witnesses' prior statements are read when they do not appear in court).

[65] UNMIK (2004).

As with the other criminal justice institutions, UNMIK arrived in Kosovo and faced a decimated correctional system. Many prisons were damaged or destroyed, and guards fled along with the Yugoslav security forces, which simultaneously transferred all the prisoners to unknown locations in Serbia.[66]

The Penal Management Division of the Department of Justice was tasked with recruiting international experts, operating Kosovo's correctional system, devising a strategy to transfer correctional authority to the Kosovo Correctional Service, and helping to reform the legal framework of the prison system to ensure its consistency with international standards.[67] In November 1999, the Penal Management Division assumed responsibility for the Prizren Detention Center. Since that time, it has instituted six additional corrections facilities: four detention facilities in Pristina, Mitrovica, Gnjilane, and Pec/Paja, and two prisons in Dubrava and Lipljan.[68] Dubrava is the largest facility, housing 67 percent of all inmates in 2003.[69]

The opening of these facilities has increased considerably the capacity to incarcerate offenders and improve security. Prison capacity in Kosovo went from 497 in 2000 to 1,358 in 2003, an increase of 173 percent.[70] During this same time, the number of correctional officers quadrupled from 350 to 1416.[71] It is clear from Figure 3.2 that the ability to capacitate and manage inmates steadily grew during the first four years of UNMIK's operation. This clearly enhanced Kosovo's ability to respond to its major security threats in that traf-

[66] Strohmeyer (2001), pp. 57–58.

[67] UNMIK (2003).

[68] UNMIK (2003).

[69] UNMIK (2003).

[70] Secretary General Reports to the Security Council: S/2000/538 (June 6, 2000); S/2000/1196 (December 15, 2000); S/2002/62 (January 15, 2002); S/2002/1126 (October 9, 2002); S2003/996 (October 15, 2003).

[71] Secretary General Reports to the Security Council: S/2000/538 (June 6, 2000); S/2000/1196 (December 15, 2000); S/2003/113 (January 15, 2002); S2003/996 (October 15, 2003).

fickers, corrupt officials, and violent criminals could be effectively removed from the community.

Correctional instructors at the Vushtrri Police Academy train recruits for the Kosovo Correctional Service. International penitentiary staff have replaced CIVPOL at the prisons and continue to assist the Kosovo Correctional Service in executive and management capacities. UNMIK appears to have been successful in developing a multiethnic correctional staff that reflects both the population of Kosovo and the population of those incarcerated in Kosovo. In 2003, Kosovo Correctional Service staff constituted about 11 percent Serbs and 4 percent other ethnic minorities such as Bosnians, Roma, and Turks. By contrast, Serbs and other ethnic minorities comprised 7 percent and 5 percent of Kosovo's residential population and 7 percent and 3 percent of Kosovo's prison population, respectively.[72]

With additional space in which to house offenders and staff to supervisor them, the number of inmates grew substantially over time. Those incarcerated in Kosovar facilities increased from 350 to 1,203, or 244 percent, from 2000 to 2003.[73] In 2003, the year in which the number of inmates was closest to reaching capacity, the correctional system operated at about 89 percent capacity. At this time, almost one in three inmates were incarcerated for homicide, with almost an additional one-third sentenced for robbery or theft.[74] Figure 3.2 depicts the steady increase in inmates and how it coincides with increases in prison capacity and correctional officers.

---

[72] UNMIK also notes, however, that the demand for additional Serb correctional staff is growing. UNMIK (2003).

[73] Secretary General Reports to the Security Council: S/2000/538 (June 6, 2000); S/2001/926 (October 2, 2001); S/2002/62 (January 15, 2002); S2003/996 (October 15, 2003).

[74] UNMIK (2003).

Figure 3.2
Prison Capacity, Guards, and Inmates in Kosovo, 2000–2003

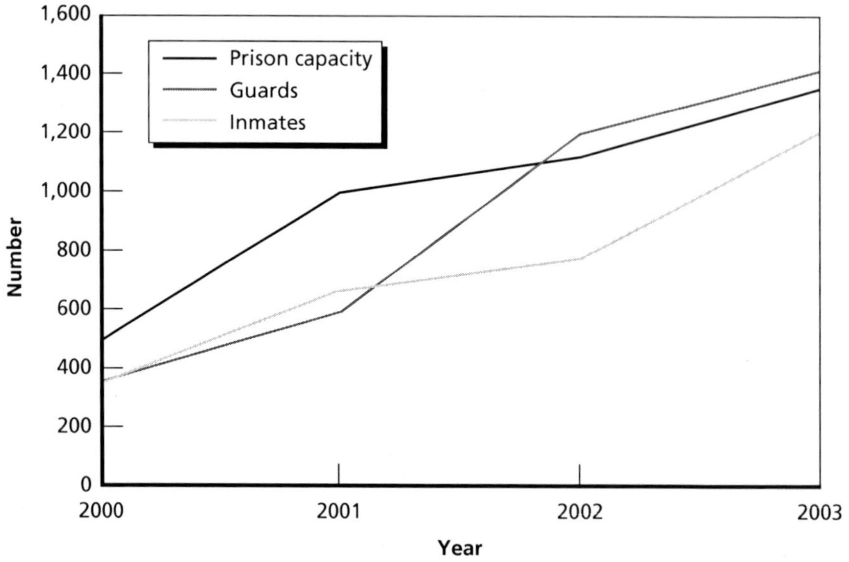

RAND *MG374-3.2*

Defense Sector

UN Security Resolution 1244 called for an international security force to be deployed to Kosovo. KFOR was established to ensure a safe and secure environment that would facilitate the return of refugees and the implementation of UNMIK's mandate. Entering Kosovo on June 12, 1999, the force initially comprised 45,000 international military personnel from 30 contributing countries.[75] KFOR consisted of five multinational brigades, each led by a major NATO partner,[76] as well as a multinational specialized unit. The 351-member multinational specialized unit was a stand-alone security force that maintained responsibility in all five areas of Kosovo for

[75] Dobbins et al. (2003), p. 115.

[76] The five NATO partners were the United States, the United Kingdom, France, Germany, and Italy.

conducting patrols, maintaining public order, crowd control, information gathering, antiterrorism activities, and gathering intelligence on organized crime.[77]

As Yugoslav military and police forces withdrew from Kosovo, the KLA, which was established when Milosevic withdrew Kosovo's autonomous status, sought to assume positions of power. One of KFOR's most fundamental and pressing tasks upon arrival was to demilitarize the KLA. KFOR quickly accomplished this task when on June 21, 1999, the KLA agreed to a 90-day demilitarization and reintegration process. During this process, the KLA relinquished 10,000 weapons, 5.5 million rounds of ammunition, and 27,000 grenades.[78] To facilitate the demilitarization, UNMIK and KFOR created the Kosovo Protection Corps. As noted above, the KPC is a mostly unarmed civilian emergency service provider engaging in activities such as rescue missions, disaster relief, and infrastructure repair. Many of those demilitarized assumed responsibilities in the KPC. There are currently more than 3,000 people in the KPC with approximately 2,000 reserves.[79] The KPC does not operate in the Serbian enclave north of the River Ibar. Although demilitarization was generally viewed as successful, many contend that remnants of the KLA still exist.

The strength of KFOR has diminished from its initial 45,000 troops in 1999 to 17,500 in 2004, although a temporary increase to 20,000 occurred because of violent outbreaks in March. On a per-capita basis, KFOR began its operation with 2,368 troops per 100,000 residents and currently has deployed 921. Figure 3.3 illustrates this trend while also comparing it to the total strength of UNMIK CIVPOL and KPS over the same period. From the figure it is evident that while police strength has yet to surpass KFOR

---

[77] Perito (2004), pp. 186–187.

[78] ICG (2000).

[79] UNSC (2004); Jane's Information Group (2004a).

Figure 3.3
Strength of KFOR and Total Police in Kosovo, 1999–2004

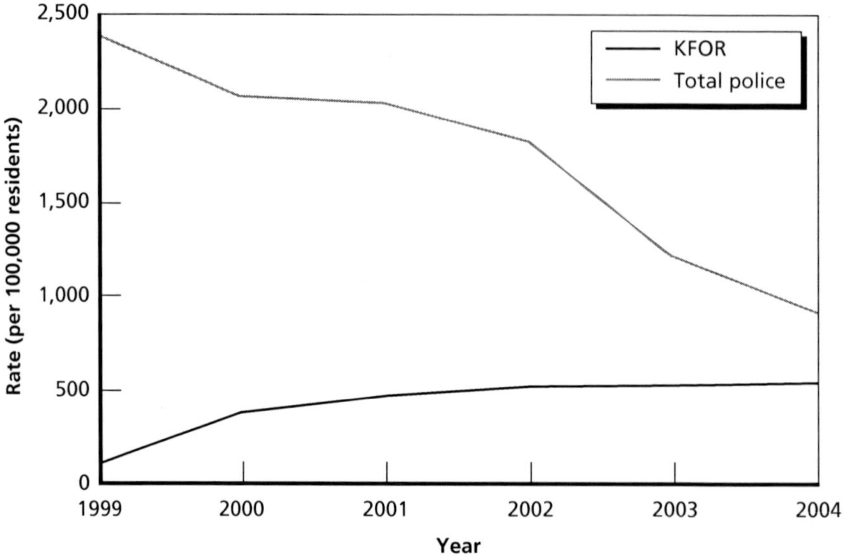

RAND *MG374-3.3*

strength, the decrease in KFOR presence coincides with an increase in police strength. This suggests that KFOR may be succeeding in transferring responsibility for law and order to civilian officials.

Outcomes

There are a number of ways to gauge the effectiveness of the internal security and justice systems. Reliable indicators of success, however, are limited. We have collected data on two types of outcomes: crime and the return of refugees.

Crime

Many violent crimes decreased throughout the first three years of reconstruction. Figure 3.4 depicts this general trend.[80] In 2000, 245 people were murdered. By 2002, this number was reduced to 68. This contrasts with the rapidly increasing murder rate during the first few months of the intervention, with up to 50 per week occurring by June 1999.[81] Per capita, the murder rate per 100,000 residents fell from 13 to 4, representing a 72 percent reduction. Over this same period, the rate of attempted murder dropped 48 percent; kidnapping, 44 percent; attempted kidnapping, 41 percent; robbery, 25

Figure 3.4
Kosovo Crime Rates, 2000–2002

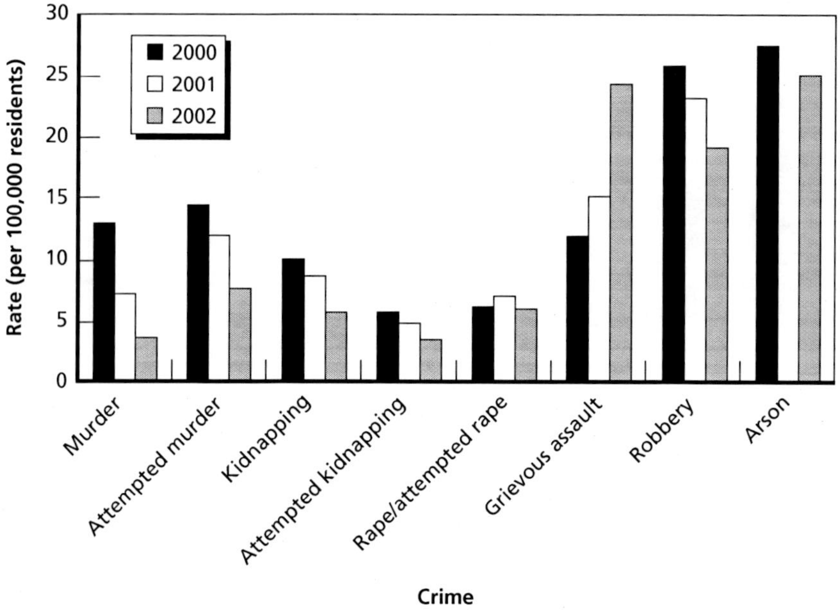

RAND *MG374-3.4*

[80] UNMIK (2002).

[81] Sabrina Ramet, *KFOR's Record in Kosovo*, Meeting Report 219, Washington, D.C.: Woodrow Wilson International Center for Scholars, November 17, 2000.

percent; and arson, 9 percent. These figures suggest that shortly after the Kosovo intervention, many forms of violence decreased. However, the reduction was not ubiquitous. The frequency of grievous assault doubled in this period from 226 (12 per 100,000 residents) in 2000 to 463 (24 per 100,000 residents) in 2002, while the rate of rape stayed roughly at six during these years.

Table 3.1 compares the frequency of crime occurring in the first six months of 2003, relative to the same period in 2002.[82] The table suggests the downward trend in homicides stopped in 2003 and actually increased by 9 percent relative to 2002. The downward trend in arson leveled off. The data for 2003 also suggest that kidnapping continued to decrease while aggravated assaults continued to increase. Theft-related offenses overall seemed to decrease during this time.

Table 3.1
Crime Statistics for Kosovo, First Six Months of 2002 and 2003

Offense	2002	2003	Percentage Change
Murder	34	37	9
Kidnapping	94	65	–31
Rape	67	69	3
Aggravated assault	224	247	10
Assault	2,525	2,389	–5
Robbery	282	219	–22
Arson	256	257	0
Burglary	2,566	2,098	–18
Theft	3,898	3,466	–11
Motor vehicle theft	842	481	–43
Criminal damage	1,172	1,258	7
Firearm discharge	173	196	13
Forged currency	217	388	79
Explosive attack	63	59	–6
Intimidation	1,229	1,448	18
Illegal weapon	744	633	–15
Trafficking in persons	21	28	33

SOURCE: Adapted from UNMIK (2003).

[82] UNMIK (2003).

Robbery decreased 22 percent, burglary dropped 18 percent, theft fell 11 percent, and motor vehicle theft declined 43 percent. By contrast, large increases occurred in intimidation (18 percent), trafficking in persons (33 percent), and forged currency (79 percent).

It is possible to break down the crime of murder by ethnicity to determine the extent to which minorities were targeted. As of 2000, Albanians represented 88 percent of Kosovo's population, with other minorities comprising the remaining 12 percent.[83] In the same year, minorities accounted for 34 percent of homicide victims, which is a far greater proportion relative to their presence in Kosovo. This disparity had reduced considerably by 2002, however, when minorities represented 9 percent of murder victims. Figure 3.5 illustrates this change over time, along with the general decline in murder. This

Figure 3.5
Murder by Victim Ethnicity, 2000–2002

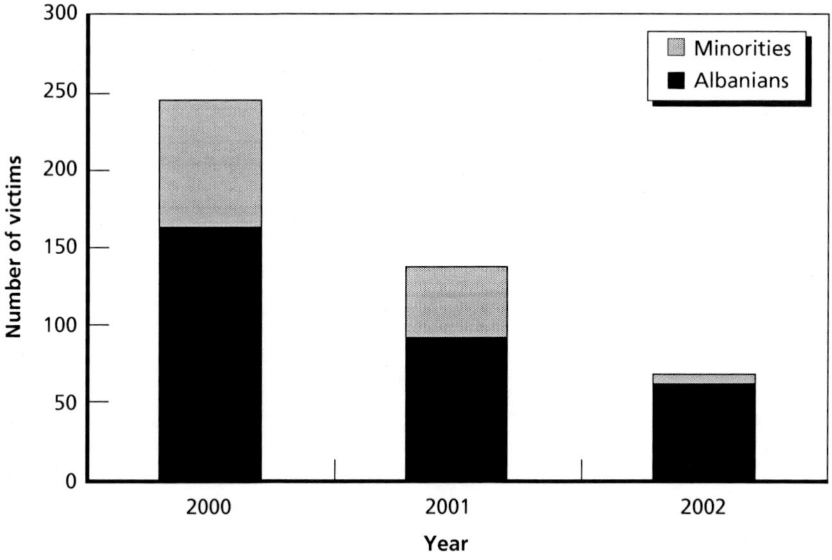

RAND *MG374-3.5*

[83] Statistical Office of Kosovo (2003).

trend appears to have changed in 2003, when murders occurring in the first six months are compared with those in the same period of 2002. Minorities accounted for about 9 percent of homicide victims in 2002, but about 22 percent in 2003. Over these periods, Albanian homicide victims dropped from 31 to 29, while Serbian and other minority homicide victims increased from two to five and one to three, respectively. The data do not permit us to examine the extent to which homicide was interethnic, that is, in which the offender was of a different ethnicity.

As a specific form of violent crime, terrorism can also be used to gauge the security environment. After initial reductions, it appears that terrorism continues to be an issue in Kosovo. As depicted in Figure 3.6, the number of terrorist incidents plummeted in 1999, the year in which the Kosovo operation began, and fell again in 2000.[84] However, the number of incidents rose from three in 2000 to 16 in 2002 and has remained somewhat close to this level since.[85] Terrorism-related deaths, and especially injuries, have also increased from their low point of one in 2000. By 2004, deaths and injuries had increased to 5 and 25, respectively, and these figures only account for incidents through September of that year.

Comparing some of the characteristics of terrorism incidents in 2000 and 2002 may provide some context for the increased security threat. In 2000, there was an assassination of a government official and a bombing of a transportation and diplomatic target. By 2002, both the targets and the tactics surrounding the terrorist incidents broadened considerably. In addition to targeting government officials (2), private citizens and their property (4), police (2), religious figures and institutions (2), utilities (1), journalists and media (1), military (1), and others/unknown (3) served as targets for terrorist attacks.

---

[84] RAND-MIPT Terrorism Incident Database.

[85] The data for 2004 only account for incidents through September 23, 2004. During the January–September time frame, 11 terrorism incidents occurred in 2002, and there were 10 incidents in 2004. This suggests that the total number of incidents in 2004 may be somewhat close to the number of incidents in 2002.

Figure 3.6
Terrorism in Kosovo, 1998–2004

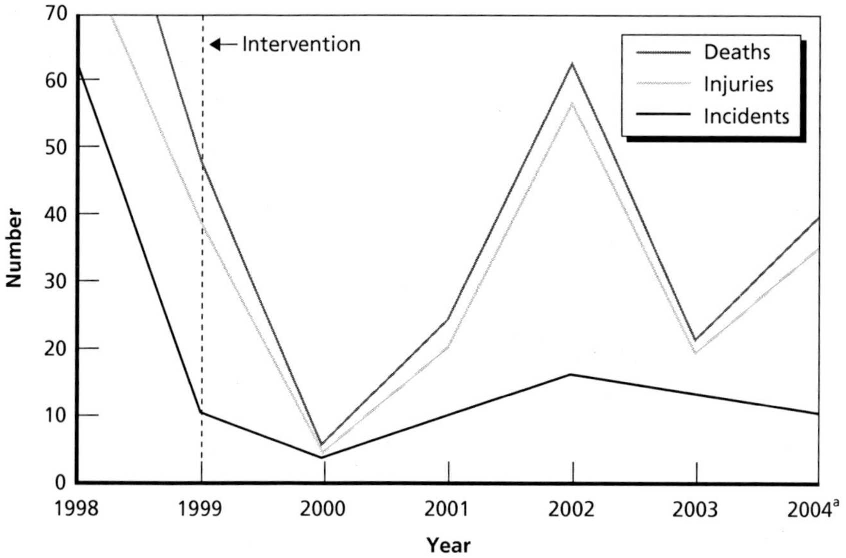

[a] Data are through September 23, 2004, only.
RAND *MG374-3.6*

These incidents included bombings (10), armed attacks (3), and assassinations (2). Although the perpetrators are unknown, the circumstances surrounding these incidents suggest a continued concern regarding Albanian-Serb relations and political and governmental progress.

It appears that considerable progress was made in reducing traditional forms of crime during the first three years of the Kosovo operation. This can likely be explained, at least in part, by the increase in police levels to detect crime and enforce the law, judges and prosecutors to process criminal cases, and prison capacity and correctional staff to incapacitate and manage those found guilty of crimes. However, the limited data available for 2003 suggest that, at least for some offenses such as murder, the trend may have reversed. The explosive interethnic violence that occurred from March 17 to March 20, 2004, provides additional evidence of this. Over these three days, 19 people were murdered and 954 people were injured; 730 houses belonging to minorities and 42 Serbian Orthodox churches and monasteries were damaged or destroyed; 65 UNMIK CIVPOL, 58 KPS, and 61 KFOR personnel were injured; and 3,800 Serbs were displaced.[86] This magnitude of violence indicates that simply setting up a criminal justice system is not enough to ensure stability; grappling with fundamental security threats and other factors that lead to crime are also important.

Return of Refugees

Instability may or may not lead to the displacement of indigenous people. Whether it does may depend on a number of factors such as likelihood of improved conditions, the targets of violence, existence of better conditions in nearby nations, and the ability to emigrate there. Kosovo was a case in which conditions were not improving, ordinary citizens faced discrimination and death, and surrounding countries provided a viable opportunity for refuge. As such, the return of refugees provides an indication of how safe individuals felt about security in Kosovo.

Ethnic cleansing significantly reduced the ethnic Albanian population in Kosovo prior to the operation. About 400,000 people were forced from their homes in 1998 as a result of the conflict between Serbian military and police and Albanian forces.[87] In early April 1999, about 384,000 refugees had sought safety in Albania, the former Yugoslav Republic of Macedonia, and Montenegro. By the end of May, about 90 percent of Kosovo's population had been expelled from their homes. Refugees numbered more than 430,000 in Albania, 230,000 in the former Yugoslav Republic of Macedonia, 64,000 in Montenegro, 21,500 in Bosnia, and 61,000 in other countries. In addition, within Kosovo, about 580,000 people were rendered homeless and 225,000 Kosovars were missing.

---

[86] UNSC (2004).

[87] NATO (1999).

Upon commencement of the Kosovo operation, refugees quickly returned. Within the first three weeks of June 1999, approximately 480,000 refugees had returned to Kosovo,[88] which translates into an average of 23,000 per day during this short period. By August 1999, about 90 percent of Kosovar Albanians who fled Kosovo during the previous year had returned. Complete stability was not reached, however. By the end of July, roughly 40 percent of the 2,000 Serbs living in Kosovo had fled.

Conclusions

This chapter noted three main challenges to the development of Kosovo's security and described specific ways in which UNMIK has addressed them. In general, the detailed planning of the KPS and the development of the justice system significantly helped to counter Kosovo's security threats. Several specific measures were taken as well. Regarding organized crime, UNMIK developed several organizational units within the UNMIK Police Organization and the Department of Justice to focus specifically on organized crime. UNMIK also codified new legislation aimed at combating organized crime and introduced internationals as prosecutors and judges to reduce the chances of intimidation. Data limitations preclude the ability to determine whether these efforts have been successful. We know that trafficking in persons increased 33 percent in the first six months of 2002 and 2003, but we do not have estimates for trafficking in persons prior to this period or direct measures for drug or gun trafficking.

We identified corruption of public officials as Kosovo's second major security threat. UNMIK did not weave corruption suppression into the institutional fabric of the Police and Justice Pillar as it did with organized crime. UNMIK CIVPOL made several high-profile arrests; however, the limited data make unclear the extent to which UNMIK has been successful in curbing corruption.

---

[88] Ramet (2000).

Perhaps the most vexing security threat facing Kosovo relates to interethnic strife, which permeates Kosovo's history. Integrating the Serb and ethnic Albanian populations is a critical component of Kosovo's future. A key way in which UNMIK has addressed this is by creating a multiethnic criminal justice system. UNMIK has done well in creating a police and correctional system that reflects Kosovo's population but have been less effective in creating a judiciary that is representative of Serbs. A multiethnic police and justice system may help to establish a more equitable application of law and serve as an example for other public institutions. But it will not by itself resolve interethnic differences. Instead, such a system could help reduce interethnic disparities and violence through effective prevention and enforcement of the rule of law. In this endeavor, UNMIK has been, at best, partially successful. The proportion of homicide victims that were an ethnic minority declined steadily from 2000 to 2002 but then reversed in 2003. It is not evident from the data, however, the proportion of homicides that had an offender and victim of different races, which would be a better indicator of interethnic conflict. The large-scale interethnic violence that broke out in March 2004 and the rise in terrorism since UNMIK assumed responsibility for Kosovo suggest that there is continued strain between ethnic Albanians and Serbs.

The experience in Kosovo provides a number of lessons that can be used to improve future stabilization and reconstruction efforts. One of the most important is the need for an immediately deployable, comprehensive criminal justice system. When UNMIK arrived in Kosovo, all aspects of internal security and justice were essentially nonexistent. There was no rule of law, police and justice personnel, equipment, or supplies. It was a significant challenge to develop security swiftly. The lesson here is that the very elements that took time to create and implement are those that could have been anticipated and at least partially developed prior to the intervention. This is particularly important given the increasing occurrence of nation-building efforts.

One way to improve future operations is to anticipate and plan ahead for potential internal security needs. Police experts developed comprehensive plans for a first-responder system and a police force prior to the initiation of Kosovo's reconstruction. This significantly enhanced the ability to establish stability. Yet the difficulty of ensuring that all necessary pieces were in place (e.g., rule of law, police and justice personnel, equipment, and supplies as noted above) in a timely manner indicates that operationalizing these plans proved somewhat of a challenge. Additional logistical planning may therefore be necessary prior to initiating security reconstruction. This may best be accomplished by establishing a national reconstruction office in each country. The primary responsibilities of this office would be to plan and coordinate post-conflict reconstruction efforts with international partners.

One of the first issues to consider in preparing for reestablishing security in a country is the appropriate rule of law. It must be determined whether it is appropriate or possible to draw on a previous rule of law that governed the country or whether it is necessary to create or adopt a new one. This encompasses a provisional criminal and procedural code. These codes may be changed as the country progresses over time or as the proper parties agree on which laws and procedures to adopt. But there is an immediate need to put into effect a rule of law at the onset of reconstruction.

A fully recruited, trained, and ready-to-deploy pool of criminal justice personnel is a second necessary aspect the national reconstruction offices must consider. Lack of immediate personnel slowed stabilization and security reconstruction in Kosovo. It took time to recruit, test, and then train those willing and able to serve as police officers, judges, prosecutors, and corrections staff. The United States and its international partners can anticipate the need for such personnel. This calls for creating and having on-call domestic and international criminal justice professionals who are qualified by international standards and trained in the application of their profession. These personnel can assume immediate responsibility for enforcing the rule of law until it can be determined how and when to reconstruct indigenous counterparts. The national reconstruction offices of each country can recruit, screen, and train criminal justice professionals who are willing and able to deploy on short notice. This on-call force would require only minimal training regarding the particular area to which its members are deployed.

Once police officers were deployed in Kosovo, a lack of equipment and supplies hampered their ability to function properly. Authorities can foresee such needs. When the national reconstruction offices anticipate an intervention, they may begin locating and storing items such as safety gear, weapons, desks, and communications devices. This will provide instant access to them when their use is required.

Finally, the goal of most nation-building missions is to reconstruct and train personnel to comprise an indigenous criminal justice system. Knowing this, the United States and its international partners, through their reconstruction offices, could devise a training curriculum and then recruit and train a set of international trainers. The trainers, like the criminal justice personnel noted above, would be available for immediate assignment and require only site-specific training. This would ensure that all police officers, judges, prosecutors, and corrections staff would receive proper training in their vocation and be assigned at the onset of reconstruction.

There are additional lessons. Kosovo provides an example of a stabilization and reconstruction effort in which the United States and its international partners attempted to develop all aspects of the criminal justice system early in the process. They quickly implemented a structure for the police and judicial system, deployed increasing numbers of police officers and judicial officials, enhanced prison capacity, and attempted to counter significant security threats such as organized crime and corruption through various organizational and legal vehicles. Consistent with this ability to enforce the rule of law was a general decline in many forms of violent and property crime and corruption, and improved government effectiveness.

While there appears to be an association between the development of a comprehensive criminal justice system and security enhancement, a deeper look into the effectiveness of the process provides additional insight. Notably, structure and personnel are not enough to ensure an efficient, effective, and equitable justice system. While Kosovar judges were in place, for example, they often acted in a discriminatory fashion and did not follow proper procedures, which led to various forms of violations of individuals' rights. Criminal justice systems are based on justice and fairness. Kosovo demonstrates the need to ensure that those assigned to specific positions are properly vetted, trained, and free of external influences. International staff can be employed in these capacities until it is clear that indigenous personnel can effectively execute their responsibilities. Moreover, it is necessary for a proper rule of law upon which to adhere. This can be enhanced by immediately adopting provisional codes of crime and procedure with which the international staff would be trained.

Addressing keystone issues takes time and planning. One such issue in Kosovo is ethnic discrimination, which has long existed between the ethnic Albanians and Serbs. While violent crimes fell steadily in the first few years following the operation, some indicators suggest this trend may have reversed. A poignant example of this is the explosive violence and uprising that occurred in March 2004. Responding to the primary underlying issues is a significant challenge that requires long-term planning, assistance, and persistence. This suggests that developing and implementing a criminal justice system is a necessary but not the only component of reconstructing security and justice.

A final lesson is the critical need for data regarding the reconstruction process. Data can help determine progress toward achieving goals and identity factors that can facilitate or impede such progress. Relative to other recent operations, more data regarding the inputs invested in Kosovo and the resultant outcomes are available. Having these data enhances the ability to evaluate the process of stabilizing and reconstructing Kosovo. Even with this case, however, there are data limitations. These include a lack of consistent data over time, the length of time for data to become available, variable estimates of the same characteristic, and minimal detail regarding criminal offenses. There is no doubt that it is difficult to collect data while consumed with reconstruction activities. Nonetheless, the success of operations can be improved if decisionmakers couple data collection plans with their operational objectives so that performance can be gauged and corrections made. Like the other components mentioned above, many important metrics and collection plans can be agreed upon prior to intervention to limit effort in this area once on site.

The primary implication for not adhering to the lessons learned in this case study is that establishing internal security will take longer than necessary. This leads to additional reconstruction costs in terms of personnel, equipment, and infrastructure rebuilding. However, the most significant cost comes in the form of needless violence, death, and injury. Planning for future operations based on past experience can help reduce the overall trauma associated with these complex and important efforts.

CHAPTER FOUR

Afghanistan

In 2001, the United States orchestrated the overthrow of the Taliban regime using a combination of special operations forces, air power, and support from indigenous allies.[1] While fighting continued over the next several years, the United States, European allies, and United Nations began assisting Afghanistan with reconstruction efforts in December 2001. Afghan leaders signed the Bonn Agreement on December 5, 2001, which established a timetable for achieving peace and security, reestablishing key government institutions, and reconstructing Afghanistan. However, the Bonn Agreement was not a peace accord; significant violence continued on the part of the Taliban, al Qaeda, and many regional commanders.

This chapter examines reconstruction efforts in Afghanistan by asking several questions: How successful have U.S. and international efforts been in reconstructing Afghanistan's internal security system? How effective are Afghanistan's police, justice system, and military in dealing with the most pressing internal threats to state stability? What are the most important implications for current and future operations? To answer these questions, we compile U.S. and other international "inputs" and "outputs" into reconstructing internal security and assess security and justice "outcomes." The country's long-term

---

[1] On the overthrow of the Taliban regime, see Stephen Biddle, *Afghanistan and the Future of Warfare: Implications for Army and Defense Policy*, Carlisle, Pa.: Strategic Studies Institute, U.S. Army War College, November 2002, and Bob Woodward, *Bush at War*, New York: Simon & Schuster, 2002.

stability to a great extent depends on the central government's ability to establish peace and order throughout Afghanistan.[2] Reconstructing the internal security system—including the police, justice system, and military—has been one of the most immediate and important tasks in Afghanistan. In particular, this means dealing with the country's major internal security threats: al Qaeda and Taliban insurgents, Afghan warlords and regional commanders, drugs and drug traffickers, and the absence of a rule of law.[3]

The core argument is that while there has been significant progress in some areas of security sector reform, reconstruction efforts have not curbed several critical security threats to the state. One of the major reasons is the low level of resources: Afghanistan continues to be one of the lowest staffed and funded U.S., UN, or European nation-building operations since World War II. Several significant trends are not encouraging:

- Terrorist attacks have increased considerably against Afghan civilians and foreign workers since January 2002, as well as the number of deaths from terrorist attacks.
- The cultivation and production of opium poppy have risen since 2001, and in 2004 Afghanistan produced approximately 87 percent of the world's illicit opium.
- Warlords and regional commanders still control substantial territory, although the central government has made progress in curbing the power of some warlords.
- There is still no functioning justice system.

The United States, Europe, and the United Nations have made notable progress in some areas of reconstruction. They have helped establish a central government with a democratic constitution, new

---

[2] For a contrasting view that a strong central government would cause more war and instability, see Anonymous, *Imperial Hubris: Why the West Is Losing the War on Terror*, Washington, D.C.: Brassey's, 2004, pp. 21–58.

[3] The term "warlord" is used to describe the various ethnic and regional leaders who possess their own militias, control and govern territory, and even collect taxes.

currency, and a new army and police force. The 2004 election of President Hamid Karzai was the first ever democratic election of an Afghan leader. The U.S. military has pioneered the establishment of provincial reconstruction teams: groups of military and civilian personnel assigned to Afghan provinces to further reconstruction efforts. Afghan women enjoy far greater freedom than they did during the Taliban period, and millions of children, including girls, have now returned to school.

But unless there is notable improvement in stemming critical security threats, it is unlikely that Afghanistan will become a viable and stable country. The Afghan National Security Council's *National Threat Assessment*, which identifies the principle strategic threats to Afghanistan, concludes: "Sustained insecurity created by the activities of non-statutory armed forces, terrorism, the drugs trade and organized crime undermines the establishment of good governance. This has a direct impact on the ability of the [Afghan Transitional Administration] to maintain public support and establish the political, economic, and institutional framework needed for future stability."[4] The long-term security of the United States also depends on the ability of Afghanistan's central government to meet these challenges. As the 9/11 Commission Report concluded, a U.S. failure to stabilize Afghanistan would decrease America's security if the country becomes a safe haven for terrorists and criminals.[5] Even though the responsibility for providing security, law, and order throughout ultimately resides with Afghans, international efforts are critical.[6]

This chapter is divided into four sections. First, it outlines the historical context of Afghanistan's police, justice system, and military. Second, it examines international efforts to reconstruct the Ministry

---

[4] Afghan Presidential Office of National Security (2004), pp. 7–8.

[5] National Commission on Terrorist Attacks Upon the United States, *The 9/11 Commission Report: Final Report of the National Commission on Terrorist Attacks Upon the United States*, New York: W. W. Norton, 2004, pp. 369–371.

[6] United Nations, Agreement on Provisional Arrangements in Afghanistan Pending the Re-Establishment of Permanent Government Institutions (The Bonn Agreement), December 5, 2001, article I, paragraph 1.

of Interior and the police, justice system, and defense sectors. Third, it assesses the overall effectiveness of reconstruction efforts by analyzing outcome measures. Fourth, it offers several lessons learned.

Initial Conditions

Afghanistan's history has had a profound effect on security sector reform after the overthrow of the Taliban. The country's security and justice systems have been characterized by two challenges. The first is the existence of a weak central government. This has made it difficult for successive Afghan leaders to establish order and justice across the country. The second is Afghanistan's dependence on foreign assistance and intervention for stability and solvency.[7] These historical developments have significantly affected Afghan, U.S., and international efforts to reconstruct security and justice since the overthrow of the Taliban regime.

First, Afghanistan has historically lacked a central government. Following the second Anglo-Afghan war in 1880, Amir Abdul Rahman Khan seized power after the departure of British troops. With British financial and military assistance, he ruthlessly attempted to defeat or manipulate tribal and ethnic groups such as the Hazaras, Aimaqs, Nuristanis, and various Pashtun tribal coalitions. However, Khan was unable to destroy tribal power and establish a strong centrally controlled state.[8] Successive efforts over the next century also failed. Instead, Afghan territory has been controlled by tribes and local strongmen, and its inhabitants have generally pledged loyalty to

---

[7] On rentier states, see Barnett R. Rubin, *The Fragmentation of Afghanistan: State Formation and Collapse in the International System*, New Haven, Conn.: Yale University Press, 2002, pp. 81–105; Charles Tilly, *The Formation of National States in Western Europe*, Princeton, N.J.: Princeton University Press, 1975; and Hazem Beblawi and Giacomo Luciani, eds., *The Rentier State*, New York: Croom Helm, 1987.

[8] Rubin (2002), pp. 48–52.

those with similar kinship ties and patrilineal descent, rather than the state.[9]

This development had at least two major consequences. One is that Afghan governments have never successfully established a monopoly of the legitimate use of force over the country. A series of violent civil wars beginning with the 1979 Soviet invasion and continuing through the Taliban conquests in the 1990s increased Afghanistan's decentralized political structure. By 2001, Afghanistan included a number of actors who controlled at least some territory: the Pashtun-dominated Taliban, who controlled most of the country; the opposition National Islamic United Front for the Salvation of Afghanistan (or Northern Alliance); and various other factions and tribes scattered across the country. The other consequence is that Afghan governments have never established a formal justice system in the country. In the absence of a central government, local *shuras* (village councils) and tribal elders developed an informal legal system that incorporated a wide range of Islamic and customary laws.[10]

Second, successive Afghan governments have depended on foreign assistance to remain politically, economically, and militarily viable. A number of states have provided aid to Afghan governments and opposition groups. The Soviet Union provided Afghanistan with a total of $1.3 billion in economic aid and $1.3 billion in military aid between 1955 and 1978, and roughly $5 billion per year between 1979 and 1989. The United States provided $533 million in economic aid between 1955 and 1978, and between $4 billion and $5 billion to the mujahideen (Islamic resistance fighters) between 1980

---

[9] Richard Tapper, "Anthropologists, Historians, and Tribespeople on Tribe and State Formation in the Middle East," in Philip S. Khoury and Joseph Kostiner, eds., *Tribes and State Formation in the Middle East*, Berkeley, Calif.: University of California Press, 1990.

[10] Olivier Roy, *Islam and Resistance in Afghanistan*, 2nd edition, New York: Cambridge University Press, 1990; Ahmed Rashid, *Taliban: Militant Islam, Oil and Fundamentalism in Central Asia*, New Haven, Conn.: Yale University Press, 2000, pp. 1–13; Barnett R. Rubin, "(Re)Building Afghanistan," *Current History*, Vol. 103, No. 672, April 2004a, pp. 165–170.

and 1992.[11] Both the United States and the Soviet Union suspended military aid at the end of 1991. Pakistan, and especially its Directorate of Inter-Services Intelligence, has played a particularly active role in Afghan politics. It provided weapons, financial aid, and other assistance such as wheat and petroleum to the Taliban and other groups during the 1990s and through 2001.[12] Saudi Arabia gave nearly $4 billion in official aid to the mujahideen between 1980 and 1990, as well as unofficial aid from Islamic charities, foundations, the private funds of Saudi princes, and mosque collections. Saudi Arabia also provided aid to the Taliban and al Qaeda in Afghanistan until 1998.[13] Finally, Iran has provided assistance to various factions, especially to the Afghan shia groups such as the Hazaras. Iranian military aid to the anti-Taliban alliance escalated after the fall of Kabul in 1996 and again after the fall of Mazar in 1998. The involvement of foreign governments has not changed since September 11, 2001. Pakistan, Russia, Iran, wealthy Saudis, and Western countries such as the United States continue to provide economic and military assistance to the central government and various factions.

Afghanistan's history of a weak central government and dependence on foreign assistance affected efforts to reconstruct the police, military, and justice system after the overthrow of the Taliban regime. During the 1980s and 1990s, there was no national civilian police force in Afghanistan. Instead, local militia and tribal forces enforced the rule of law in much of the country. Among the majority Pashtun population, the traditional military institution has been the *lashkar*,

---

[11] Rashid (2000), p. 18; Rubin (2002), p. 20; Henry S. Bradsher, *Afghanistan and the Soviet Union*, Durham, N.C.: Duke University Press, 1985, pp. 24–25; Giacomo Luciani, "Allocation vs. Production States: A Theoretical Framework," in Beblawi and Luciani (1987), p. 72.

[12] Tim Judah, "The Taliban Papers," *Survival*, Vol. 44, No. 1, Spring 2002, pp. 69–80; Rubin (2002), pp. 196–225; Ahmed Rashid, "Pakistan and the Taliban," in William Maley, ed., *Fundamentalism Reborn? Afghanistan and the Taliban*, New York: New York University Press, 2001, pp. 72–89.

[13] Samuel P. Huntington, *The Clash of Civilizations and the Remaking of World Order*, New York: Simon & Schuster, 1996, pp. 246–248; National Commission on Terrorist Attacks Upon the United States (2004), pp. 63–67, 371–374; Rashid (2000), pp. 48, 54; SIPRI, *SIPRI Yearbook 1991: World Armaments and Disarmament*, New York: Oxford University Press, 1991, p. 199.

or the armed tribe. Each family contributed its male members and weapons to the lashkar, which was further enriched by whatever booty it took in battle. There are no precise figures for the number of militia fighters. Estimates during the 1990s ranged from about 200,000 to 600,000.[14] Most were untrained, ill equipped, illiterate, and owed their allegiance to local warlords and military commanders, not to the central government.[15] As a German delegation in January 2002 concluded:

> The police force is in a deplorable state just a few months after the dissolution of the Taliban regime. There is a total lack of equipment and supplies. No systematic training has been provided for about 20 years. At least one entire generation of trained police officers is missing. Next to constables, former Northern Alliance fighters are being put to work as police officers.[16]

While Afghanistan has lacked a trained civilian police force, it has had secret police agencies. During the Soviet era, the Afghan government established a powerful secret police body, the State Information Services, to suppress opponents of the regime and establish order. The Taliban established the Ministry of Enforcement of Virtue and Suppression of Vice to enforce decrees regarding moral behavior, such as those restricting women's employment, education, and dress; enforcing men's beard length and mosque attendance; and regulating the activities of the United Nations and NGOs.[17]

---

[14] Ali A. Jalali, "Afghanistan: The Anatomy of an Ongoing Conflict," *Parameters*, Vol. 31, No. 1, Spring 2001, p. 86; IISS, *The Military Balance, 1995/96*, London: Oxford University Press, 1995, pp. 155–156; IISS, *The Military Balance, 1998/99*, London: Oxford University Press, 1998, pp. 153–154.

[15] Laurel Miller and Robert Perito, *Establishing the Rule of Law in Afghanistan*, Washington, D.C., United States Institute of Peace, Special Report 117, 2004.

[16] German Federal Ministry of the Interior, *Assistance in Rebuilding the Police Force in Afghanistan*, Berlin: Federal Foreign Office and Federal Ministry of the Interior, March 2004, p. 6.

[17] Rubin (2002), p. xv; Rashid (2000), p. 106.

The Afghan army has traditionally been an internal security force with little control over the country. During the 1980s, the Moscow-backed Democratic Republic of Afghanistan and its successor, the Republic of Afghanistan, recruited a large number of tribal and local militias. During the Taliban era, the army was an assortment of armed groups with varying degrees of loyalties and professional skills. There was no formal military structure. The army was not organized, armed, and commanded by the state.[18] Mullah Mohammed Omar was head of the armed forces and ultimately decided on military strategies, key appointments, and military budgets. The military shura, or Islamic council, sat below Omar, helped plan strategy, and implemented tactical decisions. Individual Taliban commanders were responsible for recruiting men, paying them, and looking after their needs in the field. They acquired much of the money, fuel, food, transport, and weapons from the military shura. The Taliban's military structure also included Pakistani officers and al Qaeda members such as the elite Brigade 055, which consisted of Pakistani, Sudanese, and other foreign fighters.[19]

Finally, Afghanistan has historically lacked a formal justice system. The Taliban established a nationwide judiciary with sharia courts at all levels. But there was no genuine justice system. The Kandahar Islamic Supreme Court was the most important court because of its proximity to Taliban leader Mullah Omar. It appointed Islamic judges and assistant judges in the provinces. A parallel system existed in Kabul, where the Ministry of Justice and the Supreme Court were located. The Kabul Supreme Court, which handled about 40 cases a week, was composed of eight departments that dealt with laws related to commerce, business, criminal, and public law.[20] Courts adopted the traditional *hudud* punishment, which included amputations, floggings, and death by stoning and live burial. Judicial appointments were routinely made on the basis of personal or politi-

[18] Jalali (2001), pp. 86–89.

[19] Rashid (2000), pp. 98–100.

[20] Rashid (2000), p. 102.

cal connections; judges had no legal education (secular or sharia); there were few legal texts available; and corruption was rampant. Outside of major cities such as Kandahar and Kabul, village councils or tribal elders were the most important actors in resolving disputes and delivering justice.[21]

Inputs and Outputs

Building internal security since the overthrow of the Taliban has required an integrated approach to security sector reform. As the following sections argue, however, input and output levels have been low. The levels of assistance and troops have been among the lowest of any nation-building operation since World War II. In addition, the police-to-population ratio in Afghanistan is smaller than the ratios of most governments in the region; the number of combatants that have been through the DDR process is low; and reconstruction in the justice sector has largely been in the capital region.

Afghanistan's current security structure includes the ministries of Defense, Interior, and Justice; the National Security Directorate, which serves as Afghanistan's intelligence agency; the Supreme Court and Attorney General's Office; and executive bodies such as the Presidential Office of National Security. There have been three major categories of security sector reform:

- Establishing a viable Ministry of Interior, including police and counter-narcotics capabilities
- Defense sector reform, such as building an Afghan National Army (ANA) and demobilizing, demilitarizing, and reintegrating ex-combatants
- Constructing a workable justice system.

---

[21] Miller and Perito (2004), pp. 5–10; Charles H. Norchi, "Toward the Rule of Law in Afghanistan: The Constitutive Process," in John D. Montgomery and Dennis A. Rondinelli, eds., *Beyond Reconstruction in Afghanistan: Lessons from Development Experience*, New York: Palgrave Macmillan, 2004, pp. 115–131.

In addition, the United States and the United Kingdom have assisted with the construction of an Afghan intelligence agency, the National Security Directorate. Because its primary role is external, it is not dealt with at length in this chapter. But it does perform some police functions and has domestic arrest and detention power.

There was little prewar planning because of the short time horizon. Less than three months transpired between the September 11, 2001, terrorist attacks in New York and Washington, and the December 5, 2001, Bonn Agreement that jump-started reconstruction. Most of this time was devoted to emergency response efforts in New York and Washington, collecting information on who was responsible, and planning and executing the combat phase of the operation. There was virtually no time to plan for reconstruction. The civil command structure for reconstruction in Afghanistan was significantly different from most contemporary nation-building operations. The United States did not establish a central body to ensure unity of command, like the Coalition Provisional Authority (CPA) in Iraq or the UN Transitional Administration in East Timor. Instead, security sector reform centered on a "lead nation" approach. The United States was the lead donor nation for reconstructing the ANA; Germany for the police; the United Kingdom for counter-narcotics; Italy for justice; and Japan (with UN assistance) for the DDR of ex-combatants. In theory, each lead nation was supposed to contribute significant financial assistance, coordinate external assistance, and oversee reconstruction efforts in its sector. In practice, this approach did not always work as envisioned.

The United States, which has been the largest external donor to Afghanistan, contributed nearly half of its reconstruction assistance in 2004 to the security sector. As Figure 4.1 highlights, this included \$549 million for building the ANA, \$160 million for the police, \$123 million for counter-narcotics, \$45 million for DDR, and \$10 million for justice, out of a total of \$2.1 billion. In relative terms, assistance to Afghanistan has been fairly low compared with other operations. Figure 4.2 shows the total amount of assistance during

Figure 4.1
U.S. Development Assistance to Afghanistan, 2004

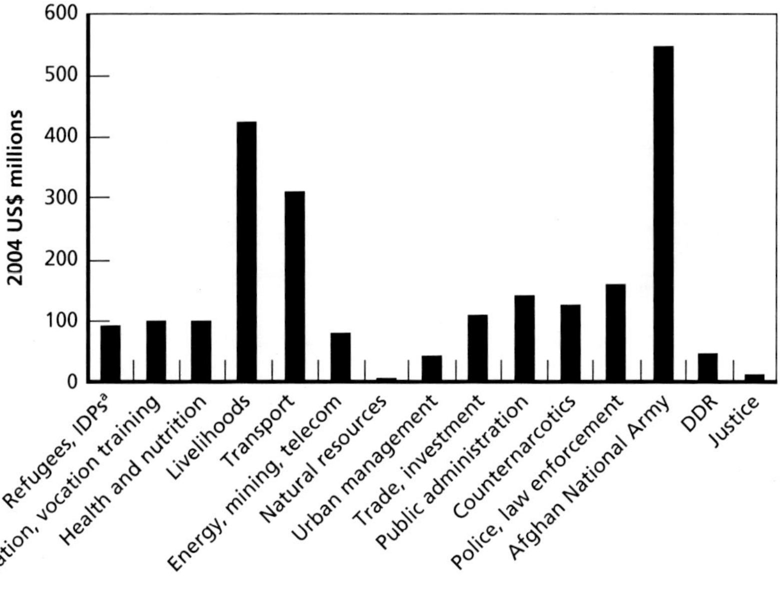

[a]Internally displaced persons.
SOURCE: United States Mission to Afghanistan (2004).
RAND *MG374-4.1*

nation-building operations since World War II. Foreign assistance to Afghanistan has been lower than all other operations except for the U.S. effort in Japan and the UN missions in the Congo, Cambodia, and Sierra Leone. U.S. government officials strongly opposed providing more resources for reconstruction efforts as far back as 2001, despite the fact that Afghanistan was a safe haven for al Qaeda and other terrorists.[22] By 2002 and 2003, U.S. resources that might have

[22] Interview with Ambassador James Dobbins, former U.S. envoy to Afghanistan, Washington, D.C., September 21, 2004. Furthermore, Richard Clarke, former National Security Council terrorism advisor, argues that the United States did not provide more resources to Afghanistan because (1) it did not want to get involved in Afghanistan to the same degree

Figure 4.2
Average Annual Per-Capita Assistance

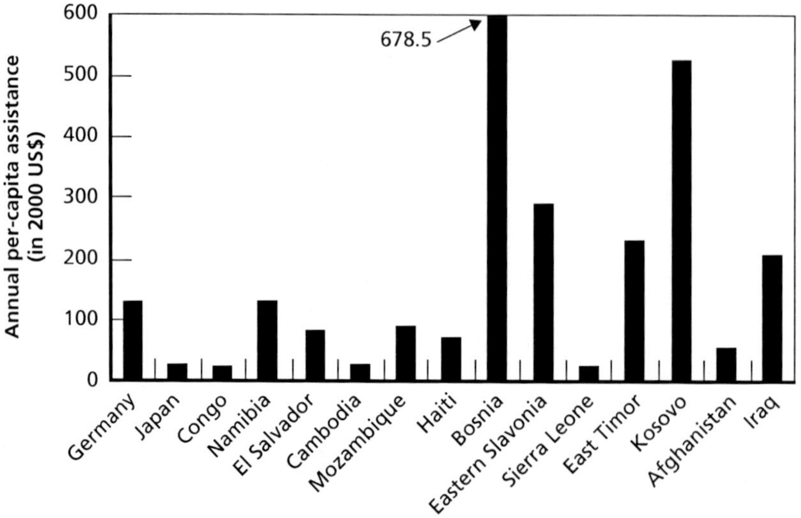

SOURCES: Killick (1997), p. 72; United Nations, Department of Peacekeeping Operations (www.un.org/Depts/dpko); World Bank (1999); World Bank (2004); GAO (2004b); GAO (2004a). Population data source: U.S. Census Bureau, International Data Base (www.census.gov).
NOTE: The data are an average over the first two years of reconstruction, which were 2002 and 2003 in Afghanistan.
RAND *MG374-4.2*

been devoted to Afghanistan went to Iraq for combat and counterinsurgency operations.

The Ministry of Interior and the Police

Creating a viable national police force has been a critical step in curbing Afghanistan's major internal security threats. The reconstruction of Afghanistan's police began in earnest in February 2002, when Germany convened a conference to discuss international support for

---

that Russia had, (2) it was saving forces for Iraq, and (3) Secretary of Defense Donald Rumsfeld believed that small numbers of ground troops, coupled with airpower, were sufficient to ensure stability. Seymour M. Hersh, "The Other War: Why Bush's Afghanistan Problem Won't Go Away," *The New Yorker*, April 12, 2004.

the Afghan police. One month later at a donors' conference in Berlin, the German government introduced a comprehensive plan to create a national police force.[23] A number of other countries—especially the United States—have also been involved in reconstructing the police. International efforts can be divided into two categories: (1) inputs, such as financial assistance and equipment, and (2) outputs, such as training police recruits, reforming the Ministry of Interior, and developing a counter-narcotics capability.

In 2004, the United States provided $160 million to the police and $123 million to counter-narcotics. Unlike other nation-building operations as Haiti, Bosnia, or Kosovo, however, the United States and European countries did not deploy international civilian police with executive authority. This meant that most training and mentoring of police had to come from either private contractors or the military. International donors have also provided significant amounts of equipment. The United States and Germany have supplied police graduates from the training academies with a standard uniform and a belt that includes basic police equipment such as handcuffs. The German government donated police cars, trucks, and motorcycles to the Ministry of Interior. The United States contracted DynCorp to install Codan high-frequency radio systems in all provincial police headquarters to facilitate communication between the Ministry of Interior and its provincial offices. Several countries have supplied handguns and ammunition to the Afghan police, and the U.S. military has provided more-lethal weapons such as AK-47s.

Training was critical, since Afghan police had not had formal training for at least two decades.[24] The first team of German police trainers arrived in Kabul in March 2002 to train police instructors. Germany has focused on training officers at the Police Academy in

---

[23] German Federal Ministry of the Interior (2004), p. 10; Afghan Ministry of Defense, *Securing Afghanistan's Future: Accomplishments and the Strategic Path Forward, National Army*, Kabul, January 2004, p. 4.

[24] German Federal Ministry of the Interior (2004), p. 6; Asian Development Bank and World Bank, *Afghanistan: Preliminary Needs Assessment for Recovery and Reconstruction*, Kabul, January 2002, p. 7.

Kabul. Officers go through a five-year training course in Kabul and take classes on tactical operations, narcotics investigations, traffic, criminal investigations, computer skills, and Islamic law.[25] The United States has concentrated on training constable-level recruits at the Central Training Center in Kabul, as well as at regional training centers in such cities as Kandahar, Mazar-e Sharif, Gardez, and Jalalabad. The U.S. State Department Bureau for International Narcotics and Law Enforcement Affairs contracted DynCorp to oversee and train the police, as well as help build training facilities.[26] The United States and Germany had trained approximately 33,000 police by the end of 2004 out of a target of 50,000. The U.S. Department of Defense has also deployed police mentoring teams to assist police personnel once they return to their local areas.

While it is not clear how Afghan and international officials decided on the target of 50,000 police, this works out to a ratio of approximately 175 Afghan police per 100,000 inhabitants.[27] As Figure 4.3 highlights, this level is low compared with other police-to-population ratios in the region. For example, Jordan's ratio is approximately 600 police per 100,000 inhabitants, Kazakhstan is 464, Kyrgyzstan is 340, and Russia is 1,222. Afghanistan's police ratio is also small compared with such developed countries as the United States and Germany, with ratios of 244 and 292, respectively.

Germany, the United States, and the United Nations Development Programme (UNDP) have helped build infrastructure and reorganize the Ministry of Interior. Since most police facilities were in extremely poor condition following the overthrow of the Taliban regime, the United States and Germany provided assistance to build infrastructure. Examples include the police officer training academy in Kabul, a number of regional training centers across the country,

---

[25] Interview with Jochen Rieso, Training Branch, German Project for Support of the Police, Kabul, June 27, 2004.

[26] Interview with members of DynCorp, Kabul and Gardez, June 25, 2004.

[27] This ratio assumes an Afghan population of 28,513,677. U.S. Census Bureau, International Data Base (www.census.gov/ipc/www/idbprint.html).

Figure 4.3
Number of Police Per Capita

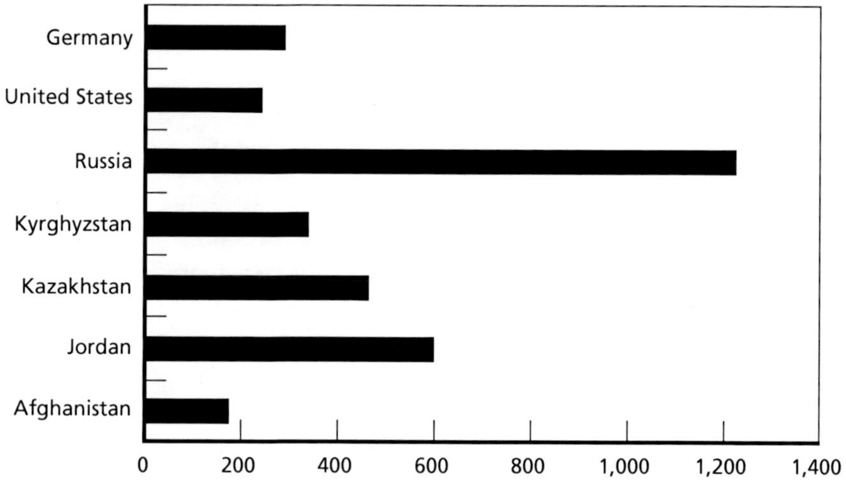

SOURCE: UNODC (2000).
NOTE: The years are from Germany (2000), the United States (1999), Russia (1994), Kyrghyzstan (2000), Kazakhstan (2000), and Jordan (1994).
RAND *MG374-4.3*

the Kabul Police Headquarters, police stations, and a criminal investigations facility in Kabul. In addition, they have embedded advisors into the ministry to help establish a driver's license and traffic system, rationalize the ministry's chain of command, and provide management training to senior staff.[28] These advisors also include private contractors, especially from DynCorp.[29] UNDP and a number of EU countries have helped the Ministry of Interior harmonize salary payment procedures, assess the existing payroll system, and review expenditure reporting procedures.

Finally, the United States, the United Kingdom, and contractors such as DynCorp have assisted the Afghan Ministry of Interior in

[28] Afghan Ministry of Defense (2004), p. 5.

[29] Interview with members of DynCorp, Kabul and Gardez, June 25, 2004.

counter-narcotics efforts. In the late 1990s, Afghanistan became the world's largest producer of opium and the source of 70 percent of illicit poppy grown worldwide.[30] The drug trade is fueled by a lack of government control over much of the country and the involvement of provincial governors, warlords, and corrupt government officials. In response, the Afghan government approved an Afghan National Drug Control Strategy in May 2003 and enacted a national narcotics control law in October 2003. To improve its institutional capacity, the government created a Counter Narcotics Directorate in the National Security Council to coordinate, monitor, and evaluate implementation of its drug strategy; a Counter Narcotics Police force; and an Afghan Special Narcotics Force to conduct interdiction operations.[31]

Reliable data on interdiction, eradication, and other steps are difficult to acquire because of the sensitivity of counter-narcotics operations. However, international assistance has included a broad strategy that has involved eradication, interdiction, alternative livelihoods, investigation and prosecution of drug traffickers, and public affairs. British forces and U.S. special operations forces under the command of Combined Forces Command–Afghanistan (CFC-A) have been involved in interdiction efforts against drug traffickers, stockpiles, and laboratories. DynCorp has also assisted in eradication efforts against opium poppy cultivators.[32] Germany, the United Kingdom, and the UN Office on Drugs and Crime have helped the Ministry of Interior build and train the border police and Counter Narcotic Police in Kabul and several provincial locations.[33] In addition, several countries have provided assistance to alternative liveli-

---

[30] Barnett R. Rubin and Andrea Armstrong, "Regional Issues in the Reconstruction of Afghanistan," *World Policy Journal*, Vol. 20, No. 1, Spring 2003, p. 32.

[31] Government of Afghanistan, *Berlin Conference Security Paper*, Kabul, March 2004b, pp. 2–5; Michael Bhatia, Kevin Lanigan, and Philip Wilkinson, *Minimal Investments, Minimal Results: The Failure of Security Policy in Afghanistan*, Kabul: Afghanistan Research and Evaluation Unit, June 2004, pp. 9–10.

[32] Government of Afghanistan (2004b), p. 5; interviews with members of DynCorp, Kabul and Gardez, June 25, 2004; UNODC, *Afghanistan: Opium Survey 2003*, 2003a, pp. 53, 95–96.

[33] UNODC, *Afghanistan: Counter Narcotics Law Enforcement*, Kabul, January 2004b.

hood and information awareness programs.[34] In late 2004, the United States pledged nearly $800 million for "Plan Afghanistan" to decrease the drug trade by implementing a public affairs campaign, improving Afghan law enforcement capabilities, encouraging farmers to grow other crops, and conducting eradication and interdiction operations.[35]

Justice System

There was no justice system existing in Afghanistan when the U.S. and allied forces overthrew the Taliban in December 2001. As a UNDP assessment mission concluded:

> The physical infrastructure of [the justice] institutions has been destroyed during the past decades of war and political upheaval and requires rehabilitation. In addition, and more critically, the country's legal "software"—the laws, legal decisions, legal studies, and texts of jurisprudence—are largely lost or scattered across the world.[36]

The December 2001 Bonn Agreement requested that the interim Afghan government establish a Judicial Commission to "rebuild the domestic justice system in accordance with Islamic principles, international standards, the rule of law, and Afghan legal traditions."[37] Consequently, the Afghan government established a Judicial Reform Commission in May 2002 to oversee and coordinate reconstruction of the justice system. The commission was disbanded several months later because of concerns about its composition and

---

[34] Government of Afghanistan (2004b), p. 2.

[35] John P. Walters, "Afghans' Drug War: U.S. Plans to Assail Several Fronts," *Washington Times*, November 26, 2004. (Walters is the director of the U.S. Office of National Drug Control Policy.)

[36] UNDP, *Rebuilding the Justice Sector of Afghanistan*, Kabul: United Nations Development Programme, January 2003, p. IA.

[37] The Bonn Agreement (2001), article II, paragraph 2.

agenda, and was reestablished in December 2002.[38] Italy has assisted the government as lead nation for justice sector reform, with the aid of the United Nations and United States. Judicial reform efforts can be divided into at least four major categories: establishing a body of laws; training prosecutors, lawyers, and Ministry of Justice officers; building physical infrastructure; and improving detention and prison capacity. We were not able to find reliable quantitative data on justice outputs, such as the number of prisons, detentions centers, and other judicial facilities refurbished or built. Instead, we relied on a qualitative assessment.

The United States provided approximately $10 million to justice sector reform in 2004, out of a total of $2.1 billion in assistance. In addition, international donors supplied a substantial amount of equipment. Examples include replenishing and refurbishing libraries in 20 law and sharia schools, as well as providing computers, communications equipment, and other basic equipment to the Supreme Court, Attorney General's offices, and Ministry of Justice.[39]

One of the Italian government's most significant goals was to develop a new, streamlined interim code of criminal procedure, which was established by presidential decree in February 2004. The interim code was the subject of some controversy. It was prepared by Italian officials with help from U.S. military lawyers but had relatively little input or support from the Afghan justice institutions. In addition, libraries and legal collections were largely depleted or destroyed during several decades of civil war, erasing a rich and elaborate legal tradition. No comprehensive collection or official record of laws survived, and institutions and lawyers had little or no access to most texts. This absence presented a serious challenge to reconstructing the justice system, since the compilation and indexing of legislation is essential to reestablishing a rule of law. Consequently,

---

38 Interviews with Carlos Batori, Counselor and Deputy Head of Mission, Italian Government, Kabul, June 22, 2004, and with Col. Gary Medvigy, Office of Military Cooperation–Afghanistan, June 24, 2004.

39 Government of Afghanistan, *Justice Public Investment Programme*, Kabul, February 2004a, p. 9.

the Italian government hired the International Development Law Organization to assemble and index more than 2,400 Afghan laws. This collection represented much of the legislation produced during the last century; it was digitalized and saved for the Ministry of Justice and other bodies on CD-ROMs.[40] Consequently, the establishment of a code of criminal procedure has been slow.

One of the greatest justice needs has been to improve the quality of judicial personnel.[41] The Judicial Reform Commission established two training programs for sharia faculty graduates and Ministry of Justice prosecutors and judges. In addition, the Italian Ministry of Foreign Affairs contracted the International Development Law Organization to train judges in civil and commercial law. It also asked the International Institute of Higher Studies in Criminal Sciences to provide training in criminal justice and human rights. Both organizations coordinated with the Judicial Reform Commission and the Italian government to train 450 judges and prosecutors from Kabul and the provinces. Each participant received 300 hours of training on judicial skills, human rights, and on civil, criminal, commercial, and international law matters. Topics included contracts and contractual liability, company law, and evidentiary techniques in comparative criminal justice systems.

As noted earlier, the judicial infrastructure was virtually nonexistent. Italy, the United States, and UNDP assisted the Afghan government in reconstructing and refurbishing courthouses, prosecutor's offices, and other justice infrastructure. UNDP took a leading role through its project on "Rebuilding the Justice Sector of Afghanistan." The project rehabilitated provincial justice buildings (including courts), Attorney General's offices, Ministry of Justice buildings, and prisons in the provinces of Kunduz, Badakhshan, Baghdis, Herat, Nangahar, Paktia, and Kabul.[42]

---

[40] Interview with Carlos Batori, Counselor and Deputy Head of Mission, Italian Government, Kabul, June 22, 2004.

[41] Miller and Perito (2004).

[42] Interview with senior official, UNDP, Kabul, June 23, 2004.

Finally, there have been some efforts to improve detention and prison capacity. In March 2003, the Afghan government shifted prison responsibility from the Ministry of Interior to the Ministry of Justice to minimize the likelihood of torture and human rights violations.[43] The UN Office on Drugs and Crime has been involved in rehabilitating prison facilities in Kabul, establishing a Prison Administration Department within the Ministry of Justice, and drafting a new penitentiary law in accordance with UN Standard Minimum Rules of the Treatment of Prisoners.[44] UNICEF (the UN Children's Fund) and the Afghan Ministry of Justice also led a joint assessment of the juvenile-justice system, created pilot programs of alternatives to custody and rehabilitation, and undertook capacity-building programs regarding juvenile-justice standards.[45] However, there are major challenges. One is the absence of prison and detention infrastructure outside of the capital region. Other challenges include substandard prison conditions and the use of torture.[46] As one Amnesty International report concluded:

> Prisons, an essential component of [the criminal justice] system, are crumbling after years of neglect and lack trained and qualified staff ... Prisoners are being held for months in overcrowded cells, some of them shackled, with inadequate bedding and food. Staff have received no training and have not been paid for

[43] Interview with Dr. Mohammad Qasim Hashimzai, Afghan Deputy Minister of Justice, Kabul, June 26, 2004.

[44] Interview with Carla Ciavarella, chief technical advisor for prisons, UNODC, Kabul, June 24, 2004; UNODC, *Programme of the Government of Afghanistan in Co-operation with the Office on Drugs and Crime, Progress Report*, Kabul, June 2004c.

[45] United Nations, *Civil and Political Rights, Including the Questions of Independence of the Judiciary, Administration of Justice, Impunity*, E/CN.4/2004/51, February 27, 2004a, p. 13.

[46] Carla Ciavarella, *Reform of the Penitentiary System in Afghanistan*, Kabul: United Nations Office on Drugs and Crime, 2004, pp. 3–4; interview with Afghan National Security Council official, Kabul, June 24, 2004; Human Rights Watch, *All Our Hopes Are Crushed: Violence and Repression in Western Afghanistan*, New York, 2002.

> months. Prisoners and detainees are not being held in safety, some are suffering ill-treatment or even torture.[47]

The Defense Sector

Efforts to reconstruct the Afghan military have included three major activities: building the ANA; reforming the Ministry of Defense; and disarming, demobilizing, and reintegrating ex-combatants. Afghan Ministry of Defense documents have explicitly noted that the military's major objective is to combat internal security threats to the state: "A trained, well equipped, and professional army will reduce the threat from terrorists, defend against insurgency, will free the regions from undisciplined and abusive militias, and will secure the country's borders against foreign foes."[48] The military currently has little external security function and no meaningful power-projection capabilities. For the next several years, U.S. and allied forces will act as the security guarantor against external attacks.

In FY 2004, the United States provided $549 million to the ANA and $45 million to DDR. In addition, the United States and other countries have provided equipment to the ANA, including assault rifles, machine-guns, mortars, antitank grenade launchers, radio sets, and ammunition. The United States has deployed a peak of approximately 20,000 soldiers under CFC-A to combat al Qaeda and Taliban insurgents, train ANA soldiers, and assist with reconstruction efforts. This translates into approximately one soldier per thousand inhabitants in Afghanistan. In addition, NATO has deployed a peak of 8,000 soldiers as part of the International Security Assistance Force (ISAF).[49] While most of the NATO forces have been deployed to Kabul to maintain security of the capital region, some have gone to provincial reconstruction teams in Meymana, Mazar-e

---

[47] Amnesty International, *Afghanistan: Crumbling Prison System Desperately in Need of Repair*, New York, 2003, p. 1.

[48] Afghan Ministry of Defense (2004a), p. 3.

[49] ISAF numbers come from U.S. Department of State, *Capitol Hill Monthly Update*, September 2004c.

Sharif, Konduz, Baghlan, and Feyzabad. By the end of 2004, there were 19 provincial reconstruction teams. These included thirteen under U.S. command, one under New Zealand command, and five under NATO command. These teams consist of between 60 and 100 personnel and are composed of civil affairs units, special operations forces, force protection, psychological operations personnel, military and security observers, and, for U.S. teams, USAID and State Department personnel.

Figure 4.4 shows the peak military presence levels in nation-building operations since World War II. The number of international troops per capita in Afghanistan is significantly less than almost every

Figure 4.4
Peak Military Presence Per Capita

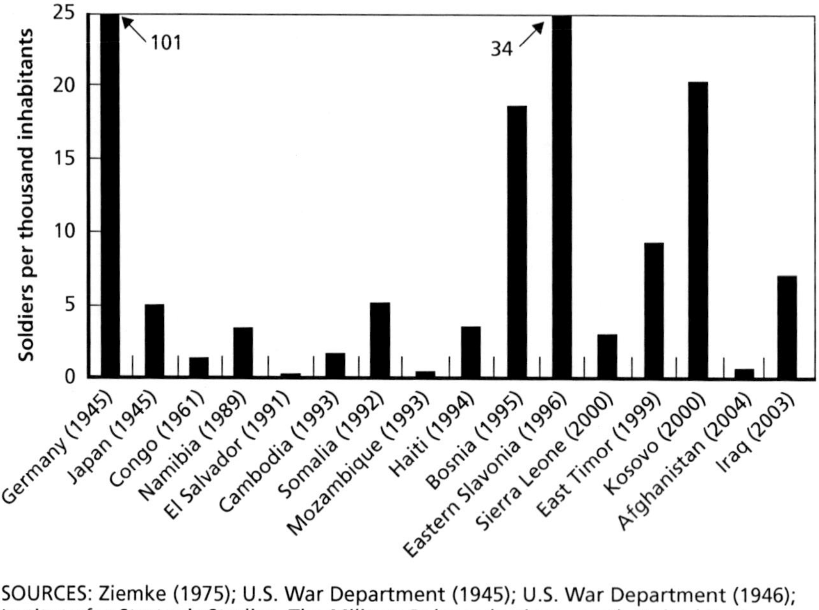

SOURCES: Ziemke (1975); U.S. War Department (1945); U.S. War Department (1946); Institute for Strategic Studies, *The Military Balance* (various years); United Nations, Department of Peacekeeping Operations (www.un.org/Depts/dpko); Jane's Information Group, Jane's Online (www.janes.com); Ramsbotham and Woodhouse (1999); United Nations Department of Public Information, *Yearbook of the United Nations* (various years). Source of population data: U.S. Census Bureau, International Data Base (www.census.gov).

RAND *MG374-4.4*

nation-building operation since World War II, except for the UN missions in El Salvador and Mozambique. The United States and other actors adopted a "light footprint" approach largely because Afghanistan had a history of resistance to foreign intervention. The concern was that a large deployment of international forces might trigger a destabilizing insurgency.[50] However, several U.S. government officials, such as General James Jones, Supreme Allied Commander, Europe, have acknowledged that the level of NATO and U.S. military forces has been low and under-resourced.[51]

The United States has been the lead nation for building the ANA, although French, British, Turkish, and other military instructors have also been involved.[52] Training began in May 2002, when the ANA's first regular army battalion commenced 10 weeks of infantry and combat training at the Kabul Military Training Center. U.S. Special Operations Forces, assigned to 1st Battalion, 3rd Special Forces Group, provided the initial training.[53] Combined Joint Task Force Phoenix and the Office of Military Cooperation–Afghanistan currently oversaw ANA training in areas ranging from recruiting to combat operations. New Afghan recruits received training on basic rifle marksmanship, platoon and company-level tactics, use of heavy weapons, and engineering, scout, and medical skills. Attrition rates

---

[50] Simon Chesterman, *You, the People: The United Nations, Transitional Administration, and State-Building*, New York: Oxford University Press, 2004, pp. 89–92; Simon Chesterman, "Walking Softly in Afghanistan: The Future of UN State-Building," *Survival*, Vol. 44, No. 3, Autumn 2002, pp. 37–46; United Nations, *Report of the Secretary-General on the Situation in Afghanistan and Its Implications for International Peace and Security*, A/56/875-S/2002/278, 2002a, paragraph 98.

[51] *Afghanistan Stabilization and Reconstruction: A Status Report*, Hearing Before the Committee on Foreign Relations, United States Senate, 108-460, January 27, 2004, pp. 14, 17–18.

[52] On training of the ANA, see Anja Manuel and P. W. Singer, "A New Model Afghan Army," *Foreign Affairs*, Vol. 81, No. 4, July/August 2002, pp. 44–59, and Luke Hill, "NATO to Quit Bosnia, Debates U.S. Proposals," *Jane's Defence Weekly*, Vol. 40, No. 23, December 10, 2003, p. 6.

[53] Anthony Davis, "Kabul's Security Dilemma," *Jane's Defence Weekly*, Vol. 37, No. 24, June 12, 2002, pp. 26–27; Mark Sedra, *Challenging the Warlord Culture: Security Sector Reform in Post-Taliban Afghanistan*, Bonn, Germany: Bonn International Center for Conversion, 2002, pp. 28–30.

were initially high; Afghanistan's 1st Battalion had an attrition rate of approximately 50 percent. But the rate eventually dropped to 10 percent per month by the summer of 2003, and between 2 percent and 3 percent per month by 2004.[54]

The United States and coalition forces had trained approximately 16,000 ANA recruits by the end of 2004, out of a target of 70,000.[55] As Figure 4.5 shows, the ANA is larger than most—though not all—warlord militias. The first ANA graduates went into the

Figure 4.5
Power of the Afghan National Army, Major Warlords, and Other Factions

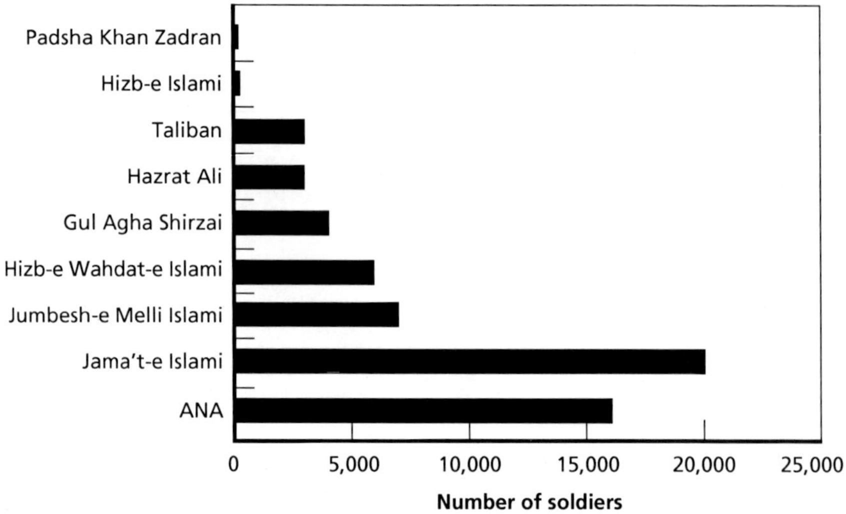

SOURCE: The number of soldiers is from IISS (2003), p. 134, and Jane's Information Group (2004b).
RAND *MG374-4.5*

---

[54] Attrition has been caused by a number of factors, such as low pay rates and apparent misunderstandings between ANA recruits and the U.S. military. For example, some Afghan soldiers believed they would be taken to the United States for training. On attrition rates, see Afghan Ministry of Defense (2004), pp. 6–8; U.S. State Department (2004b), p. 2; The White House, *Rebuilding Afghanistan*, 2004.

[55] Interview with Maj. Gen. Craig P. Weston, Chief, Office of Military Cooperation–Afghanistan, Kabul, June 23, 2004.

Central Corps and its supporting garrisons. The Central Corps included 23 battalions, or *kandaks*, and was deployed primarily to the Kabul area.[56] U.S. and Afghan officials plan to train approximately 70,000 soldiers by 2009 and deploy them to four regional commands: First Regional Command in Kandahar, Second Regional Command in Gardez, Third Regional Command in Mazar-e Sharif, and Fourth Regional Command in Herat.[57] Units of the Central Corps have been deployed throughout the country to conduct combat operations against Taliban and al Qaeda forces, oversee the collection of heavy weapons, stem inter-factional fighting, and enhance security for loya jirga delegates. In July 2003, for example, the ANA launched "Operation Warrior Sweep" with U.S. forces in the Paktia province against Taliban and al Qaeda forces. This was followed in November 2003 by "Operation Mountain Resolve" in the Nuristan and Kunar provinces. The ANA has deployed outside of Kabul to stem factional inter-fighting in such areas as Herat and Maimana. During the constitutional loya jirga in December 2003, the ANA was deployed in the capital region to enhance security for the delegates. In 2004, the ANA conducted combat operations in a number of provinces in the east and south, such as Kunar, Uruzgan, Helmand, and Paktia. In other areas, such as Herat, the government deployed ANA and police forces to patrol roads, secure government and UN buildings, and institute a curfew following the removal of Ismail Khan.

The Ministry of Defense began the DDR of ex-combatants in October 2003. It asked UNDP to oversee the process, officially referred to as the "Afghan New Beginnings Program." The overall objective is to decrease the supply of armed combatants in Afghanistan, create income-generating opportunities for them, and provide economic support to their communities. Reintegration areas include agriculture, teaching, information technology, small business, carpentry, and public works. A referral service for those wishing to join the

---

[56] A kandak consists of approximately 750 to 800 soldiers.

[57] Government of Afghanistan (2004b), pp. 8–9.

ANA or police was also established.[58] The United Nations and Afghan Ministry of Defense inaugurated a pilot phase to disarm, demobilize, and reintegrate 1,000 ex-combatants in late 2003 in six areas: Kunduz, Mazar-e Sharif, Kabul, Gardez, Kandahar, and Bamyan. Herat and Jalalabad were added later. As Figure 4.6 illustrates, approximately 30,000 combatants out of an initial target of 100,000 went through the DDR program by the end of 2004. The target has since been reduced to 60,000 combatants. Estimates of the actual number of militia and other non-statutory armed forces in Afghanistan range from a low of 60,000 to as many as 200,000.[59]

Figure 4.6
Number of Ex-Combatants Who Completed DDR Program

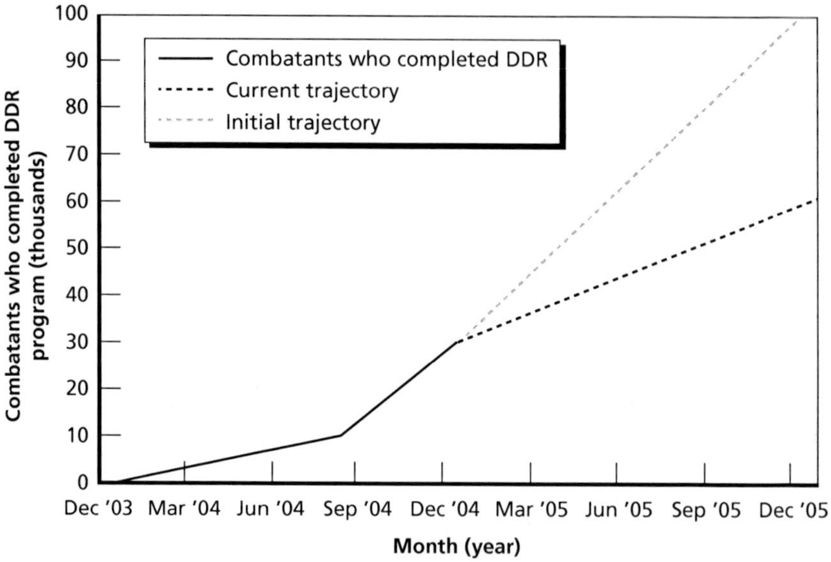

SOURCE: Interview with officials from Afghanistan's New Beginnings Program.
RAND *MG374-4.6*

---

[58] Afghanistan Government Inter-Ministerial Reintegration Team, *Disarmament, Demobilization, and Reintegration (DDR) in Afghanistan*, working draft, Kabul, April 2004, p. 17.

[59] Interview with senior officials, U.S. State Department, U.S. Defense Department, and Afghanistan National Security Council, Washington, D.C., June–August 2004.

There is little indication that the Afghan New Beginnings Program will be able to meet its target goal, leaving thousands of combatants at large throughout the country.

The DDR program has presented several challenges. First, warlords have refused to demobilize many of their fighters. The Bonn Agreement did not contain an agreement on DDR. UN drafters initially included a paragraph calling for the DDR of non-statutory forces, but Northern Alliance and other delegates strongly objected.[60] The final text simply stated that "all mujahidin, Afghan armed forces, and armed groups in the country shall come under the command and control of the Interim Authority, and be reorganized according to the requirements of the new Afghan security and armed forces."[61] Since many warlords and regional commanders perceived Defense Minister Mohammed Fahim as a rival faction leader, they viewed demilitarization and demobilization as a zero-sum game that would increase Fahim's relative power at their expense. Second, many of the officers and soldiers listed on the rolls of units to be disbanded or downsized have not existed. Some commanders have inflated the number of soldiers or created "ghost forces" to receive DDR funds from the Ministry of Defense.[62] Third, weapons collected by the United Nations and Afghan government have not been destroyed but have been sent to armories such as the one in Kabul. Several UN officials have expressed concern that they are not secure and may end up on the black market.[63] During the UN operation in Mozambique in the early 1990s, for example, weapons collected during the DDR process were stolen from government stockpiles and ended up on the black

---

[60] Barnett R. Rubin, "Identifying Options and Entry Points for Disarmament, Demobilization, and Reintegration in Afghanistan," working paper, Center on International Cooperation, New York University, March 2003.

[61] The Bonn Agreement (2001), article V, paragraph 1.

[62] Afghanistan Government Inter-Ministerial Reintegration Team (2004), pp. 7–8; Bhatia, Lanigan, and Wilkinson (2004), p. 16. Interview with Afghan National Security Council official, Kabul, June 24, 2004.

[63] Interview with UN officials, Kabul, June 22–24, 2004.

market.[64] Finally, significant poverty in Afghanistan has made it difficult to reintegrate ex-combatants and ensure steady work.

The United States, coalition forces, and such U.S.-based firms as MPRI have also assisted in reforming the Ministry of Defense. This included developing a national military strategy, organizing the Ministry of Defense and General Staff, training senior ministry officials, and improving management systems in such areas as personnel, logistics, acquisition, operational command and control, and budgeting systems. Finally, in 2003, the U.S. government established a new strategy titled "Accelerating Success" to achieve more ethnic and religious balance in staffing major ministries, speed up construction of the ANA and other security forces, and increase the pace of economic and social reconstruction.[65]

Outcomes

How successful have U.S. and allied efforts been in reconstructing Afghanistan's internal security system? In particular, how effective have Afghanistan's police, military, and justice systems been in dealing with the most pressing security threats to the state? The information presented in this section strongly suggests that there is little security in notable parts of the country and that the justice system is poorly functioning. The number of terrorist attacks and the number of deaths caused by terrorism have increased significantly. Public opinion polls show that many Afghans believe that security is the most significant problem facing the country. Warlords and regional commanders are still powerful, although there has been success in decreasing the power of some of them. The cultivation of poppy has increased significantly since 2002. And Afghanistan still lacks an effective rule of law.

---

[64] Eric Berman, *Managing Arms in Peace Processes: Mozambique*, Geneva: United Nations Publications, 1996, pp. 72–73; Christopher Smith, "The International Trade in Small Arms," *Jane's Intelligence Review*, Vol. 7, No. 9, 1995, p. 427.

[65] S. Frederick Starr, *U.S. Afghanistan Policy: It's Working*, Washington, D.C.: Central Asia–Caucasus Institute, Johns Hopkins University, 2004, pp. 4–18.

Reliable data on security sector reform are extremely limited. In the absence of a viable central government or a central statistics agency, little data have been systematically collected since 2001. We were not able to find any viable crime statistics (including homicide rates). We found only two public opinion polls: one conducted by the Asia Foundation and the other by the International Republican Institute. In the justice sector, we found no quantitative data on such indicators as the recidivism rate or the average number of days a prisoner is in detention before an adjudication hearing. We also found no reliable data on security sector indicators before 2001, making it difficult to compare levels of violence before 2001 with levels during the post-Taliban era. In the absence of such measures, we have relied on five proxy measures for the level of security and the effectiveness of the rule of law:

- Terrorist attacks and deaths from terrorist attacks
- Public perceptions of security
- Power of warlords and regional commanders
- Drug cultivation
- Perceptions of the rule of law.

Terrorist Attacks and Deaths from Terrorist Attacks

Figures 4.7 and 4.8 show that the number of terrorist attacks increased from January 2002 to December 2004. One of the most significant events was the September 2004 rocket attack against President Karzai in Gardez. The data, which come from the RAND-MIPT Terrorism Incident Database, capture the number of terrorist attacks and deaths.[66] Terrorism is defined as the use of political vio-

---

[66] Based on a review of data collected from such sources as the Afghanistan Non-Governmental Organization Security Office, it appears that the RAND-MIPT Terrorism Incident Database underestimates the number of attacks and deaths. It is not clear, however, the degree to which it underestimates the actual numbers. Nonetheless, the RAND-MIPT database is still the most comprehensive collection of terrorist and insurgent incidents since January 2002.

Figure 4.7
Number of Terrorist Attacks, 2002–2004

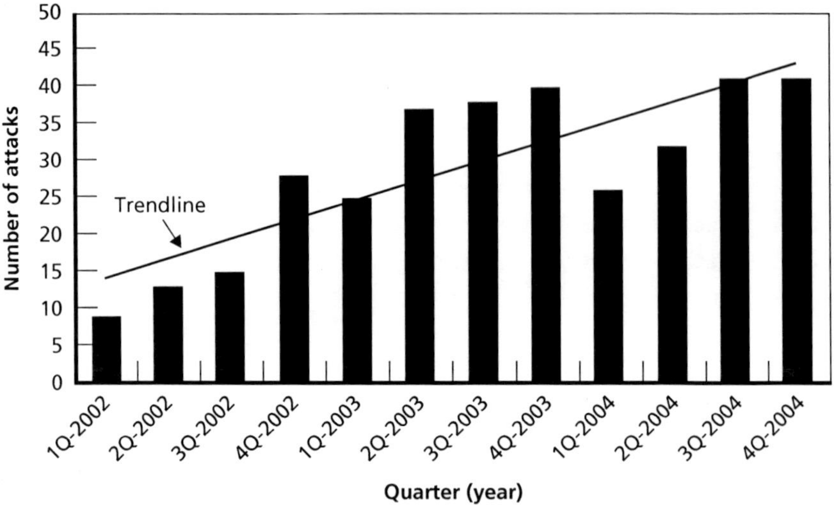

SOURCES: RAND-MIPT Terrorism Incident Database; Afghanistan Non-Governmental Organization Security Office, *ANSO Security Situation Summary* (various reports).
RAND *MG374-4.7*

Figure 4.8
Number of Deaths from Terrorist Attacks, 2002–2004

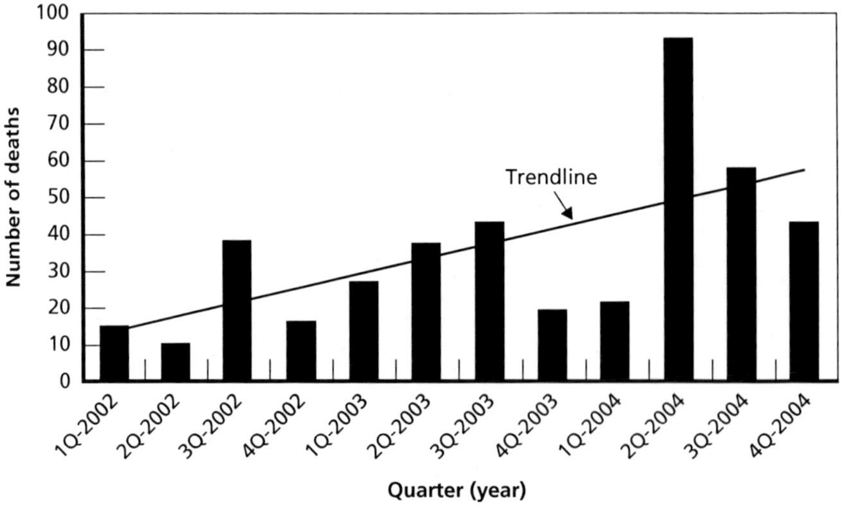

SOURCES: RAND-MIPT Terrorism Incident Database; Afghanistan Non-Governmental Organization Security Office, *ANSO Security Situation Summary* (various reports).
RAND *MG374-4.8*

lence, or the threat of violence, to create an atmosphere of fear; it can include efforts to coerce others into actions they would not otherwise undertake or to deter them from actions they would otherwise have taken.[67] The data include terrorist attacks on Afghan civilians, international aid workers, and coalition forces. The data do not capture military combat between coalition forces and insurgents, unless it comes under the definition of terrorism. Nor does it capture crime rates.

In contrast to the increase in terrorism, U.S. government data show a significant *decrease* in the number of terrorist attacks against U.S. and other coalition forces in 2004.[68] This suggests that the Taliban, al Qaeda, and other groups such as Gulbuddin Hekmatyar's Hizb-e Islami have shifted their strategy from targeting coalition forces to attacking Afghan civilians and personnel of NGOs. Part of the reason for this shift may be that the number of U.S. forces involved in Operation Enduring Freedom increased from less than 10,000 in 2003 to nearly 20,000 by late 2004.[69] Faced with a larger and more viable fighting force, Taliban and other insurgent forces shifted toward softer and easier targets. Examples include Afghans organizing or otherwise involved in election work, NGO workers, and Afghan citizens believed to be cooperating with coalition forces or the Afghan government. In October 2004, Jaish-e Muslimeen abducted three UN staff members in Kabul. Attacks have occurred throughout the country, although most have been in the south and east in such provinces as Nangarhar, Paktia, Paktika, and Khowst.[70]

---

[67] On the definition of terrorism, also see Bruce Hoffman, *Inside Terrorism*, New York: Columbia University Press, 1998, pp. 13–44.

[68] Interview with United States Army officials, November 2004.

[69] Michael O'Hanlon and Adriana Lins de Albuquerque, *Afghanistan Index: Tracking Variables of Reconstruction and Security in Post-Taliban Afghanistan*, Washington, D.C.: Brookings Institution, November 15, 2004.

[70] "Country Risk Assessment: Afghanistan," *Jane's Intelligence Review*, Vol. 16, No. 5, May 2004, pp. 38–41; Bhatia, Lanigan, and Wilkinson (2004), pp. 1–8; Anthony Davis, "Afghan Security Deteriorates as Taliban Regroup," *Jane's Intelligence Review*, Vol. 15, No. 5, May 2003, pp. 10–15.

The result has been a decrease in security for Afghans and foreigners, especially those living in the east and south. Road travel in many areas is dangerous, and crime continues to be a major problem. As one security assessment concluded: "The level of criminal activity —characterized by increasing numbers of armed robberies, abductions, and murders even in areas controlled by the ANA and police patrols—is still high."[71] Inter-factional fighting continues among regional commanders in such provinces as Herat, Nangarhar, Nuristan, Logar, Laghman, and Badghis.[72]

The increasing number of terrorist attacks is caused by at least three factors. First, ANA forces are not strong enough to defeat Taliban and Hizb-e Islami forces by themselves. They have been tenacious fighters in battle.[73] But they are not yet self-sufficient, and still rely on embedded U.S. special operations forces and U.S. air support during combat. There are no reliable statistics on the numerical strength of Taliban forces, although most indicators suggest they are weaker than they were in 2001. They have only been able to mount a low-grade insurgency, and they control little territory in the sense of taking and holding land. Data extrapolated from several sources suggest that the Taliban may possess between 2,000 and 4,000 full-time fighters.[74] Second, although the number of U.S. and coalition war-fighting forces in Afghanistan has increased, it is low—at one soldier per thousand inhabitants. This contrasts, for example, with the more than seven U.S. soldiers per thousand inhabitants in Iraq. Third, Taliban and Hizb-e Islami forces continue to benefit from porous borders along the Afghan-Pakistani frontier and assistance from

---

[71] *ANSO Security Situation Summary*, Weekly Report 039, September 24–30, 2004, p. 15.

[72] Carlotta Gall, "21 Killed in Afghanistan Attacks Directed at Provincial Governor," *New York Times*, August 15, 2004; *ANSO Security Situation Summary*, Weekly Report 039, September 24–30, 2004, p. 7; *ANSO Security Situation Summary*, Weekly Report 036, September 3–9, 2004, p. 5; *ANSO Security Situation Summary*, Weekly Report 038, September 17–23, 2004, pp. 7–8.

[73] Interview with Maj. Gen. Craig P. Weston, Chief, Office of Military Cooperation–Afghanistan, Kabul, June 23, 2004.

[74] Jane's Information Group (2004b).

sources in Pakistan and the Muslim world, channeled through Pashtun tribesmen on the Afghan-Pakistani border. A key question to defeating insurgents is whether the Taliban will continue to enjoy sanctuary in Pakistan.

Public Perceptions of Security

Public opinion polls show that the Afghan population considers the absence of security as the most significant problem facing the country. Opinion polls are a useful outcome measure for the security environment. Ideally, we would analyze opinion poll results over time and identify changing patterns in public views of the security environment. However, we were aware of only two public opinion polls following the collapse of the Taliban regime: one commissioned by the Asia Foundation and the other by the International Republican Institute.[75]

Public opinion data demonstrate at least two major trends. First, as Figure 4.9 highlights, approximately two-thirds of Afghans believe that security is the biggest problem facing the country, which includes threats from warlords, insurgent attacks, and other violence such as crime. The International Republican Institute poll also indicates that the most important priority of the Afghan government should be to disarm commanders and warlords. Other important security priorities have included strengthening the army and police, eliminating the Taliban, and removing al Qaeda.[76] The withdrawal in July 2004 of Médecins Sans Frontières, which had been in Afghanistan for nearly three decades, was a testament to the deteriorating security environment. A month earlier, five Médecins Sans

---

[75] The Asia Foundation, *Voter Education Planning Survey: Afghanistan 2004 National Elections*, Kabul, 2004; International Republican Institute, *Afghanistan: Election Day Survey*, Kabul, October 9, 2004.

[76] International Republican Institute (2004), p. 16.

Figure 4.9
Perceptions of Security

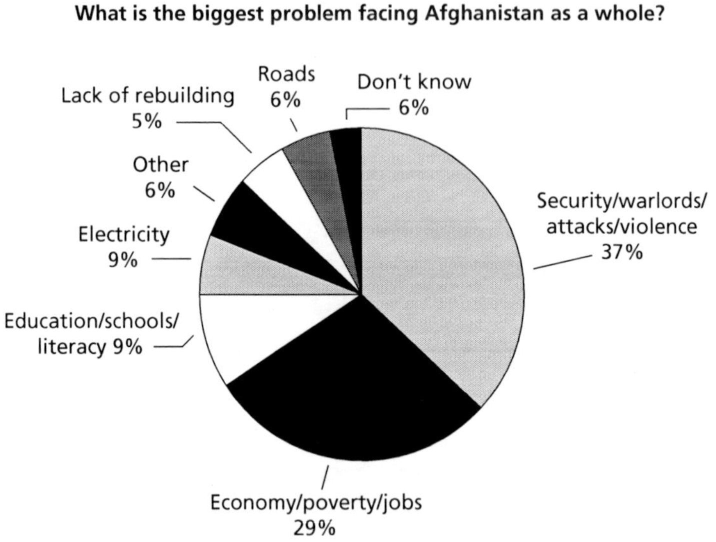

SOURCE: The Asia Foundation (2004), p. 104.
RAND *MG374-4.9*

Frontières workers were ambushed and shot dead in the northwestern province of Badghis. Second, the data also suggest that most Afghans believe the security situation is somewhat better than under Taliban rule. The Asia Foundation poll shows that approximately 35 percent feared for their personal safety in 2004, compared with 41 percent during the Taliban period.[77]

Power of Warlords and Regional Commanders

Warlords and regional commanders still remain strong throughout the country, although the Afghan government has made notable progress in curbing the power of several warlords. Examples of the latter

---

[77] The International Republican Institute poll also shows that more than 80 percent of Afghans believe that their living standard have improved since the end of the Taliban government (2004, p. 13).

include the removal of Herat Governor Ismail Khan and Kandahar Governor Gul Agha Shirzai.[78] Figure 4.10 illustrates the location of several major warlords and factions throughout the country. Pashtun warlord Pasha Khan Zadran has a force of several hundred militia and controls much of the Khost province. The northern part of the country has become a scene of rivalry between two major United Front factions, Jama't-e Islami and Jumbesh-e Melli Islami. Their leading figures, Abdul Rashid Dostum and Atta Mohammad, respectively, have been affiliated with the Karzai government. Other major warlords include Shirzai, who still retains some militia forces, and Shia

Figure 4.10
Geographic Distribution of Warlords and Factions

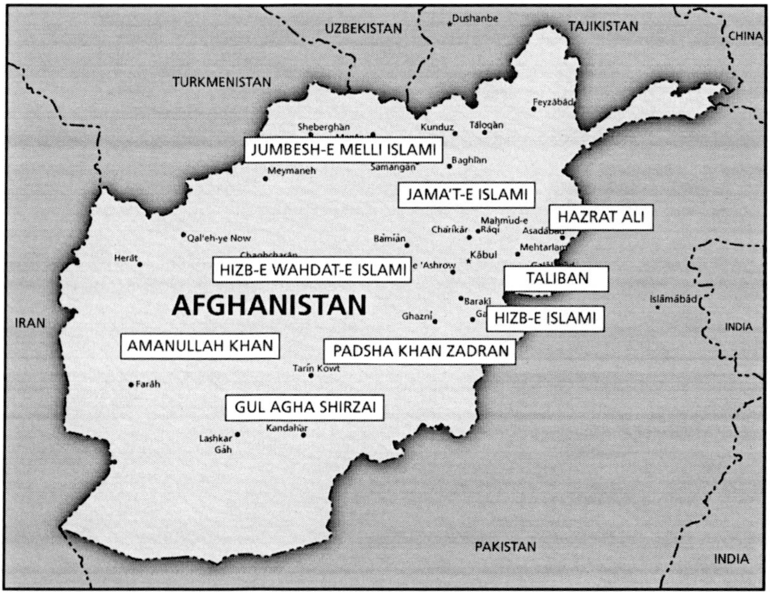

RAND *MG374-4.10*

[78] Starr (2004), pp. 4–5.

leader Karim Khalili. Khalili's Hizb-e Wahdat-e Islami dominates the Bamiyan province and the central Hazarajat region. The Taliban, remnants of al Qaeda, and members of Gulbuddin Hekmatyar's Hizb-e Islami faction have also been active along the Afghan-Pakistani border. In the Herat province, there are a number of commanders who control smaller factions, such as Amanullah Khan, Abdul Salam, and Zaher Naibzada.

Neighboring states and other outside powers have contributed to the power of warlords and to the weakness of the central government by providing financial assistance, weapons, and political support. There is some evidence that Russia has provided military equipment directly to Afghanistan's former defense minister, Abdul Qasim Fahim, instead of supplying the ANA. Iran has provided assistance to warlords in the west.[79] Pakistan has provided assistance to Pashtun factions, such as Gulbuddin Hekmatyar's Hizb-e Islami, through its Inter-Service Intelligence Directorate.[80] In addition, the U.S. and coalition forces have supplied assistance to warlords and military commanders in the south and east as part of Operation Enduring Freedom.[81] U.S. support has been a double-edged sword, though. The United States allied with a number of warlords beginning in 2001, such as Hazrat Ali and Mohammed Fahim, to defeat the Taliban and other insurgent forces.[82] However, a continuation of this policy weakens the central government by preserving the power of warlords.

Drug Cultivation

The cultivation of opium poppy has significantly increased since 2002. This contributes to security problems by strengthening the power of warlords, insurgents, and drug traffickers at the expense of

---

[79] Rubin and Armstrong (2003), p. 34; Sedra (2002).

[80] Davis (2003), p. 13.

[81] "Country Risk Assessment: Afghanistan," pp. 38–41; Bhatia, Lanigan, and Wilkinson (2004), p. 6; Davis (2003), pp. 10–15.

[82] Interview with Ambassador James Dobbins, former U.S. envoy to Afghanistan, Washington, D.C., September 21, 2004.

the state. As Antonio Maria Costa, executive director for the UN Office on Drugs and Crime, warned: "There is a palpable risk that Afghanistan will again turn into a failed state, this time in the hands of drug cartels and narco-terrorists."[83] Since at least 1980, mujahideen, warlords, and the Taliban regime used drug money to help fund their military campaigns and to earn a profit. In 1997, the United Nations and United States estimated that 96 percent of Afghan heroin came from areas under the Taliban control. The Taliban expanded the area available for opium production, as well as increased trade and transport routes through such neighboring countries as Pakistan.[84] In July 2000, Mullah Omar banned the cultivation—though not the trafficking—of opium poppy, which the Taliban effectively enforced. The ban caused a temporary decrease in the cultivation and production of opium in 2001. But much of the damage had already occurred, since Afghanistan steadily became a major producer of opium poppy during the Taliban regime.

Figure 4.11 shows that the cultivation of opium poppy has increased markedly since reconstruction efforts began in 2002. Poppy cultivation rose from 74,045 hectares in 2002 to an estimated 131,000 hectares in 2004. In addition, the income of Afghan opium farmers and traffickers was equivalent to nearly two-thirds the legal gross domestic product of the country. The number of provinces where opium poppy cultivation was reported increased from 18 in 1999, to 24 in 2002, to 28 in 2003, and to all 32 provinces in 2004. The main bazaar prices of opium increased from $65 per kilogram in 1995 to more than $350 per kilogram in 2002, and then fell to around $283 in 2003 and even further to $92 in 2004.[85] Even though the Taliban ban on opium poppy cultivation in 2000

---

83 UNODC (2003a), p. 1.

84 Rashid (2000), p. 119–120.

85 UNODC, *Afghanistan: Opium Survey 2004*, Vienna, 2004. UNODC, *The Opium Economy in Afghanistan: An International Problem*, 2nd edition, Vienna, 2003b; UNODC (2003a), pp. 1–10; Barnett R. Rubin, *Road to Ruin: Afghanistan's Booming Opium Industry*, New York: Center on International Cooperation, October 2004b.

Figure 4.11
Opium Cultivation, 1986–2004

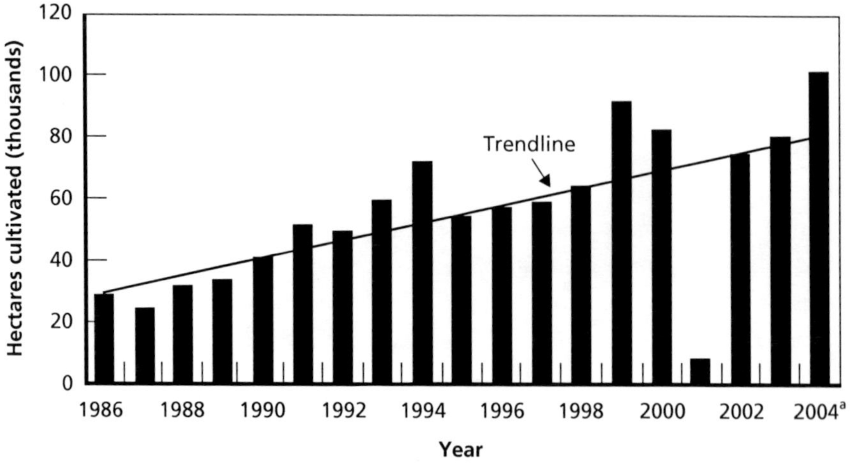

a Estimated.
SOURCE: UNODC (2000a).
RAND *MG374-4.11*

decreased the 2001 crop, Afghanistan became the world's largest producer of poppy during the Taliban rule and the source of 70 percent of global illicit poppy. The income from opium helped sustain the Taliban, al Qaeda, and the Islamic Movement of Uzbekistan, as well as some components of the Northern Alliance. The drug trade is a major source of revenue for warlords and insurgents in control of Afghanistan's border regions, as well as members of the Afghan government.[86] A leaked memo to U.S. Secretary of State Condoleezza Rice argued that the rise in drug cultivation and trafficking has been caused by British failure to eradicate more acreage and President Karzai's unwillingness "to assert strong leadership, even in his own province of Kandahar."[87]

---

86 Rubin and Armstrong (2003), p. 34.

87 David S. Cloud and Carlotta Gall, "U.S. Memo Faults Afghan Leader on Heroin Fight," *New York Times*, May 22, 2005. Frederick Starr (2004, p. 24) places most of the blame on European countries where most of the drugs are exported to: "Serious progress against the

Perception of the Rule of Law

Afghanistan's justice sector continues to face severe problems. Measuring the effectiveness of Afghanistan's judicial system is problematic in the absence of reliable data. However, World Bank data suggest that Afghanistan's rule of law is viewed as one of the least effective in the world. This measures the extent to which populations have confidence in, and abide by, the rules of society. It includes perceptions of the incidence of crime, the effectiveness and predictability of the judiciary, and the enforceability of contracts.[88] Figure 4.12 illustrates Afghanistan's rule of law from 1996 to 2004 in comparison to other countries in the region. The data allow us to make two tentative conclusions. First, Afghanistan's justice system started from a low base. When the United States helped overthrow the Taliban regime in 2001, Afghanistan had the lowest ranking justice system in the world. Furthermore, in comparison to other countries in the region—such as Iran, Pakistan, Russia, Tajikistan, Turkmenistan, and Uzbekistan—Afghanistan's justice system has been viewed as one of the least effective. Second, the justice system improved following the overthrow of the Taliban regime but deteriorated slightly between 2002 and 2004. Today, Afghanistan still has one of the most ineffective justice systems in the world.

There have been several challenges to improving justice sector outcomes. First, the central government's inability to decrease the power of warlords and exert control over the country has affected justice sector reform. Warlord commanders, who have been allowed to maintain de facto control over areas seized following the overthrow of the Taliban regime, established authority over local courts. The factional control of courts has led to intimidation of centrally appointed judges. Second, the Afghan government's inability and unwillingness

---

drug production in Afghanistan will begin only when the European Union admits that the problem traces directly to its own citizens' demand for heroin and that this places on Europe the obligation to provide the kind of massive help to the Afghans that the US has extended to Colombia."

[88] Daniel Kaufmann, Aart Kraay, and Massimo Mastruzzi, *Governance Matters III: Governance Indicators for 1996–2002*, Washington, D.C.: World Bank, 2003, p. 4.

Figure 4.12
Perception of the Rule of Law

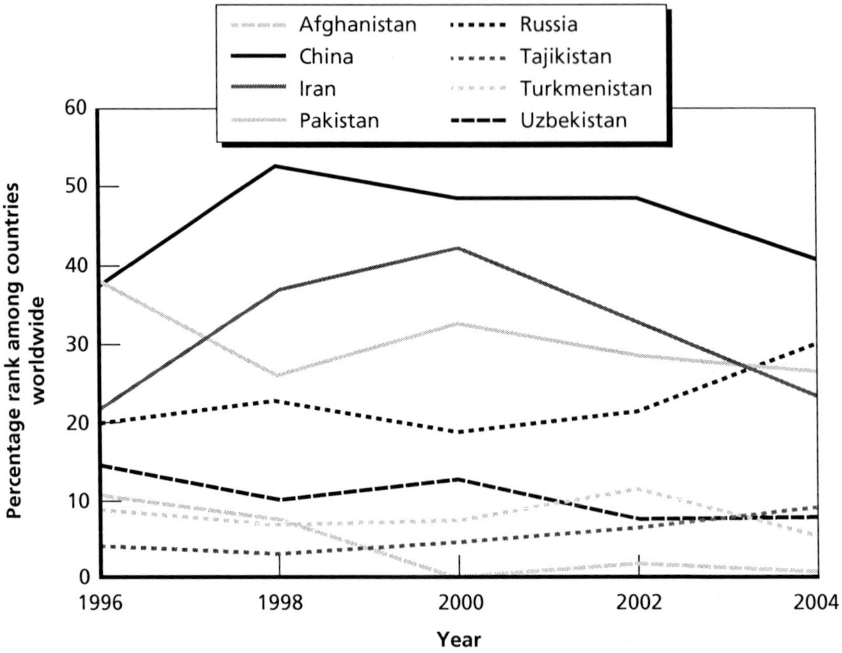

SOURCE: World Bank (2005).
RAND *MG374-4.12*

to address widespread and deep-rooted corruption has decreased the effectiveness of the justice system. Corruption is endemic in the justice system, partly because unqualified personnel loyal to various factions are sometimes installed as court officials. The Supreme Court and Attorney General's Office have been accused of significant corruption.[89] The World Bank concludes that Afghanistan is one of the most corrupt governments in the world; only Haiti and Equatorial

[89] Interview with Deputy Minister of Justice Mohammad Qasim Hashimzai, Kabul, June 26, 2004. Rama Mani, *Ending Impunity and Building Justice in Afghanistan*, Kabul: Afghanistan Research and Evaluation Unit, 2003, p. 2.

Guinea had lower corruption rankings in 2002.[90] A corrupt judiciary is a serious impediment to the success of Afghanistan's ability to establish a viable rule of law, since it cripples the legal and institutional mechanism designed to curb corruption.

Conclusions

What are the most important implications for current and future operations? American, European, and UN efforts to reconstruct internal security in Afghanistan have encountered numerous challenges. When reconstruction efforts began in 2001, Afghanistan ranked 89th out of 90 developing countries on the UN development index for human and income poverty.[91] America's military efforts were successful in curbing the use of Afghanistan as a launchpad for international terrorist groups, at least compared with the country's infiltration during the 1990s. But there are a number of broad implications:

- Providing a low input of financial, military, and other resources will yield a low outcome in security and justice indicators.
- Provincial civilian-military reconstruction teams can be useful in facilitating reconstruction and helping to win "hearts and minds."
- Establishing an independent and functioning justice system is equally as critical as training and equipping police and internal security forces.
- Security sector reform needs to involve the collection and assessment of input, output, and outcome measures, and to ultimately tie success to outcomes.
- Centralized "unity of command" is critical for coordinating security sector reform.

---

[90] Kaufmann, Kraay, and Mastruzzi (2003), pp. 113–115.

[91] UNDP, *Human Development Report 2001: Making New Technologies Work for Human Development*, New York, 2001, p. 151.

Afghanistan has been one of the lowest staffed and funded U.S., UN, or European nation-building operations since World War II. U.S. and other international civilian and military personnel accomplished much with the resources they were given. But the United States deployed one soldier per thousand Afghans and provided nearly $30 per person per year. Only the UN operations in El Salvador and Mozambique had lower levels of military forces, and only the UN operations in the Congo, Cambodia, and Sierra Leone had lower per-capita assistance levels. In addition, the target of 50,000 trained Afghan police will leave Afghanistan with a much smaller police-to-population ratio than most of its neighbors or developed countries. It is hard to imagine that the United States or European countries will devote substantially more resources to Afghanistan. U.S. government officials have strongly opposed providing more resources for reconstruction efforts as far back as 2001, despite the fact that Afghanistan was a safe haven for al Qaeda and other terrorists. However, if there is no increase in resources, Afghanistan will have a difficult time defeating its major internal security threats such as insurgents, warlords, and drugs traffickers.

The "golden hour" is a critical time for security sector reform during stability operations because it can prevent security from quickly spiraling out of control. In Afghanistan, significant levels of resources were not provided during the golden hour, the period immediately following the overthrow of the Taliban regime. Future efforts should be particularly mindful of the period following major combat operations. While follow-on steps will vary from operation to operation, they should involve training indigenous police and other internal security forces to take over the primary responsibility of ensuring stability. They should also involve civil-military reconstruction efforts. Indeed, the introduction of provincial reconstruction teams was an innovative development to reconstruct the country and win Afghan hearts and minds. In future operations, the military, in coordination with indigenous and international civil-sector planners, should consider deploying reconstruction teams to a variety of geographic regions to assist civilians, ensure stability, improve economic development, and provide other assistance.

Afghanistan demonstrated that reforming the police and security forces is not enough to create a secure environment. This seems to be a recurrent lesson of nation-building operations. Effective internal security forces require a functioning justice system, including courts and prisons. Arbitrary or politicized sentencing, an incompetent judiciary, and decrepit prison conditions quickly corrode and undermine whatever benefits come from better policing. A weak justice system also increases the prevalence of organized crime and can lead to a spiral of corruption, extrajudicial killings, and petty crime. The inability to establish a viable justice system has plagued most reconstruction efforts, such as Somalia, Haiti, El Salvador, Panama, and Afghanistan. The elements that underpin any internal security system—the police, military, and justice system—should be regarded as interlinked and interdependent. While it may be necessary to focus on reconstructing the police and security forces during the golden hour, substantial resources should quickly be devoted to the justice system. The United States, Italy, UNDP, and other international personnel needed to dedicate more resources to justice sector reform. In FY 2004, for example, the United States spent 55 times more on the ANA than on reconstructing the justice system, 16 times more on the police, and 12 times more on counter-narcotics. As Simon Chesterman has argued: "It seems fair to say that rule of law was not seen as a priority by either the Interim Authority, UNAMA [United Nations Assistance Mission in Afghanistan], or the donor community."[92]

Policymakers have not systematically collected and assessed input, output, and outcome measures. Too often, internal security assistance programs assess progress by compiling measurements such as financial assistance or the number of personnel trained. In Afghanistan, for instance, the State Department compiled and tracked an impressive list of quantitative and qualitative metrics for reconstruction. However, as far as we were aware, most were input and output measures. Examples include the number of ANA and police soldiers trained, number of combatants demobilized and rein-

[92] Chesterman (2004), p. 180.

tegrated, and number of judicial facilities constructed or rehabilitated. While important, these metrics provide little information about the security environment or the viability of the rule of law. Much better measures would be to compile crime rates (especially violent crime rates), key prosecutions, and public perceptions of security and justice —and to link these with inputs.

Finally, reconstruction efforts in Afghanistan were organized much differently than in other nation-building operations such as Iraq, East Timor, or Kosovo. Security sector reform centered on a lead-nation approach. In theory, each lead nation was supposed to contribute significant financial assistance, coordinate external assistance, and oversee reconstruction efforts in its sector. In practice, this approach did not work well. In too many areas—such as police training, counter-narcotics, and justice sector reform—participating countries did not perform adequately. In addition, the absence of unity of command created enforcement problems and led to what economist Mancur Olson famously referred to as a "collective action problem."[93] The need to overcome these problems makes it important to establish institutional arrangements that improve coordination. The establishment of the Afghan Reconstruction Group, which assisted the U.S. ambassador in such areas as political and economic sector reform, was an important step. In hindsight, security sector reform and overall reconstruction led and coordinated by one entity, perhaps the United States or United Nations, would have been preferable to the lead-nation approach.

---

[93] Mancur Olson, *The Logic of Collective Actions: Public Goods and the Theory of Groups*, Cambridge, Mass.: Harvard University Press, 1971, p. 2.

CHAPTER FIVE

Iraq

An international coalition led by the United States and the United Kingdom invaded Iraq on March 21, 2003, captured Baghdad on April 9, and declared an end to major combat operations on May 1, 2003. The declared reasons for the invasion were the failure of the Saddam Hussein regime to comply with UN Security Council Resolutions calling for Iraq to be disarmed of weapons of mass destruction. The United States and its coalition partners had concluded that only regime change would ensure this disarmament. Their expectation was that the removal of the senior layers of the Saddam regime would allow a reformed Iraqi government to come to power and to oversee a transition to democracy and economic reform. In reality, though, the unexpected weakness of the Iraqi civil and economic infrastructure, exacerbated by widespread insurgency and terrorism, led to a collapse of governance and order. The United States and the United Kingdom responded by establishing the Coalition Provisional Authority in May 2003 and taking on the responsibilities of occupying powers until the creation of a sovereign Iraqi Interim Government (IIG) on June 28, 2004.

Reconstituting the Iraqi security sector, which disintegrated in the wake of the defeat of the regime, has been one of the most critical challenges facing the United States and coalition forces in Iraq. The absence of security has threatened all aspects of the political and economic transition as well as the reconstruction of essential services. In particular, the Iraqi Police Service (IPS), which must form the cornerstone of a secure, stable, and democratic society, remains unable to enforce the rule of law in most of the country. Until the IPS becomes capable of enforcing order, troops from the Multi-National Force–Iraq (MNF-I), including the Iraqi military, will remain on the front line of Iraqi security, a situation acceptable neither to Iraqis nor to contributing nations. Without viable internal security institutions, the legitimacy and sovereignty of an already weak Iraqi government will remain in doubt.

This chapter examines the development of the Iraqi internal security sector by examining U.S., Iraqi, and other "inputs" into reconstructing internal security, assessing the security and justice "outputs," and examining security "outcomes" for Iraq and the international presence in the country. It concludes that, two years after the fall of the Saddam regime, political violence and crime remain unacceptably high, and the fear of crime and violence among Iraqis and foreigners threatens the political and economic reconstruction of Iraq. These outcomes are in part attributable to the fact that efforts to reconstruct and transform the Iraqi security sector, and in particular the police, have been hampered by a lack of preparation and planning, as well as delays in the mobilization of financial resources, deployment of personnel, and delivery of equipment. A worse-than-expected security situation has forced already-overstretched coalition forces to take on much of the responsibility for building Iraq's security sector. By the time of the transfer of authority to a sovereign Iraqi government, on June 28, 2004, the Iraqi security forces remained unable to enforce public order or the rule of law. It is clear that MNF-I will have to retain the leading internal security role throughout the planned schedule for Iraq's political transition, into 2006.[1]

The data available in post-conflict operations to assess performance and effectiveness are often poor. In Iraq, inferior data quality is a particular problem. The immaturity of Iraqi government institutions means that one is forced to rely on international, primarily U.S. gov-

---

[1] That is, when an elected, sovereign government is scheduled to be in place.

ernment, sources. Unfortunately, even the quality of these data is poor and uncertain. For instance, throughout the life of CPA reporting, the numbers of employed police sometimes varied by a margin of several thousand on a weekly basis. On one notable week in October 2004, the figures for the numbers of "in-service" police personnel being used by the Iraqi senior police officer and the coalition forces differed by some 60,000 people.[2] Serious data discrepancies were evidenced in the records of equipment being distributed among IPS stations. Calculating accurate and comprehensive figures for investment in Iraq's security sector is also problematic.[3] These data problems should be kept in mind when assessing performance in Iraq and, in particular, when undertaking comparisons with other cases.

This chapter is divided into five sections. First, it sketches the historical background to the Iraqi security sector. Second, it puts the Iraqi security sector into the wider, postwar context. Third, it outlines the steps taken by the coalition to build the Iraqi security sector from May 2003 to June 2004. This section focuses in turn on national security architecture, the police, the judiciary and prisons, the armed forces, and the intelligence services. Fourth, it examines security sector "outcomes" such as crime and violence. Fifth, it provides some conclusions and lessons identified.

---

[2] Interviews in Baghdad, October 2004.

[3] There were four main sources of funding for the Iraqi security sector: Iraq budgets, the Development Fund for Iraq, U.S. supplemental funds, and other donor assistance. The former can be accounted for in a reasonably transparent manner, and the latter is insignificant in financial terms. The problem comes when accounting for the Development Fund for Iraq (DFI), which was established by UN Security Council Resolution 1483 and administered by the CPA. The DFI provided the core of long-term Iraqi government financing from oil and other revenues as well as from transferred oil-for-food program assets. The amounts spent from DFI on security are unclear. Documentation obtained and our interviews with CPA personnel involved in the DFI allocation process, the Program Review Board, have been inconclusive. For the purposes of this study, we make the assumption that around $1 billion was allocated from DFI to the security sector during the course of 2003 and 2004, divided equally between police and armed forces programs.

Initial Conditions

After the British carved Iraq out of disparate provinces of the Ottoman Empire and installed the Hashemite monarchy in the aftermath of the First World War, they worked with the new ruling elite to build both a modern Iraqi state and a unified nation. The state-building project achieved some success by the 1958 revolution that overthrew the monarchy. Iraq had the trappings of a modern government, including ministries, police, and armed forces. The nation-building effort had been less successful as power had been concentrated in the hands of one community, the Sunni elite. Neither Sunni pan-Arabists, the Kurds, nor the Shiite religious establishment were reconciled to the nature of the Iraqi polity.

The 1958 revolution ushered in an era of coups and counter-coups in which power came increasingly to be held by minority cliques working through the armed forces. Politics was dominated by various strains of Arab nationalism, flavored with socialism. Kurds and Shiites were excluded, but Sunni communities were empowered at the expense of the landed elite. The second Ba'athist coup in 1968 consolidated in power a minority, conspiratorial party that proceeded to impose authoritarian rule that, by the late 1970s and 1980s, had many of the features of totalitarianism. This state was never all-powerful. It had at times used force or conciliation against the Kurds, the Shiite politico-religious movement, and against powerful tribes. But it did succeed in maintaining itself in power despite numerous internal and external challenges. It also destroyed most vestiges of the incipient civil society and, admittedly elitist, democracy that had begun to emerge under the monarchy.[4]

---

[4] Toby Dodge, *Inventing Iraq: The Failure of Nation-Building and a History Denied*, New York: Columbia University Press, 2003; Charles Tripp, *A History of Iraq*, 2nd edition, Cambridge, UK: Cambridge University Press, 2002; Nazih Ayubi, *Over-Stating the Arab State: Politics and Society in the Middle East*, London: I. B. Tauris, 1996.

Saddam's Mukhabarat State

By 2003, Iraq had become perhaps the epitome of the Mukhabarat state: one in which intelligence and security services linked to the ruling clan dominated politics and society. Because Saddam Hussein had come to power via the Ba'ath Party's security apparatus, it is perhaps not surprising that it was this network of agencies that held real power and imposed order on society. This made Iraq significantly different from states that may have appeared similar in nature, such as Syria and Egypt, in which the army played a greater role in domestic order—the praetorian model.[5]

Saddam created a number of overlapping internal security services, part of whose role was to monitor one another. Although the number and roles of the agencies changed over time, by 2003, the key agencies were the Special Security Organization, the Directorate of General Security, the Directorate of General Intelligence, the Directorate of Military Intelligence, and the Military Security Service. The Special Protection Apparatus and Special Republican Guard were part of this system but were concerned more with the regime's physical security than with deploying extensive policing or intelligence networks. All these agencies were overseen by the National Security Council, nominally headed by Saddam, and reported into the Presidential Secretariat around Saddam himself.[6]

These organizations had the lead on internal security. In addition, the Ba'ath Party had a variety of enforcement organizations that also undertook political policing and neighborhood security tasks. Iraqi Ministry of Interior (MoI) forces, including the police, had low status and low prestige.

The IPS, which had originally been formed under the British mandate, suffered from low professional standards, insufficient

---

[5] Andrew Rathmell, "Syria's Intelligence Services: Origins and Development," *Journal of Conflict Studies*, Vol. 16, No. 2, Fall 1996, pp. 75–96.

[6] UK Cabinet Office, "Iraq: Its Infrastructure of Concealment, Deception and Intimidation," February 3, 2003; Ibrahim al-Marashi, "Iraq's Security and Intelligence Network: A Guide and Analysis," *Middle East Review of International Affairs,* Vol. 6, No. 3, September 2002; Andrew Rathmell, "Iraqi Intelligence and Security Services," *International Defense Review*, May 1991.

resources, a lack of quality recruits, and rampant corruption.[7] The force had a military rank structure, was highly centralized, and was confined to basic policing functions such as dealing with petty crime and traffic offenses. The Iraqi police operated on a colonial policing model rather than a modern democratic model. Police officers spent most of their time in police stations, generally venturing out only when called to an incident. When they did so, the normal procedure was to round up possible suspects, extract confessions by force, and extort bribes from family members for release of the suspects. In addition to the police, the MoI also controlled the Vital Installation Guards, which protected government buildings, and some of the border security forces.

Although under Saddam there was little concept of a rule of law, the police did operate within a fairly clear judicial framework. The Iraqi justice system was a mixture of Napoleonic and British law, along with provisions for sharia family law. Tribal judicial structures held some sway in rural areas. Special security courts provided a veneer of legality for those accused of anti-regime or other serious crimes, but there was no concept of judicial independence under the Ba'ath regime. The police investigatory role was limited to the initial phase with prosecutors, who were members of the judiciary, undertaking the bulk of any investigation. Although they worked closely with the police, the relationship between police and prosecutors appears to have been poor, with prosecutors sometimes bribing police to obtain case files. More broadly, there was no concept of independent judicial oversight of the police and security services. The prison system in Saddam's Iraq was under the control of the MoI and Ministry of Labor. The police ran detention facilities in police stations. In addition, the other security agencies administered detention

---

[7] It should be noted, however, that the IPS officer corps was, in formal educational terms, ahead of the U.S. and UK police in requiring degrees from the police academy for all its entrants.

facilities for political prisoners. Standards in Iraqi prisons were abysmal, and human rights violations were common.[8]

In addition to the internal security forces and the interior ministry forces, Iraq had a very large defense sector. Under the monarchy, the Iraqi armed forces had become a symbol of nationalism, but their primary role had been counterinsurgency and maintaining external order. They expanded massively in size during the Iran-Iraq war, but by 2003 they suffered from poor morale, desertion, and lack of equipment.[9] Although regular army units were deployed to counter internal threats to the regime, by 2003 they had ceded most internal security functions to other organizations such as the Republican Guard, Special Republican Guard, and Special Security Organization.

Security Developments After the War

Contrary to popular belief, the United States and the United Kingdom did undertake extensive planning for postwar Iraq. Unfortunately, this planning focused on humanitarian relief and was based on the assumption that the institutions of the Iraqi state, including police, could be relied upon to keep the state functioning and to maintain order after the overthrow of the regime.[10] Prewar planning did not envisage the need for an extensive program of work in Iraq's police and justice sectors.

Most of the administrative structures of central and local government had collapsed when the Office for Reconstruction and Humanitarian Assistance (ORHA) and its successor, the CPA, took over the administration of Iraq in April and May 2003. Whereas prewar planning had envisaged merely the removal of the top-level Ba'athists and regime loyalists, most of the security sector institutions

---

[8] The Saddam regime released the 38,000 inmates of Iraqi prisons before the April 2003 invasion. UNCHR, *Report of the United Nations High Commissioner for Human Rights and Follow-Up to the World Conference on Human Rights: The Present Situation of Human Rights in Iraq*, June 9, 2004 (CPA submission).

[9] Anthony H. Cordesman, *The Iraq War: Strategy, Tactics, and Military Lessons*, Washington, D.C.: Center for Strategic and International Studies, 2003.

[10] James Fallows, "Blind into Baghdad," *The Atlantic Monthly*, January/February 2004.

evaporated overnight. The intelligence and security agencies, Ba'ath Party organizations, and paramilitaries went underground. Many soldiers simply left their units, and police officers went home.[11] The disappearance of the state and party institutions left the country open to a wave of looting and disorder, exacerbated by organized sabotage.

Although coalition military planners had hoped to use some Iraqi army units for security and reconstruction tasks, the armed forces had effectively "self-demobilized," and their infrastructure was devastated both during combat and during the looting that followed the collapse of the regime. Coalition officials also decided that it would be unconscionable to retain any of the secret police agencies that were so heavily associated with Saddam's regime.

Therefore, one of the CPA's first acts in May 2003 was to formally dissolve the security and intelligence services, the defense ministry, Republican Guard, and the armed forces. In addition, the CPA dissolved the Ba'ath Party and initiated a sweeping purge of high-level Ba'athists from government positions. These reforms were part of an ambitious attempt to transform Iraqi society and build a new, democratic Iraq.[12]

However, as they began to formulate and implement their plans for the transformation of Iraq's security sector, coalition authorities simultaneously found themselves tackling a "security gap" that widened as the occupation progressed. The initial challenge was widespread looting and street crime, exacerbated by organized sabotage. The collapse of the Iraqi security services and the unpreparedness of thinly stretched coalition forces to undertake a policing role meant that this crime wave raged out of control for a period. ORHA and the CPA responded by rapidly recalling Iraqi police personnel to assist with basic law and order, with mixed results.[13]

---

[11] Williamson Murray and Major General Robert H. Scales, Jr., *The Iraq War: A Military History*, Cambridge, Mass.: Belknap Press of Harvard University Press, 2003.

[12] CPA, "Dissolution of Entities," CPA Order 2, May 23, 2003a.

[13] In some areas, coalition forces had to rebuild local police forces from scratch because they were found to be too corrupt, brutal, and incompetent to contribute to reestablishing law and order.

In addition, by the early summer of 2003, the coalition had begun to come under attack from assorted insurgents and terrorists. This escalating campaign involved former regime loyalists, often from the dissolved security organizations; domestic Sunni Islamists, sometimes linked to foreign Islamist organizations such as al Qaeda; and nationalist and tribal resistors who opposed both the foreign occupation and the central state. Although there were often tensions between these groups, they could agree on the desirability of removing the coalition presence and undermining the secular, democratic government that the coalition was trying to set up. As new Iraqi government institutions began to be established from the autumn of 2003, the insurgents and terrorists increasingly turned their fire on these targets, with a particular focus on the new Iraqi security forces (ISF). As Figure 5.1 illustrates, weekly attacks on ISF were negligible at the start of September 2003, but by May 2004 they had risen to about 30 per day.

In addition to these insurgents, the coalition and its Iraqi partners had to face an armed insurrection by Moqtada al-Sadr's Mahdi Army, a Shiite movement that mobilized poor and marginalized Shiites in eastern Baghdad and the center-south region.[14] Major armed clashes broke out in April and again in July/August 2004 between al-Sadr's militia and the coalition and then the IIG.

In addition, there were extensive networks of organized criminals engaged in smuggling, looting, extortion, robbery, and kidnapping. These criminals included many released by Saddam Hussein before the war. But they also included many groups connected to the Ba'athist "shadow state"—the networks that had benefited from their relationships with what, by 2003, had become effectively a gangster state engaging in widespread black-marketeering, corruption, and intimidation. These criminals exploited to the full the chaos of post-Saddam Iraq, including the open borders, the lack of effective police, and the easy availability of weapons.

---

[14] In describing Iraq's regions, we use the CPA's six divisions as illustrated in Figure 5.2.

Figure 5.1
Daily Attacks on Iraqi Security Forces

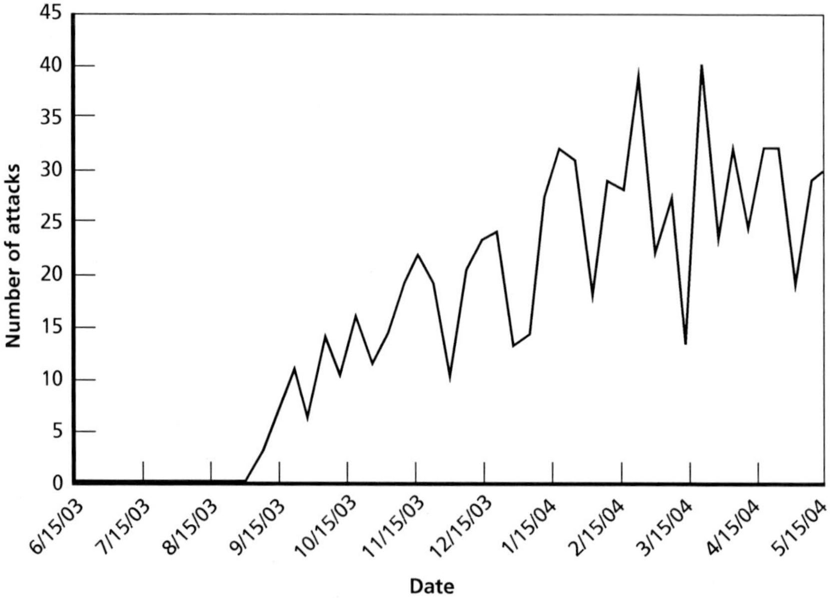

SOURCE: U.S. Department of Defense.
RAND *MG374-5.1*

In the face of this mounting violence, coalition forces and the CPA put a high priority on building ISF.[15] This was part of a broader program of preparing Iraq for self-government by building Iraqi capacity. The problem was that, unlike in other areas such as health care and municipal services, the new Iraqi security forces were starting almost from scratch. In the face of escalating violence and pressures to draw down the international troop presence, there was constant pressure to accelerate the buildup of Iraqi security forces and to transfer "local control" to Iraqis from the coalition. But the need for speed

---

[15] Building ISF was, however, never the CPA's sole priority. It simultaneously prioritized other policy areas such as the political process, local governance reform, infrastructure reconstruction, and economic reform.

Figure 5.2
CPA Regions

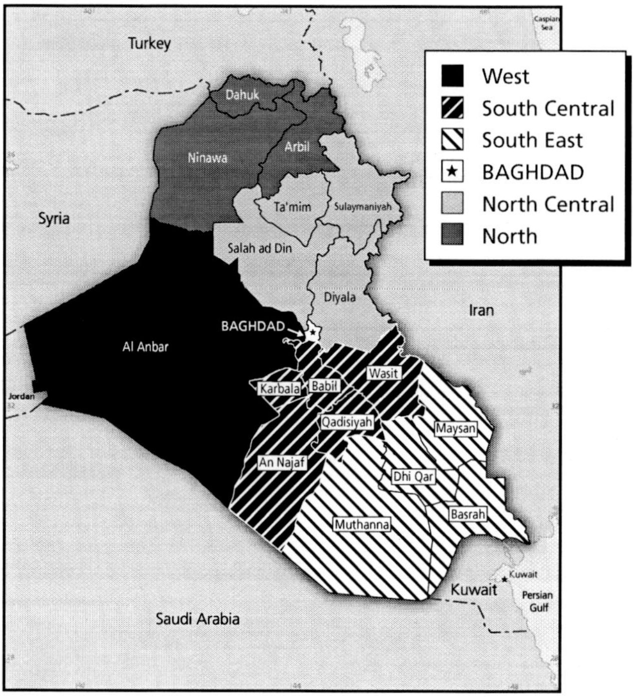

SOURCE: CPA.
RAND *MG374-5.2*

was always in conflict with the desire to undertake capacity-building at a more gradual pace in order to build sustainable, high-quality forces.

Inputs and Outputs

There were five elements to the coalition's efforts to develop Iraq's security sector: (1) the elaboration of fundamental principles and governance mechanisms; (2) the interior ministry, the police, border enforcement agencies, and Facilities Protection Service; (3) the judiciary and prisons; (4) the armed forces and defense ministry; and (5) the intelligence services.

Coalition authorities in Iraq took some steps to address the Iraqi security sector as a whole,[16] in line with international best practices.[17] However, it was not until the end of 2003 that the CPA began to develop a coordinated, coalition-wide approach to the reconstruction of the Iraqi security sector. Once a comprehensive vision had been developed, a process of dialogue was begun with the Iraqi Governing Council. During this dialogue, the concepts were refined and a process of Iraqi ownership was begun. Hence, by April/May 2004, when interim Iraqi ministers began to exercise real decisionmaking authority in preparation for the transfer of full authority, the principles and structures developed by the CPA began to be used by their future Iraqi owners. The IIG that took over on June 28, 2004, has adopted many of these principles and structures.

The security sector development program had three key elements. First was the elaboration of principles such as democratic accountability of the security services; mainstreaming respect for civil liberties and human rights in security force practice; giving the police primacy for internal security and the military primacy for external security. These principles were enshrined in the March 8, 2004, Transitional Administrative Law (TAL).[18]

Second was the affirmation of the right of the state to monopolize the means of violence. An important challenge in Iraq was the proliferation of armed militias associated with political parties. Although most of these did not overtly flex their muscles under the CPA, preferring to make gains through the political process, the

---

[16] Ambassador L. Paul Bremer III had initially brought in Walter Slocombe to act as the security sector "czar," but Slocombe's remit was rapidly restricted to building the New Iraqi Army and laying the basis for the Ministry of Defense.

[17] OECD, Development Assistance Committee, Network on Conflict, Peace and Development Co-operation (2003).

[18] CPA, Law of Administration for the State of Iraq for the Transitional Period, March 8, 2004c.

potential obviously remained for them to use force.[19] The TAL made clear that only the state had the right to use force, and agreement was reached in principle in June 2004 with all the militias that they would enter a transition and reintegration (TR) process leading to their eventual demobilization.[20] The plans for TR envisaged reintegrating some 103,000 fighters into the economy, the security forces, and the public sector. In June 2004, responsibility for implementing these plans was passed to an interministerial Transition and Reintegration Implementation Committee reporting to the Iraqi Interim Government. However, neither the IIG nor its international partners have demonstrated an interest in pursuing or resourcing this process since the demise of the CPA, leaving the TR program moribund at the time of this writing.

Third, development of national-security decisionmaking mechanisms provided a framework for the IIG to manage security policy decisionmaking in a rational and informed manner. The Ministerial Committee on National Security (MCNS) was formed, along with a Deputies Committee and a small staff, around an appointed national security advisor.[21] This decisionmaking architecture proved its worth when interim Iraqi ministers became substantively and actively involved in shaping security policy during the April 2004 uprisings in Fallujah, Sadr City, and center-south Iraq. The MCNS also worked on development of a national counterterrorist strategy and a comprehensive national security strategy.[22] Personal rivalries derailed the workings of the MCNS in the summer of 2004, but by fall it appeared that the structure was beginning to work as intended.

---

[19] As demonstrated by Muqtada al-Sadr Mahdi's Army, which staged major uprisings in April and August 2004.

[20] CPA, "Armed Forces and Militia Agreement Announced," press release, June 5, 2004j.

[21] CPA, "Ministerial Committee on National Security," CPA Order 68, April 4, 2004e.

[22] Although the national security strategy was drafted in the summer of 2004, only a much shortened version was published before the January 2005 elections.

The Interior Ministry and Police

Reconstituting and reforming the Iraqi Police Service was one of the key tasks facing the coalition after the occupation of Iraq in April 2003. Unfortunately, the immensity of the task was underestimated and was never given the priority it deserved by coalition governments, the CPA, or coalition forces. The challenge was to reconstruct the force so that it could play an immediate internal security role and transform an ineffective and corrupt institution into an effective and honest force that would serve the community rather than the regime.

In May 2004, the CPA concluded that the Iraqi police were incapable of providing security and order and that the force also required fundamental transformation.[23] Like its counterparts in the regions, the Baghdad police had to function in an environment in which most of its prewar senior officials and officers were removed, many personnel abandoned their posts, most equipment was stolen, and specialist units such as intelligence and emergency response were disbanded. More fundamentally, the disappearance of the other Iraqi internal security agencies had left the IPS on the front line against crime and political violence, a position for which it was never designed, trained, or equipped.[24]

Coalition efforts to reconstruct and transform Iraq's police can be understood by examining three elements: transformation, philosophies and models, and program delivery.

Police Force Transformation. The CPA developed a twin-track approach to police transformation. This involved rehiring Saddam-era policemen and providing a minimal level of training while beginning a full-scale recruitment and basic training program to bring new blood into the force. At the same time, the CPA sought to mod-

---

[23] CPA, *Iraq Police: An Assessment of the Present and Recommendations for the Future*, Baghdad, May 30, 2003b.

[24] While it was true that the IPS was often intimidated into inaction by insurgent forces, it is a simple fact that no democratic police force in the world would be able or expected to cope on its own with opponents routinely armed with rocket-propelled grenades, mortars, and car bombs. For instance, even the well-equipped and trained Royal Ulster Constabulary relied on the British Army to help it deal with much lower levels of violence experienced in Northern Ireland during the "Troubles."

ernize the institutional capacity of the IPS and the interior ministry, to develop specialized units, and to reequip the IPS.

The first step was for coalition military units, the only international bodies with presence outside Baghdad,[25] to either rehire Saddam-era policemen or hire new personnel, nominally under the supervision of CPA civilian police advisors.[26] The police advisors designed a three-week "transition and integration" training package. This was intended to verify the existence of police officers supposedly on the books,[27] to vet personnel, and to instill a modicum of modern policing skills and ethos.[28] The absence of civilian police advisors in most of the country, however, meant that much of the training had to be provided by military police (MP) units.

Longer-term transformation was to be achieved by gradually populating the force with new recruits brought in with higher standards.[29] These recruits were to go through an eight-week basic mandate course before embarking on a field training program in which recruits would be supervised by coalition and Iraqi field training officers.[30] This ambitious program involved an abortive attempt to undertake police training in Hungary, the construction of the Jordan International Police Training Center, the build-out of the Baghdad Public Safety Academy, and smaller training centers outside the capital. A vital part of the program was the planned deployment of up to

[25] Although the CPA rapidly deployed civilian personnel into Iraq's main regions, it did not have fully staffed and functioning governorate teams in every governorate until early 2004. Even then, most provinces did not have police advisors.

[26] The lack of records, most of which were looted or destroyed in April/May 2003, meant that it was very hard for CPA and coalition officials to determine with any certainty who had been a serving IPS member before the war.

[27] It subsequently emerged that many of the supposedly "rehired" officers in fact had no police experience at all.

[28] Many Iraqi policemen lacked even basic skills. At least one coalition MP unit refused to issue extra ammunition to its local IP unit because of concerns over lack of weapons training and firearms discipline.

[29] Many of the rehired policemen had to be weeded out due to corruption or illiteracy.

[30] The course was originally 12 weeks but was cut because of the requirement to deploy police officers onto the streets to restore order.

1,500 international police advisors (IPAs).[31] Although IPAs in Iraq were armed for self-defense (and often had to use their weapons), they did not have executive authority to enforce Iraqi law.[32]

While the initial focus of the police reform program was on recruit training, it became increasingly clear that one of the primary weaknesses of the IPS was its senior leaders and managers. Some senior officers displayed great courage and dedication. Overall, however, the professional standards and education of the IPS leadership cadre that remained after de–Ba'athification was poor. This problem became particularly evident in April 2004 when the IPS in Fallujah, Mosul, Najaf, Karbala, and other cities targeted by Sunni or Shiite insurgents melted away or went over to the insurgents. Subsequently, the police program was revamped to provide additional management and leadership training. Belatedly, a "train the trainer" program was instituted to free up scarce expatriate resources to focus on working with the senior ranks.

Policing Philosophies and Models. The CPA addressed two critical aspects of policing philosophy: (1) governance and institutional development, i.e., the "politics" of the police, and (2) the structure of the police and, specifically, the question of a constabulary-style "third force."[33]

The CPA philosophy was that the Iraqi Police Service would become the primary public safety and internal security agency. It would be democratically accountable, run according to modern principles of managerial efficiency, and adopt contemporary policing methods and technologies. The force envisaged was significantly different from the reality that existed on the ground in 2003.

---

[31] As noted later, this number was never reached. The numbers of IPAs to be deployed either at training academies or in the field varied as the program underwent a series of revisions. Likewise, the nomenclature varied. At one stage, the term "international coalition police force" was used.

[32] On several occasions the main Baghdad hotel used by expatriate police trainers came under attack from car bombs and small arms fire. On more than one occasion, police advisors were engaged in intensive firefights, both taking and inflicting casualties.

[33] See Bayley (1985), chapters 3 and 7, for comparative discussions of these topics.

To achieve this goal, two issues needed to be addressed: governance and institutional development. The Saddam-era police force had been a national force tightly controlled by the interior ministry. The CPA struggled with the tension between its desire to decentralize control to build a more accountable force and the requirement to retain central control to ensure effectiveness against insurgents and terrorists. In the end, the model chosen was a hybrid. Local police chiefs would have some autonomy but would be accountable both to the MoI in Baghdad and to local, elected councils and provincial governors.[34] National units, such as an antiterrorism branch and the Civil Intervention Force, a high-end armed response unit, would operate under the authority of the central government but could be requested by local police chiefs.[35]

Wholesale institutional development was needed for the MoI to manage the police and its other responsibilities, which included border enforcement, immigration, passport control, customs, and weapons control. The institutional development program, which would proceed along with wider reforms of the Iraqi civil service, envisaged transforming a cumbersome, patronage-based, centralized hierarchy into a "modern," service-oriented institution complete with transparent hiring practices, personnel policies, strategic plans, inspectors general, and auditors.

The second philosophical question concerned the requirement for a "third force." There was debate over the relative merits of making the IPS a community-based public safety force and building it as a paramilitary organization, able to confront high levels of organized crime and political violence. Although there were tentative efforts to promote community-policing initiatives, the CPA recognized that the IPS, armed with AK-47s as well as handguns, was always going to have a paramilitary flavor. Initially, CPA officials resisted requests from the IPS that they be armed with heavy weapons to match the

---

[34] CPA, "Local Governmental Powers," CPA Order 71, April 6, 2004f.

[35] The three Kurdish provinces remained outside this system; in 2004, the Transitional Administrative Law gave them significant autonomy over policing.

firepower of their opponents. By early summer of 2004, though, the violence had escalated to the point where the IPS began acquiring heavy weapons to defend their stations, and police pickup trucks were routinely deployed with pedestal-mounted heavy machine-guns. In addition, the IPAs developed plans for the police to have specialized local and national units to deal with "high-end" violence. These units became known as the emergency response units (a national special operations and explosive ordnance disposal unit of some 270 men) and the Civil Intervention Force (a 4,900-man force with two light-armored special police regiments and nine public-order battalions).

However, these specialized units only existed on paper through much of 2004. To fill the gap, coalition forces turned to the mainstay of occupation forces: auxiliary troops. The Iraqi Civil Defense Corps (ICDC) provided a cheap and rapidly constituted paramilitary force that could put an Iraqi face on coalition military operations.[36] Although its founding charter gave it "constabulary" duties, the ICDC was not a gendarmerie. Its personnel received basic military rather than police training, and it had a military rather than police mission. Although there was a considerable body of opinion within the coalition that argued for the ICDC to become a gendarmerie, this option was resisted by the CPA's police advisors who argued that such a move would divert resources from the IPS.[37]

The ICDC proved very popular with coalition military commanders, and it went through a number of expansions and accelerations. In September 2003, the plan was for it to reach an end strength of 15,000 by late 2004 and for its units to operate at squad or pla-

---

[36] CPA, "Establishment of the Iraqi Civil Defense Corps," CPA Order 28, September 3, 2003d.

[37] Interestingly, the following comments on a previous effort to organize an indigenous police force applied equally to the policy debates in Iraq: "[E]fforts to organize a district police were hindered by the lack of consensus on organization … [The Commanding General's] … call for a provincial constabulary seemed to contradict the earlier guidelines … which established municipal police. Officers … [were perplexed] over whether native police were to be municipal guards or part of a paramilitary district constabulary, and, as a result, suggestions for their organization ranged from battalion-sized units to small squads in each town." Brian McAllister Linn, *The US Army and Counterinsurgency in the Philippine War, 1899–1902*, Chapel Hill, N.C.: University of North Carolina Press, 1989, pp. 50–51.

toon level. By early 2004, this plan had been radically revised to a target end strength at the same time of more than 40,000, with battalion and brigade command structures. Nonetheless, even when the ICDC was put under the defense ministry and renamed the National Guard by the IIG, it remained a lightly trained light infantry force capable of providing area security and presence patrols, not of real policing or stand-alone combat operations.

Program Delivery. The fact that the United States and the United Kingdom had failed to secure explicit UN Security Council support for Operation Iraqi Freedom meant that they could not call on the UN mechanisms that had been deployed in other post-conflict zones, such as CIVPOL. Nor could they call on some of the governments who had deployed policing resources in the Balkans and Afghanistan, notably France and Germany. Although the UN Security Council did authorize an Assistance Mission[38] to Iraq and did encourage member states to assist with civil police functions,[39] the lack of international consensus and the destruction of the UN headquarters in Baghdad on August 19, 2004, by a terrorist bomb meant that little was achieved on this front.

Therefore, design and implementation of the Iraqi police program fell to the U.S. government, primarily the State Department's Bureau of International Narcotics and Law Enforcement (INL) and the Justice Department's ICITAP. They were assisted by the United Kingdom, Australia, Canada, and Spain, all of which deployed senior police officers to advise the MoI. Other EU countries also provided assistance with police training under UK auspices in the south of the country. However, delays in the arrival of civilian advisors meant that, even a year after the end of major combat operations, there were few advisors in country, and the Baghdad-based police advisors had limited visibility on the state of the IPS in many of the outlying provinces.

---

[38] In August 2003. UNSCR, S/RES/1500, 2003.

[39] In UNSCR 1483, S/RES1483, 2003.

Into this vacuum stepped the already overstretched coalition forces. MP and civil affairs units were the main day-to-day liaison with the IPS. Despite their reluctance to get involved in civil policing, the military had to undertake the selection of leaders, oversee recruitment, provide basic training, and equip and mentor the police. Helped by the presence of police officers in U.S. reserve units, many of these programs were remarkably successful. But the attention that the military could give to the police was rudimentary, sporadic, and underfunded. It was also very uneven across the country. The gap between theory and reality led to tensions between civilian agencies responsible for police reform and the military, which had primary responsibility for security. The CPA approach involved the U.S. Departments of State and Justice designing the police program and relying heavily on contractors to implement the training programs. However, it became evident by late 2003 that the standard, civilian-led approach was not delivering results. Moreover, because they had not been given the police mission, coalition forces concentrated on building up the ICDC and supporting the New Iraqi Army (NIA) rather than supporting the police.[40]

In the spring of 2004, the U.S. Department of Defense conducted an assessment of progress made in developing ISF. The assessment recommended transferring resources from the NIA program into the police and the ICDC and giving Combined Joint Task Force 7 (CJTF-7) the mission of developing the IPS. Although many of the CPA civilian advisors were wary of the concept of subordinating the police program to the military, by March 2004 the Department of Defense concluded that only the military had the resources to move forward the police program fast enough.

In March 2004, CJTF-7 established the Civilian Police Advisory Training Team (CPATT). This team was under the operational control of CJTF-7 but took policy direction from the CPA's MoI advisors. Headed by a military officer, with a civilian deputy, CPATT was staffed jointly by military and civilian personnel. It was given the mis-

---

[40] Except in the south, where the British-led Multi-National Division (South East) made security sector reform and support to the IPS its main priority in the fall of 2003.

sion of mobilizing civilian and military resources to staff, train, equip, and mentor the Iraqi police. With the transition from CJTF-7 to MNF-I in May 2004, CPATT became part of the Office of Security Transition. In June, it was renamed the Multi-National Security Transition Command–Iraq (MNSTC-I) and charged with manning, training, and equipping all Iraqi security forces.

Past cases demonstrate that placing the military in charge of police reform has potential dangers, since the two have different missions, skill sets, and rules of engagement. This was certainly the view of many civilian advisors involved in the police program. Nonetheless, CPATT was probably a sensible recognition that, given the uniquely challenging circumstances of Iraq, civilian police advisors will have to rely on the military to help deliver police reform and capacity building.

Border and Population Control.[41] In addition to delivering urban and rural policing, the MoI was tasked with implementing border and population control. In both areas, work had to begin almost from the ground up.

Iraq's borders under Saddam had been protected by a large conscript force but had never been secure against smugglers and infiltrators. In August 2003, the CPA reorganized border control assets from various ministries (Interior, Defense, and Finance) into a single Department of Border Enforcement (DBE) under the MoI.[42] The DBE was given responsibility for border policing, customs, the development of a new passport system, and immigration functions. Since the majority of the personnel previously employed in these tasks had either deserted or been dismissed because of their association with the Ba'ath Party or the intelligence services, most staff had to be recruited and trained anew. At the same time, most border facilities had been ruined either in the war or due to looting and required rebuilding. As with the IPS, the DBE program was implemented by a handful of

---

[41] The term "population control" tended to be used in line with U.S. military doctrine, but the real focus of this work was on population identification.

[42] CPA, "Creation of the Department of Border Enforcement," CPA Order 26, August 24, 2003c.

coalition personnel—some drawn from specialist agencies in the United States or United Kingdom, others drawn from the ranks of U.S. Army civil affairs units.[43] In the meantime, coalition forces had responsibility for securing Iraq's borders. The fact that they lacked the resources to effectively control the borders was evident from the widespread smuggling, infiltration, and other cross-border traffic such as returning refugees from Iran.

Population control measures such as identity cards, passports, weapons permits, and security vetting were important programs for which the interior and foreign ministries shared responsibility. Coalition advisors and their Iraqi counterparts found themselves hamstrung by the loss of most central government files and databases. However, despite numerous initiatives to deploy the latest database and biometric technologies, the CPA had failed to implement comprehensive and effective population control measures by the time of the transfer of authority.

Infrastructure Security. Although only in part a police responsibility, infrastructure security soon became a pressing issue for Iraq and the coalition. Widespread looting of government facilities was superseded by increasingly organized and widespread sabotage directed against Iraq's infrastructures. Threats ranged from insurgent bombings of oil pipelines, railroads, and attacks on aircraft to criminal theft of electrical wires and hijackings of trucks. Coalition forces, the ICDC, and police were deployed against these threats, and a range of infrastructure security forces were also created. The Facilities Protection Service (FPS) was a force of minimally trained static guards over whom the MoI had oversight for training and policy purposes. But they were controlled and funded by the individual ministries for which they worked.[44] Ministries with particular vulnerabilities, such as oil and electricity, formed their own private security

---

[43] The challenges facing this program were highlighted when the U.S. Department of Homeland Security decided in February 2004, because of the security situation, not to assign customs staff to Iraq.

[44] The FPS created a number of specialist subunits, such as the Diplomatic Protection Service, which serviced foreign embassies and international missions in Iraq.

forces, in some cases contracting out to foreign private-security companies.[45]

Inputs. The international inputs to the Iraqi police sector consisted of (1) money from the Iraqi budget, coalition forces, and donor assistance; (2) equipment; (3) expatriate civilian police advisors; and (4) advisors and mentors provided by coalition forces.

Funding. As discussed above, there were four sources of funding for the Iraqi MoI: the Iraqi budget, the Development Fund for Iraq, U.S. supplemental funding, and other donor assistance. The 2003 (July–December) Iraqi budget included $22.9 million for the MoI's capital and operating expenditures. This did not cover any salary costs and was concentrated on immediate reconstruction needs such as the MoI headquarters and border posts.[46] The revised 2004 budget allocated $490 million to the MoI.[47] The amounts allocated to MoI from the Development Fund for Iraq remain unclear. The partial data available on allocations and expenditures from the records of the CPA MoI and the Program Review Board indicate that $149 million was allocated to the MoI through June 2004.[48] However, we assume that $500 million was allocated from DFI for MoI expenses in 2003 and 2004. This means that the total allocated to the MoI from Iraqi sources during 2003 and 2004 was around $1 billion.

The FY 2004 U.S. supplemental allocated $3.24 billion to security and law enforcement and $1.49 billion to justice, public safety

---

[45] The Iraqi MoI had the responsibility for regulating private security companies, which proliferated in occupied Iraq, but the regulation process remained informal during the life of CPA.

[46] Republic of Iraq, *Budget Revenues and Expenses*, Baghdad, July–December 2003.

[47] Iraqi Ministry of Finance, *Revisions to 2004 Budget, Ministerial Allocations*, Baghdad, April 10, 2004. Original 2004 budgets in Iraqi dinars. Converted on August 26, 2004, at the rate of USD1= ID1,462.50.

[48] The allocation included $79 million noted in CPA MoI records indicate for assorted construction and equipment contracts, $47.8 million recorded in the DFI financial reporting matrix, and $22 million for development of the passport system. CPA, *MoI Finance Files*, Baghdad, September 2004; DFI Financial Reporting Matrix, June 26, 2004.

and infrastructure, and civil society.[49] The Bush administration received congressional authorization in October 2004 to reprogram these funds, leading to an increased allocation to the security sector. The budget categories used in the 2207 (*Quarterly Report to Congress*) reporting make it slightly difficult to break out spending on police. But the overall allocation to police, border enforcement, and the Civil Defense Directorate (fire and rescue) was just under $3 billion (see Table 5.1).

Table 5.1
U.S. Supplemental Spending Plan Related to the Ministry of Interior (in $ millions)

	Allocated (October 2004)	Disbursed (as of September 22, 2004)
Police training and technical assistance	1,889	196
Border enforcement	450	12
Facilities protection[a]	53	3
Facilities repair, mine removal, and fire service[b]	275	30
Public safety training and facilities[c]	220	1
National security communications network[d]	98	3
Total	**2,985**	**245**

SOURCE: *Quarterly Report to Congress* (2004).
[a] FPS costs are the responsibility of their parent departments; the MoI's role is to ensure oversight and standards, as well as to fund its own FPS.
[b] Although mostly allocated to civil defense (fire and rescue), this will fund reconstruction and repairs of 31 police stations and police coordination centers.
[c] Although largely devoted to the recruitment and training of firefighters, this element covers the operating costs of police training academies.
[d] Also known as the first responder network; designed to enable MoI agencies to communicate nationwide.

---

[49] Congress cut some police/justice items from the administration's original request, such as funding for Iraqi traffic police and the construction of extra maximum-security prisons.

With supplemental aid only really beginning to flow in the spring of 2004, many of the immediate needs of the Iraqi police had to be met by small grants administered by coalition military commanders in the field. As of September 2004, the Commander's Emergency Response Program (CERP) had spent $124.4 million on police and security programs. This funding was allocated across some 4,500 small projects and tended to cover items such as refurbishment of police stations or purchase of basic supplies such as uniforms.[50]

Non-U.S. international assistance was provided through bilateral channels. Japan provided 1,150 police vehicles and, in May 2004, allocated $5 million to provide the MoI with armored vehicles. The United Kingdom allocated an initial $40 million to police training, mentoring, equipping, and prisons advice. Canada allocated $7.3 million to support police training in Jordan.[51] The multilateral donor mechanisms were used to a limited extent to support the MoI. At the Second Donor Committee meeting in May 2004, the MoI requested support for a vehicle registration system to counter car theft and for maintenance facilities for MoI vehicles.[52]

How Much Was Spent. It is possible to estimate that total allocations[53] to the MoI, primarily for police and border forces, from May 2003 to December 2004 will have been around $4.2 billion, three-quarters of this total ($3.2 billion) coming from donor funds.[54] This overstates the amount committed in 2003 and 2004, since most of the supplemental expenditure programs will be implemented in

---

[50] *Quarterly Report to Congress*, 2207 report, October 2004.

[51] *Quarterly Report to Congress* (2004), Appendix 2, "Contributions from Other Donors."

[52] Iraqi MoI submissions to Second Donor Committee meeting, Qatar, May 25–26, 2004.

[53] For a previous estimate, see GAO, *Rebuilding Iraq: Resource, Security, Governance, Essential Services, and Oversight Issues*, GAO-04-902R, June 2004b.

[54] Funds consisted of Iraqi MoI budgets, $514 million; DFI, $500 million; IRRF 2003, $64 million; Iraq Relief and Reconstruction Fund (IRRF) 2004, $2,985 million; CERP, $150 million; and other donors, $52 million. The CERP figure assumes that MSMNF-I continues to spend CERP and ISF Quick Response Program funds at a consistent rate on the Iraqi police and border forces through the remainder of 2004.

2005. Indeed, as of November 2004, only 8 percent of the funds from the FY 2004 U.S. supplemental had been disbursed.[55]

Equipment. The IPS started off with inadequate equipment, and the postwar looting gutted many police stations. Further attrition took place as a result of assaults by insurgents and criminals. The CPA therefore had to undertake a countrywide program of reconstructing police and MoI facilities and reequipping the police. Until the spring of 2004, most investment came from local coalition military units using CERP funds.

In terms of facilities, the CPA's infrastructure plan included refurbishment of the MoI in Baghdad and the refurbishment or construction of 18 provincial police headquarters, 425 police stations, and nine training facilities. By the summer of 2004, the MoI building was ready for use, and the Jordanian and Baghdad academies were already in use. Progress had also been made with other facilities, but the main construction work was expected to begin later in 2004. In addition, eight commercial border stations and 84 other border facilities were to be developed. A computerized immigration system, PISCES (Personal Identification Secure Comparison Evaluation System), was installed at two sites, and plans were made for a nationwide rollout. It was complemented by a computerized system for collection of a 5 percent import duty, the Reconstruction Levy. A further critical part of the policing infrastructure, a nationwide communications system known as the First Responder Network, had been subject to innumerable delays but was scheduled to begin construction in the summer of 2004. However, rising security costs resulting from the growing threat to expatriate contractors threatened to delay this project even further.[56]

In terms of individual equipment, as shown in Table 5.2, by August 2004, the various Iraqi police units and the border enforce-

---

[55] U.S. Department of State, *Iraq Status Report*, November 3, 2004e.

[56] *Quarterly Report to Congress* (2004); CPA, *An Historic Review of CPA Accomplishments*, Baghdad, June 28, 2004n.

Table 5.2
Iraqi Ministry of Interior Equipment, August 2004

	Weapons		Vehicles		Communications Equipment		Body Armor	
Force/Element	**Required**	**On-Hand**	**Required**	**On-Hand**	**Required**	**On-Hand**	**Required**	**On-Hand**
Police								
Iraqi Police Service	136,054	90,073	14,895	5,447	45,065	12,769	90,000	40,391
Civil Intervention Force	11,490	0	1,002	0	10,240	0	4,800	0
Emergency response units	1,020	500	58	0	352	0	270	50
Department of Border Enforcement	17,153	8,017	3,700	1,408	3,700	1,402	12,626	4,000
Total	**165,717**	**91,590**	**19,655**	**6,855**	**59,357**	**14,171**	**107,696**	**44,441**

SOURCE: U.S. Department of State (2004d).

ment units were at 55 percent of their requirement in terms of weapons, 35 percent in vehicles, 24 percent in communications equipment, and 41 percent in body armor.

Civilian Advisors. An initial CPA assessment had recommended the deployment of some 6,500 international police advisors, but this was rapidly ruled out as unrealistic.[57] By late summer of 2003, the CPA plan called for deployment during the following year of an International Police Task Force of 1,500 IPAs. These advisors would mentor the IPS, ensure the institutionalization of the principles taught in classroom training, and assist with management of situations beyond the capability of the IPS leadership. In addition, some 600 police trainers would be required to conduct training at academies in Iraq and in Jordan.

In the spring of 2004, the proposed numbers of advisors and trainers were revised. This was in part a recognition of the difficulty of recruiting, retaining, and supporting this number in the difficult security and living conditions provided by Iraq. It was also the result of a change of direction in which CPATT chose to focus its efforts on leadership training and train-the-trainer programs as a response to the perceived weaknesses of the IPS leadership during the April 2004 confrontations with insurgents. The revised targets were 500 American IPAs, up to 500 non-U.S. IPAs, and 200 international police trainers (IPTs). By August 2004, the figures for U.S. personnel stood at 376 IPAs and 57 IPTs.[58] There were up to 50 non-U.S. IPAs and trainers in Iraq in the spring and summer of 2004.[59]

In addition to the IPAs and IPTs, expatriate civilian advisors were deployed to manage and build the MoI itself. The numbers of these advisors, mainly from the United States, varied. But by the spring of 2004, there were around 60 expatriate advisors helping to

---

57 Andrew Higgins, "As It Wields Power Abroad, U.S. Outsources Law and Order Work," *Wall Street Journal*, February 2, 2004.

58 CPATT status update, August 2004.

59 The United Kingdom had approximately 40, mainly in southern Iraq. *Quarterly Report to Congress*, 2207 report, July 2004, Appendix 2, "Contributions from Other Donors."

develop the MoI.[60] The advisors came from a variety of backgrounds: police or other law enforcement, the private sector, and the military. After the transfer of authority in June 2004, the authorized strength of this advisory team was cut to 42.[61] The majority of the advisors were from the United States, but important leadership roles were played by British staff and detailees from Spain, Australia, and Canada.

Coalition Assistance. By the summer of 2004, the U.S. Department of Defense had some 138,000 U.S. troops in Iraq, supplemented by some 24,000 coalition military personnel.[62] It is impossible to break out in any systematic manner the military resources that went into supporting the Iraqi police and border enforcement units. In general, though, MP and civil affairs units devoted a considerable proportion of their time to supporting, mentoring, training, and conducting joint operations with the Iraqi police. In addition to these specialist units, regular infantry, armor, and artillery units supported the Iraqi police in their areas of responsibility to varying degrees. This unquantifiable but widespread support had more impact on the local Iraqi police forces than did the CPA program, which tended to be Baghdad-centric. Furthermore, the advent of CPATT in spring 2004 meant that additional military officers were deployed by the United States and the United Kingdom to manage the police training and equipping program.[63]

Outputs. The programmatic outputs of the Iraqi police program comprised (1) police personnel, (2) police capability, and (3) institutional development.

Police Personnel. Both the target numbers for Iraqi police and the measurement of numbers on hand were gray areas in Iraq. CPA plans in the summer and fall of 2003 set a target number of IPS per-

---

[60] Although the authorized strength was 117.

[61] By September 2004, only a quarter of those posts had been filled.

[62] As of August 2004.

[63] However, by August 2004, only around a third of CPATT's 135 authorized slots had been filled.

sonnel at 75,000, based on a population ratio of 1:300. Subsequent revisions to the estimated Iraqi population led the CPA to raise the target to just under 90,000 in the spring of 2004.[64] Specialist police units such as the Civil Intervention Force were additional to this total. The target manning for DBE police units was just under 16,300, with a total DBE strength of 29,000.[65]

In July/August 2004, MNF-I undertook a new troops-to-task analysis that led to plans to revise the IPS target upward to some 135,000 personnel, a ratio of about 1:200. The number of planned DBE police personnel was increased to 32,000.[66] Meeting the raw numerical targets was never the problem. By the spring of 2004, the CPA recognized that simply boosting the numbers of untrained, ineffective police was unhelpful.[67] The recognition of the need to focus on quality was evident when the U.S. State Department took over from the CPA. In the summer of 2004, the State Department reported that there were some 85,000 IPS personnel "on hand."[68] As it became evident that many of these personnel either did not exist or were ineffective, the State Department began to report personnel as "trained/on-hand." In November, the State Department was reporting some 43,600 trained/on-hand Iraqi police personnel (see Table 5.3).

---

[64] There was no reliable, up-to-date census, so population figures were based on the less-than-reliable ration card system.

[65] Composed of border police, customs police, and immigration police.

[66] This analysis was reportedly based on assessments of coalition military commanders based on the perceived needs of their areas. U.S. State Department, *Iraq Weekly Status*, September 8, 2004.

[67] It was noticeable that the rebellious al-Anbar province, which included Ramadi and Fallujah, was in fact significantly over its quota of police personnel by late 2003. These numbers contributed little to stabilizing the province.

[68] By June 2004, the actual IPS numbers stood at 118,000 and $60 million had been allocated to provide severance for the approximately 30,000 police personnel who did not meet minimum employment standards, such as literacy, fitness, or age. *Quarterly Report to Congress* (2004).

Table 5.3
Iraqi Ministry of Interior Personnel, October 2004

Force/Element	Required	Trained/On Hand
Iraqi Police		
Iraqi Police Service	135,000	43,627
Civil Intervention Force	4,920	0
Emergency response units	270	100
Department of Border Enforcement	32,000	18,148
Total	**172,190**	**61,875**

SOURCE: U.S. Department of State (2004d).

Even so, the majority of the "trained" police personnel had only been through the three-week transition and integration program course. With the program getting into gear, the prospects for training output in late 2004 and 2005 were improving. The expansion of the Jordan and Baghdad academies meant that some 15,000 new recruits would be trained by 2005. In addition, 613 personnel had already gone through specialized training courses, including those on basic criminal investigation, criminal intelligence, counterterrorism, dignitary protection, management and leadership, and train-the-trainer. Another 1,845 students were scheduled to pass through these specialized courses later in 2004, with the addition of courses on organized crime, drug enforcement, kidnapping investigations, post-blast investigations, and internal controls.[69]

Police Capability. The recognition to go beyond raw numbers of police personnel encouraged CPATT in the spring and summer of 2004 to use aggregate measures such as "effective police." These measurements brought together quantitative measures, such as "trained" and "equipped," with qualitative judgments by coalition advisors, such as "capable."[70] Such measurements began to enable CPATT to better assess the real current and projected effectiveness of the police units it was supporting.

---

[69] *Quarterly Report to Congress* (2004).

[70] An important lesson learned was to measure training and equipping of the *same* officer rather than measuring these variables separately.

Institutional Development. In addition to measuring the quantitative outputs of the police program, three broad dimensions of institutional development served as important measures. The first was the development of a police command and control capability, which consisted of the training and mentoring of the Iraqi police leadership and the development of the police communications system, known as the First Responder Network. The second measure was the development of specialist police units essential to the delivery of safety and security. These specialist units included not just the Civilian Intervention Force and emergency response units, but also public order units, a criminal intelligence and records branch, criminal investigation units, and specialist crime squads dealing with terrorism, organized crime, kidnapping, and drugs. The MoI was reorganized in the fall of 2003 to provide a structure for these specialized units, and training was initiated in 2004. The third measure was the institutional development of the MoI itself, along with local governance and oversight institutions such as governors and provincial public safety committees. Although steps were taken by CPA advisors to reform and civilianize the MoI in accordance with modern technocratic practices, limited progress had been made by July 2004.

Justice System

Judicial and prison reform were the responsibility of the U.S. Department of Justice, supported by U.S. Army Civil Affairs and Judge Advocate General officers. The majority of the advisors in the field were contractors, with a leavening of detailees from agencies such as the U.S. Marshals Service. However, as with the IPS, the bulk of the work on the ground with Iraqi prisons or courts was undertaken by the military.[71] These advisors, operating in an environment in which planned-for expatriate personnel and funds never seemed to arrive on schedule, struggled to reconstruct and transform the court and prison system while operating it at the same time.

---

[71] It should be recalled that, simultaneous to this program, coalition forces and other government agencies were running their own detention program for security detainees.

The CPA implemented sweeping reforms of the judicial and correctional systems. Early CPA orders transferred responsibility for prisons to the Ministry of Justice, laid the basis for an independent judiciary, and reformed the penal code. Although the courts and judiciary had been politicized and subordinated to the intelligence services and Ba'ath Party, Iraq had a body of judges and prosecutors who were relatively honest, educated, and professional. Within a short time, most of Iraq's courthouses were functioning, and serious work had begun on reforming Iraq's penal code. By 2004, all judges had been vetted: those found to be corrupt or guilty of human rights abuses were removed from their posts, and others dismissed by Saddam were reappointed. In addition, the CPA established new institutions such as the Central Criminal Court to try the more serious cases, including attacks on coalition forces.

In reality, however, the Iraqi judiciary was a long way from being effective. Fears over their security made most judges reluctant to investigate or try the more serious cases. Three judges were murdered in November 2003, prompting emergency efforts to provide judges with bodyguards. There was little urgency among judges about processing cases, and it was common for suspects to remain in police custody for weeks without appearing before the court. A lack of nationwide communications, and the CPA's failure to publish its directives in a timely manner, meant that many courts received new legislation from Baghdad weeks or even months after it had been enacted.

The situation in Iraq's prisons was worse. Although the CPA consolidated Iraq's prisons under the justice ministry in an attempt to reduce the scope of abuses under the MoI and the Ministry of Labor, this program ran into bureaucratic wrangling between the police and corrections service. Worse, the vast majority of Iraqi Corrections Service officers were completely unfit to work in a modern prison service. Recruits and managers had to be found, trained, and mentored. The physical infrastructure of the Iraqi prisons system, inadequate before the war, was comprehensively looted in the conflict's aftermath. If minimum international standards were to be applied, Iraq did not have enough prisons to house its expected prison population.

Confronting Organized Crime and Corruption. The bulk of the CPA's efforts in the justice sector were focused on reconstituting a basic level of capability. The CPA, however, also recognized that two longer-term issues had to be addressed. First, the justice and police systems had to be given the capabilities to deal with serious organized crime and terrorism as well as ordinary crime. This would require judicial-police units with the dedication, skills, resources, and courage to tackle these threats. Only small steps were taken in this direction.

Second, the new Iraq had to tackle endemic corruption. It was evident that the corruption that pervaded the Saddam-era system would drag down the new Iraq and pose a real threat to stability and reconstruction. The November 15 agreement gave the CPA the spur to implement a number of measures that sought to tackle this problem. In January 2004, the CPA launched the Commission on Public Integrity,[72] which was set up as an independent investigative commission that would focus on major cases of corruption. At the same time, all Iraqi ministries were instructed to appoint an Inspector General and a staff.[73] Further oversight was provided by the reconstitution of Iraq's Board of Supreme Audit.[74]

Transitional Justice. Transitional justice issues fell outside the strict remit of the Iraqi Ministry of Justice (MoJ). But the CPA recognized the importance of beginning to address these issues as part of a process of promoting reconciliation and stabilization. The two key initiatives were the establishment of the Iraq Special Tribunal (IST) and the Iraq Property Claims Commission (IPCC). The IST was set up by CPA order in December 2003 and provides for a court to try

---

[72] CPA, "Commission on Public Integrity to Combat Government Corruption," press release, January 31, 2004.

[73] CPA "Iraqi Inspectors General," CPA Order 57, February 10, 2004b.

[74] CPA, "Board of Supreme Audit," CPA Order 77, April 25, 2004h. The sensitivity of the corruption issue was highlighted in July 2004, when Ihsan Karim, chair of the Board of Supreme Audit, who was investigating corruption in the oil-for-food program, was assassinated in a bomb attack. BBC News Online, "Bomb Kills Oil-for-Food Auditor," July 3, 2004.

members of the former Iraqi regime for war crimes and crimes against humanity. The U.S. government established a Regime Crimes Liaison Office to provide international legal, investigative, and prosecutorial expertise to the IST. The CPA also undertook initial forensic work on mass gravesites and built a secure document storage facility to hold and process documentation from the former regime, to be used in trials. The IPCC, meanwhile, was established in January 2004 to resolve property claims among the estimated one million internally displaced people across Iraq.[75] The IPCC provided a judicial mechanism whereby competing claims, often resulting from Kurds returning to areas that had been "Arabized" by the Saddam regime, could be adjudicated and compensation provided. However, as Human Rights Watch reported in August 2004, delays in the implementation of this program meant that "a crisis of serious proportions is brewing in northern Iraq, and may soon explode into violence."[76]

Inputs. The key external inputs to the Iraqi justice sector were (1) funding, (2) expatriate advisors, and (3) coalition assistance.

Funding. The 2003 and 2004 Iraqi budgets included $204.6 million for the MoJ's capital and operating expenditures.[77] The reprogrammed FY 2004 U.S. supplemental allocated $1.95 billion to justice, public safety infrastructure, and civil society.[78] Within this total, the allocation to justice and prisons was just under $520 million (see Table 5.4).

As with the police, many of the immediate needs of the judiciary had to be met by small grants administered by coalition military commanders in the field. As of June 2004, the CERP had spent

---

[75] The Saddam Hussein regime released the 38,000 inmates of Iraqi prisons before the April 2003 invasion. UNCHR (2004).

[76] Human Rights Watch, *Claims in Conflict: Reversing Ethnic Cleansing in Northern Iraq*, New York, August 2004.

[77] Republic of Iraq (2003); Iraqi Ministry of Finance (2004). DFI allocations to the MoJ were negligible, totaling some $1 million, according to DFI records. DFI Financial Reporting Matrix (2004).

[78] *Quarterly Report to Congress* (2004).

Table 5.4
U.S. Supplemental Spending Plan Related to the Ministry of Justice (in $ millions)

	Allocated (October 2004)	Disbursed (As of September 22, 2004)
Technical investigative means[a]	5	0
Witness protection program[b]	40	0
Penal facilities[c]	100	1
Reconstruction and modernization of detention facilities[d]	137	1
Rule of law[e]	30	1
Investigations of crimes against humanity[f]	75	1
Judicial security and facilities[g]	133	5
Total	**520**	**9**

SOURCE: *Quarterly Report to Congress* (2004).
[a] Allocated to the Commission on Public Integrity for use of electronic surveillance equipment and advanced accounting techniques.
[b] $5 million of this was diverted to start up the Commission on Public Integrity; the remainder on hiring and training Iraqis to establish a Witness Protection Program and providing safe houses.
[c] Devoted to the construction of a single maximum-security prison near Nasiriyah.
[d] Allocated to the reconstruction of one regional detention facility at Khan Bani Saad and the deployment of 107 civilian prison experts to train and mentor the Iraqi Corrections Service and undertake the institutional development of the service.
[e] Allocated to judicial training, increasing access to the legal system and capacity building in the Ministry of Justice.
[f] To assist the establishment and operations of the Iraqi Special Tribunal.
[g] To support reconstruction and physical security of Iraqi courthouses; provide personal security for judges and fund a U.S. Department of Justice Overseas Prosecutorial Development Assistance & Training (OPDAT) judicial training program in Iraq.

$27.3 million on rule-of-law and government programs. This was allocated across some 1,670 small projects and was used in large part for refurbishment or reequipping of courthouses.[79]

Non-U.S. international assistance was channeled both through the international trust funds and through bilateral channels. The United Kingdom and the European Commission have both been

---

[79] *Quarterly Report to Congress* (2004).

interested in aiding reform to Iraq's justice sector.[80] The UK Department for International Development (DFID) provided a few million dollars to support judicial training, through the International Legal Assistance Consortium (ILAC).[81] Justice sector reform has been prominently featured on the international donor agenda. At the May 2004 Donor Committee meeting, the MoJ lodged requests for $6 million worth of courthouse refurbishment, $25 million for information technology (IT) infrastructure and training for judicial and support staff, and $4 million for the construction of two prison clinics.[82]

How Much Was Spent. Making realistic assumptions about the continued use of CERP funds, it is possible to estimate that total allocations to the MoJ, from May 2003 to December 2004 will have been around $826 million, of which some three-quarters, or $560 million, came from donors.[83]

Expatriate Advisors. The CPA employed up to 35 expatriate advisors to manage and develop the MoJ, including several dedicated to founding new institutions such as the Commission on Public Integrity and the Central Criminal Court. After June 28, 2004, the authorized number of U.S. advisory posts fell to 13, dedicated to providing training and advice in areas such as judicial education, judicial security, and witness protection. Up to 31 advisors were also sought to support the Commission on Public Integrity. The advisors were drawn heavily from U.S. Army Civil Affairs and Judge Advocate General units, supplemented by contracted lawyers, prosecutors,

---

[80] Europe's 2004 aid strategy has allocated Eur10 million ($12 million) to governance and civil society, including aid to the judicial system. European Commission, *Iraq Assistance Programme*, Brussels, COM(2004) 667, March 4, 2004.

[81] ILAC, "Lawyers Call for International Role in Iraq," undated.

[82] Iraqi Ministry of Justice, submissions to Second Donor Committee meeting, Qatar, May 25–26, 2004.

[83] This overstates the amount that will be obligated in 2003–2004, since some of the supplemental expenditure programs on prisons will continue into 2007. These expenditures include Iraqi MoJ budgets, $265 million; additional DFI, $1 million; IRRF, $520 million; CERP, $30 million; UK and EU donations: notional, $10 million. The CERP figure assumes that MSCs and the MNSTC-I continue to spend CERP funds in part on the Iraqi judiciary through the remainder of 2004.

investigators, and U.S. Marshals Service personnel. A small number of British advisors supplemented the team. Seven British prisons advisors were deployed in southern Iraq, and Denmark provided some advice to courts and judges in this region.

In addition to the judicial advisors, the need to purge and rebuild the Iraqi Correctional Service (ICS) led the prisons department to contract for 107 expatriate prisons experts. These experts' task was to help take over the operations of the prisons from the CJTF-7 MPs and to train and mentor ICS personnel. These U.S. contractors tended to be retired corrections personnel. The team did not begin deploying in strength until spring of 2004, but the initial handful of staff deployed in the fall of 2003 made an impact on reforming the ICS.[84]

Coalition Assistance. The key role played by U.S. Army personnel in managing and advising the MoJ in Baghdad has been noted above. Outside Baghdad, the CPA justice advisors had very little reach; support to the local judicial system was provided almost exclusively by coalition military lawyers attached to CJTF-7's major subordinate commands (MSCs).[85] The CPA did endeavor to recruit and deploy additional legal experts who would form regional legal advisory teams to build the capacity of courts in the provinces; however, it was never able to recruit the required staff.[86] In relation to the prisons throughout the life of the CPA, coalition MP units undertook the task of running Iraq's jails. This posed problems in the spring of 2004, when the rotation of U.S. forces left a far smaller number of MP units in country, a loss compensated for only by the recruitment of civilian prisons experts.

---

[84] The challenges facing this program were highlighted in April 2004, when the 53 advisors were "locked down" for much of the month because of security concerns and so were unable to work closely with their Iraqi counterparts or to undertake site visits.

[85] The difficulties in this mission were illustrated in January 2004, when a judicial assessment team was mortared near Baquba. Three members of the team were injured.

[86] A proposal to deploy military legal assistance teams to the regions never progressed through the U.S. Department of Defense system.

Outputs. The programmatic outputs of the justice program can be defined in terms of (1) judicial human capital (personnel vetting and training), (2) judicial infrastructure, (3) judicial systemic reform and judicial capability, (4) corrections service human capital, and (5) prisons capacity and infrastructure.

Judicial Human Capital. During the life of the CPA, the Judicial Review Committee[87] reviewed the files of all 860 judges and prosecutors in Iraq, removed 176 staff, reappointed 82 judges and prosecutors who had been removed by Saddam, and appointed 123 new judges and prosecutors.[88] To counter corruption, judicial salaries were doubled. Short training courses were provided both in Iraq and in the Hague for some 185 judges and prosecutors. Another aspect of the CPA's justice program was to institute the regular practice of appointments by courts of defense counsel. By June 2004, the CPA could report that such appointments were being made in "a sizeable proportion of cases."[89]

Judicial Infrastructure. After the fall of the Saddam regime, the CPA and coalition forces assessed that 10 percent of Iraq's 128 courthouses had been destroyed and that another 70 percent had been badly damaged. The CPA focused on Baghdad, where it rehabilitated courthouses and the judicial college. Outside Baghdad, coalition forces took charge of the rehabilitation of many courthouses using CERP funds; the real investment in courthouse reconstruction via U.S. supplemental funds was scheduled to begin later in 2004. In addition to buildings, the judicial system suffered from the lack of a communications system and computerization. Coalition forces provided IT equipment and training on an ad hoc basis, but it was only in the early summer of 2004 that MoJ advisors developed a detailed plan to implement a justice sector–wide IT network.

---

[87] Grounds for exclusion were corruption, malfeasance, and high-level membership of the Ba'ath Party. CPA, "Establishment of the Judicial Review Committee," CPA Order 15, June 23, 2004.

[88] CPA (2004n); CPA, *Strategic Plan*, Baghdad, June 25, 2004m.

[89] CPA (2004m).

An additional, urgent judicial need was for security. A number of judges and courthouses were attacked, and most judges were reluctant to put their lives at risk by prosecuting well-connected defendants. The CPA responded by initiating a program of relocating or fortifying courthouses across the country, as well as deploying FPS guards at all courthouses. In addition, the CPA initiated a program to provide personal security details for 400 judges and criminal prosecutors. Because of funding delays, training was scheduled only to begin in July 2004 and to produce 1,600 security personnel by January 2005.[90] Likewise, an ambitious program to have an Iraqi witness protection program operational by January 2005 was delayed by U.S. government funding wrangles. As of the end of June 2004, only one witness was being protected.[91]

Judicial Systemic Reform. The focus of the CPA's judicial reform efforts was to institutionalize the independence of the judiciary. The Council of Judges, abolished by Saddam in 1979, was reestablished in September 2003 under the leadership of the Iraqi Chief Justice. The council was separated from the MoJ and given authority over court budgets, personnel, security, and property.[92] In addition, the CPA established the Central Criminal Court of Iraq with nationwide jurisdiction and a mandate to concentrate on the more serious crimes that other courts were often reluctant to deal with, such as terrorism, organized crime, and governmental corruption.[93] Work was also initiated to assist in the establishment of an Iraqi Supreme Court.

Corrections Service Human Capital. The existing ICS staff had to be extensively purged in 2003 because the standards of behavior and management were unacceptably low.[94] A recruitment and five-week training program meant that, by June 2004, 4,000 of the target

---

[90] *Quarterly Report to Congress* (2004); CPA (2004m).

[91] CPA (2004m).

[92] CPA, "Re-Establishment of the Council of Judges," CPA Order 35, September 15, 2003e.

[93] CPA, "The Central Criminal Court of Iraq (Amended)," CPA Order 13, April 22, 2004g.

[94] On more than one occasion, CPA prison advisors came across ICS staff routinely using Saddam-era torture techniques on prisoners.

5,000 staff were employed, including 3,300 corrections officers. By June, plans were also being implemented for a management training course at the ICS training academy, and expatriate advisors were developing a program of in-service training and mentoring.[95]

Prisons Capacity and Infrastructure. The CPA prisons advisors and coalition forces renovated the 17 facilities managed by the ICS, providing some 5,500 prison beds.[96] Conditions in the renovated prisons were improved, for instance, by guaranteeing 25 square feet per inmate, the provision of food, and family visits. The overall target was for 50 percent of prisons to be compliant with UN standards by March 2005, with 100 percent compliance to be achieved by September 2007.[97] In addition, the CPA developed plans for the renovation and construction of three large prisons; these were scheduled to provide an additional 11,000 prison beds by the end of 2005. In addition to the ICS-run prisons, the MoJ initiated a program to transfer control of police detention facilities from the IPS to the ICS while at the same time raising the standards in these often-appalling police lockups.[98]

In addition to the prisons themselves, the CPA had to acquire a fleet of vehicles to enable the ICS to transport prisoners between the jails and the courts. It also sought to develop a computerized prison records system to improve prisoner management.

Defense Sector

Prewar coalition planning had envisaged making some use of the existing Iraqi armed forces and instituting a comprehensive program of disarmament, demobilization, and reintegration. By May 2003, coalition officials concluded that the Iraqi armed forces had effectively "self-demobilized" and restricted the DDR program to paying

---

[95] CPA (2004n); CPA (2004m).

[96] By June 2004, the ICS held some 4,000 criminal detainees.

[97] However, these "UN standards" were never precisely defined. CPA (2004m).

[98] In its Annual Human Rights report published in February 2005, the U.S. Department of State singled out these police detention facilities for particular criticism.

stipends to former military personnel. Instead, attention turned to building new armed forces.

The program to build the New Iraqi Army, subsequently renamed the Iraqi Armed Forces (IAF), envisaged forming a small, professional force that could form the nucleus of a larger military establishment, if so desired, by a future Iraqi government. Under CPA supervision, the program was implemented by the Coalition Military Assistance Training Team (CMATT), an international team of military officers under a U.S. general.[99] CMATT's task was to recruit, train, and equip the NIA, much of whose actual implementation was undertaken by U.S. contractors. Plans for the NIA changed a number of times during the life of the CPA. Revised plans in September 2003 called for training of 40,000 personnel and the production of 27 battalions organized into three divisions by the end of 2004.[100]

These plans were revised again in the spring of 2004, in part because of the diversion of some $200 million in funding to support the police and ICDC program. The new plans called for the development of a 27,000-person force, organized into two motorized infantry divisions, by March 2005.[101] These units would be supplemented by an air wing equipped with transport aircraft and helicopters; a coastal defense force equipped with six patrol boats; and special operations units consisting of a counterterrorist force and a commando battalion. In addition, the 1st Brigade, Iraqi Intervention Force, of some 6,600 soldiers, became operational on June 24, with specialized training in internal security operations in urban areas.[102] In addition to these units, the ICDC was to be formally brought

---

[99] CMATT was incorporated into its successor organizations from the spring of 2004: Office of Security Cooperation, Office of Security Transition, and MNSTC-I.

[100] Report to Congress Pursuant to Section 1506 of the Emergency Wartime Supplemental Appropriations Act, 2003 (Public Law 108-11), *Update Report on United States Strategy for Relief and Reconstruction in Iraq*, October 14, 2003.

[101] This delay from September 2004 was due to the diversion of effort to the IIF, which was tasked with internal security operations.

[102] This third battalion brigade was constituted from the first four battalions of the NIA program.

under the Iraqi Ministry of Defense (MoD). The ICDC, which was planned to expand to 45 battalions during 2004,[103] was characterized as a "mobilized reserve" force that would continue to function as a locally recruited, lightly armed, and trained force dedicated to internal security missions in support of the police and coalition forces.[104] The ICDC was renamed the Iraqi National Guard (ING) by the Interim Iraqi Government in July 2004.

The roles and missions of the armed forces were an important issue for the military program. The philosophy adopted by the CPA was to design the NIA for the defense of Iraq against external enemies.[105] Unlike the old Iraqi army, the intention, as enshrined in the TAL and the CPA order that established the army, was to keep the army out of domestic security tasks as far as possible. However, the worsening security situation led to an erosion of this principle. Over time, recruit training began to focus more on internal security tasks; the air wing was given the task of infrastructure surveillance; and a counterterrorist force was developed within the NIA. This change in direction was controversial. The first NIA battalion to be deployed against insurgents in Fallujah in April 2004 refused to deploy after being ambushed on its way to the rebel stronghold. Coalition and interim government policymakers sought to lay down a legal basis for such internal use, stipulating that the police could call on the army for assistance under clearly defined circumstances.

At the same time the armed forces were being built, the CPA had to build a new defense ministry. The new MoD was formally established on March 21, 2004.[106] By June 2004, it was being operated by a small but growing number of carefully recruited civilian officials. Operating within a ministerial structure devised by the CPA, these officials underwent short training courses in Washington and

---

[103] In addition to fielding bomb disposal companies.

[104] CPA, "Transfer of the Iraqi Civil Defense Corps to the Iraqi Ministry of Defense," CPA Order 74, April 25, 2004i.

[105] However, the CENTCOM vision had always been to use the NIA for internal security as part of CJTF-7.

[106] CPA, "Ministry of Defense," CPA Order 67, March 21, 2004d.

were mentored by international officials in areas such as administration, personnel, finance, acquisition, and intelligence. The new ministry was designed to provide democratic accountability, civilian control, and efficient management of all aspects of defense affairs.

Inputs. The international inputs to the Iraqi military sector comprised (1) funds from the Iraqi budget, coalition forces, and the United States; (2) equipment; and (3) advisors provided by the CPA and coalition forces.

Funding. The 2003 and 2004 Iraqi budgets allocated $268 million to the MoD.[107] DFI and CPA records on the MoD break down allocations of only about $25 million to the MoD and CMATT in 2003–2004.[108] However, we have assumed that the MoD and CMATT received some $500 million between them in DFI funding during the course of the CPA.[109] Out of the 2003 supplemental, the U.S. Department of Defense allocated $48 million to pay for CMATT to employ civilian trainers.[110] The reprogrammed FY 2004 U.S. supplemental allocated $2,448 million to the Iraqi military and National Guard (see Table 5.5).

Non-U.S. international assistance to the defense sector was mainly in the form of advisors and military trainers provided by the United Kingdom, Australia, Italy, and Spain. However, at the Second Donor Committee meeting in Qatar in May 2004, the MoD requested $200 million worth of assistance with establishing an Iraqi Veterans Agency.[111]

---

[107] Derived from Republic of Iraq (2003); Iraqi Ministry of Finance, *2004 Budget*, Baghdad, October 2003; and Iraqi Ministry of Finance (2004).

[108] See International Advisory and Monitoring Board, "Development Fund for Iraq Statement of Cash Receipts and Payments for the period from 22 May 2003 to 31 December 2003 (with Independent Auditors' Report)," June 29, 2004; DFI Financial Reporting Matrix (2004).

[109] A significant proportion of this was spent via the CERP program on the ICDC.

[110] Report to Congress (2003).

[111] Iraqi MoD, submissions to Second Donor Committee meeting, Qatar, May 25–26, 2004.

Table 5.5
U.S. Supplemental Spending Plan Related to Iraqi Military (in $ millions)

	Allocated (July 2004)[a]	Disbursed (as of September 22, 2004)
IAF facilities, equipment, training, and operations	1,765	332
ING operations and personnel, equipment, and facilities	683	81
Total	**2,448**	**413**

SOURCE: *Quarterly Report to Congress* (2004).
[a] CPA and MNF-I altered allocations slightly during the course of implementing the supplemental.

How Much Was Spent. It is possible to estimate that total allocations to the MoD and Iraqi Armed Forces, including the ING, from May 2003 to December 2004 was around $3.3 billion, of which three-quarters ($2.5 billion) came from donors.[112]

Equipment and Infrastructure. Funding and contractual delays dogged the IAF equipment program, which was meant to be mainly funded out of the FY 2004 U.S. supplemental (see Table 5.6).[113] Allocation of DFI funds bridged some of the gap, but the April 2004 uprisings in center-south Iraq and in the Sunni triangle caused further logistical delays. This meant that, by August 2004, the NIA had on hand 76 percent of its required weapons but only 63 percent of its required vehicles, 4 percent of required communications equipment, and 37 percent of required body armor. These delays had a particular impact on the ING, which was thrust into the front line against insurgents—often without body armor, radios, or vehicles.

---

[112] This overstates the amounts to be obligated and disbursed in 2003–2004, since some of the supplemental funding will continue to be spent for programs in 2005. This comprises Iraqi MoD budgets, $267.9 million; DFI, $500 million; IRRF 2003, $48 million; and IRRF 2004, $2,448 million. It is not clear what CERP funds will be expended on supporting the IAF in the remainder of 2004.

[113] Notably the need to re-solicit bids when a contract for battalion sets of equipment was challenged by a losing firm.

Table 5.6
Iraqi Armed Forces Equipment, August 2004

	Weapons		Vehicles		Communications Equipment		Body Armor	
Force/Element	**Required**	**On-Hand**	**Required**	**On-Hand**	**Required**	**On-Hand**	**Required**	**On-Hand**
Army								
Army	18,909	15,432	1,980	1,728	3,596	0	27,000	6,137
Iraqi National Guard[a]	42,576	36,055	1,311	658	6,963	0	41,088	18,900
Iraqi Intervention Force	8,850	3,300	583	152	1,798	594	6,584	2,741
Special Operations Forces	1,898	824	180	42	1,212	12	1,620	924
Air Force	383	0	34	4	21	0	502	0
Coastal Defense Force	486	12	15	15	156	1	409	0
Total	**73,102**	**55,623**	**4,103**	**2,599**	**13,764**	**607**	**77,203**	**28,702**

[a] Formerly ICDC.
SOURCE: U.S. Department of State (2004d).

By the summer of 2004, the funding and contractual issues seem to have been worked out, and the Bush administration reported to Congress in July 2004 that equipment on order would arrive in time to equip the 27 NIA battalions and that communications systems were beginning to be installed at military bases across the country. In addition to equipment, the FY 2004 U.S. supplemental allocated more than $600 million for construction and refurbishment of NIA facilities across the country. These projects included recruiting centers, training facilities, garrisons, airbases, naval facilities, and the joint headquarters.[114]

Advisors. Although their numbers varied during the life of the CPA, there were some 48 CPA expatriate advisors supporting the MoD in early 2004. It was planned that some 20 advisors would remain in the ministry after the transition from the CPA, but by the summer of 2004, it appeared there were fewer than 10 advisors, largely from the United Kingdom. In support of the NIA, CMATT had some 200 coalition military staff, but its strength varied over time, as did the number of civilian contractors employed.[115] In addition, CJTF-7 MSCs had the responsibility for recruiting, training, and mentoring ICDC/ING units in their area of operations. This meant that the assistance provided by coalition forces to the development of the NIA was substantial during and after the life of the CPA.

Outputs. The programmatic outputs of the NIA program consisted of (1) military personnel and (2) institutional development.

Military Personnel. In the summer of 2004, MNF-I revised the required end strengths for the Iraqi National Guard from 41,000 to 62,000 (see Table 5.7). By October 2004, some two-thirds of the required personnel were reported as being "on hand and trained." The quality of the ING should not, however, be overemphasized.

---

[114] *Quarterly Report to Congress* (2004).

[115] Fifty-seven NATO trainers from 12 countries under a Dutch general were also deployed to CMATT after the transfer of authority. Dow Jones International News, "Tiny Iraq NATO Mission Sticks to Training, Not Fighting," August 26, 2004.

Table 5.7
Iraqi Military Personnel, October 2004

Force/Element	Required	Trained/On Hand
Iraqi Police		
Iraqi Police Service	27,000	3,887
Iraqi National Guard	61,904	41,261
Iraqi Intervention Force	6,584	1,794
Special operations forces	1,967	604
Air Force	502	167
Coastal Defense Force	582	409
Total	**98,539**	**48,122**

SOURCE: U.S. Department of State (2004e).

The ING training consisted of minimal two- to three-week recruit training followed by on-the-job mentoring by coalition forces. In addition, doubt had been thrown on the effectiveness of the ICDC during the April 2004 uprisings, when the numbers of personnel reporting to duty across the country dropped from 32,000 to 17,500.[116] Although most personnel returned to work after the uprisings had subsided, this experience demonstrated the risks associated with relying on a lightly trained and locally recruited force.

The more thorough training that would build a truly professional army was being delivered at a slower pace to regular army personnel. By October 2004, the regular armed forces had recruited and trained some 18 percent of their target end strength (6,861 of a target 36,635 personnel). In addition to recruit training, several thousand soldiers had passed through a two-month-long noncommissioned officer course, and more than 1,500 officers were graduated from the Jordanian military academy. In addition, more than 40 officers were graduated from brigade/battalion staff officer courses.[117] By the summer of 2004, the emphasis was very much on train-the-trainer programs rather than relying on contractors or coalition military personnel for recruit training.

116 *Quarterly Report to Congress* (2004).

117 CPA (2004n).

Institutional Development. Institutional development of the IAF included building command structures and control structures, reforming the uniform code of military justice, and transforming the armed force's logistical tail. By the summer of 2004, preparations were under way to build an Iraqi joint headquarters capable of commanding Iraqi military operations under the direction of the MoD. The CPA had also reformed the military legal codes to end the privileged status of military personnel and to bring the IAF into line with the civil legal system. Likewise, the logistical tail of the armed forces was made reliant on the civil sector. This was intended to have the effect of both integrating the military with the civil economy and making the military unable to deploy for large-scale offensive operations.

Institutional development of the MoD, critical to ensure civilian control of the military, was nascent at best by June 2004. The MoD's policy processes, command and control capabilities, management systems, and intelligence structures were well planned but provided the new minister of defense with limited capabilities to run Iraqi defense policy after the resumption of sovereignty.

Intelligence Services

One of the CPA's first acts was to dissolve the multiple entities that made up Iraq's Mukhabarat state. The range of these entities was indicated by those listed by name in CPA Order 2, issued on May 23, 2003. Primarily, they included the National Security Bureau, the Iraqi Intelligence Service, the Directorate of National Security, the Special Security Organization, and Saddam Hussein's bodyguard organizations (Murafaqin, Himaya al-Khas). In addition, the following intelligence and security military forces were dissolved: Directorate of Military Intelligence, al-Quds Force, Emergency Forces, Saddam Fedayeen, Friends of Saddam, Saddam's Lion Cubs, and Ba'ath party militia.[118] The personnel from these organizations were dismissed as of April 16, 2003.

---

[118] CPA (2003a).

The U.S. Central Intelligence Agency was given the mission of standing up Iraq's new intelligence agencies, and it worked closely with British intelligence. The Iraqi National Intelligence Service (INIS) was made public on April 1, 2004, by CPA Order 69, in which the CPA delegated authority to the Iraqi Governing Council to promulgate a statute adopting the Charter of the INIS. In line with the March 8, 2004, TAL, the INIS's role was to "collect information, assess threats to national security, and advise the Iraqi government. This Service shall be under civilian control, shall be subject to legislative oversight, and shall operate pursuant to law and in accordance with recognized principles of human rights."[119] The INIS charter made clear that the INIS Director General,[120] appointed in April 2004 for a period of five years, should serve as the Iraqi government's principal intelligence advisor. This mirrored the U.S. model of a Director of Central Intelligence. From April 2004 to the transfer of authority, the INIS Director General reported directly to the Ministerial Committee on National Security. The INIS provided the regular intelligence briefings that this committee came to rely on to conduct its business.

The INIS was envisioned as primarily an internal security intelligence service, focused on countering insurgent and terrorist threats to the government. Although former agents of the dissolved Saddam-era intelligence services were recruited, the INIS's British and U.S. mentors also sought to ensure that new blood was brought in and that serious human rights violators did not serve in the new agency.

An important feature of the INIS that distinguished it from its predecessors was its lack of arrest authority. Although the INIS's agents were authorized to carry weapons for self defense, this provision was inserted to prevent it from taking on a secret police role. This also meant that the INIS would have to work closely with the Iraqi Police Service to take action on intelligence collected. This

---

[119] CPA (2004c).

[120] Mohammed Abdullah Mohammed al-Shehwani, a former Iraqi Air Force general who had been active in covert opposition to Saddam during the 1990s was appointed by the CPA.

reflected the success of advocates of the British "special branch" model. This model, however, depended on the creation and deployment of a police unit with security-cleared officers able to liaise with the INIS. In the British model, these officers would also have been the security intelligence first line in Iraq's regions. In fact, by July 2004, the MoI had not developed this capability, and the INIS was establishing regional offices in Iraq's major cities and exercising executive authorities.

Although the MoI made little progress on establishing a "special branch," it did push ahead with plans for more general police intelligence capabilities. This focused on developing a nationwide criminal intelligence system and a national counterterrorism investigation section. The criminal intelligence system had to be built from a very basic level, including the development of crime record databases and the collection and collation of crime statistics.

Meanwhile, the coalition personnel in charge of developing the embryonic Iraqi armed forces came to recognize the need to provide these forces with tactical-, operational-, and strategic-level defense intelligence assessment capabilities. These requirements were built into the MoD structure, which included an intelligence analysis and management branch. The NIA plan called for an intelligence function in the military staffs. At the same time, however, there was a push to provide the military with its own human intelligence capabilities, based in part on the desire to maintain and exploit the human intelligence networks that the coalition forces had built up while in country.

The critical challenge that the CPA was never able to resolve was how the various elements of the Iraqi intelligence community would coordinate and cooperate. Although numerous models and organizational schema were developed, the CPA never managed to implement a program to build a joined-up Iraqi intelligence community with clear demarcations of roles and responsibilities.[121] The intelligence situation became even more confused when the IIG took over in June

---

[121] For instance, although the INIS was not given an external intelligence function, it was always assumed that a foreign intelligence service would one day grow out of the INIS core.

2004, with interim Prime Minister Iyad Allawi's announcement that he would reconstitute the old General Security Directorate, with powers of arrest. There seemed to be a real danger that Iraq would fall into its traditional pattern of building competing, stovepiped, and overlapping intelligence services.

Outcomes

The ongoing instability and violence in Iraq that make international headlines are indicators that the Iraqi security sector cannot yet enforce the rule of law. Further, the reported delays in building the capacity of the Iraqi security forces have led some observers to lambaste the U.S. government and the CPA for their "inexcusable failure" to develop the Iraqi security forces.[122] This chapter uses four measures to understand the security outcomes that have been achieved:

- Political violence and crime rates
- Fear of crime and perceptions of security
- Judicial effectiveness
- Ability of coalition forces to withdraw from providing security.

These data paint a bleak picture of the outcome of coalition efforts to provide security or to make the Iraqi security sector effective. The data that have been consistently collected on political violence, which concentrate on attacks against coalition forces and the CPA, demonstrate an increase in the number and sophistication of insurgent attacks since the summer of 2003. While systematic data on political violence that targets Iraqi civilians or officials are not publicly available, the partial data available demonstrates an upward trend in such attacks. The partial data on "ordinary" crime, murders, and

---

[122] Anthony H. Cordesman, *Inexcusable Failure: Progress in Training the Iraqi Army and Security Forces as of Mid-July 2004*, Washington, D.C.: Center for Strategic and International Studies, July 20, 2004a.

major property crimes support the public perception of a dramatic increase in such crimes since April 2003. Although major property crimes have declined since their peak in the summer of 2003, there is no evidence yet of a downward trend in reported crimes or an upward trend in clear-up rates.[123]

Perceptions of security among Iraqi citizens more or less match the trends in reported crimes and attacks. Polls indicate that security and public safety were even higher in the public's agenda in May 2004 than they had been in January, when they were still top priority. Although there was growing concern at the civilian toll taken by terrorist attacks, street crime was the top priority for most Iraqis. Meanwhile, there is strong evidence that the unstable security situation has affected the operations and perceptions of foreign contractors working on Iraqi reconstruction. This has contributed to the CPA's failure to achieve key objectives such as boosting electrical power output.

As far as the effectiveness of the criminal justice system is concerned, the evidence from Baghdad indicates that, just to ensure a minimal standard of performance (detention-to-trial period of one month), coalition advisors had to intervene extensively to operate the system themselves. The weakness of the justice system is evidenced by the fact that relatively few judges, prosecutors, or police officers have been willing to take the risk of confronting serious criminals in court. Those with tribal, family, or political connections are therefore unlikely to stand trial.

Finally, and perhaps most damning, are the internal assessments that coalition forces in Iraq have made since the occupation. Based on a systematic, region-by-region assessment of security sector outputs (strength and capability of forces) and threats, CJTF-7 had originally planned to hand over responsibility for security in most urban areas

---

[123] It may be that detection rates, the Iraqi term for "clear-up," are higher than official figures indicate. Under the current reporting system, crimes solved outside the month in which they are reported are not counted as "detected."

to Iraqi forces by early 2004, but this schedule had to be delayed to late 2004. The violent uprisings of April and summer 2004, combined with poor ISF performance, have delayed this schedule even further.

The positive news from the data is that Iraqi public support for the IPS and, to a lesser extent, for the IAF are high. Poll respondents repeatedly express their support for and faith in the IPS as the leading agency capable of providing law and order in Iraq.

Political Violence and Crime Rates

The most comprehensive source of data on political violence and resultant casualties in Iraq is that collected by coalition forces in their Significant Activities (SIGACTS) database, derived from unit reporting. This reports all manner of attacks (including small arms fire, antiaircraft fire, indirect fire, improvised explosive device, and complex attacks) against coalition forces, as well as against civilian "neutrals" and Iraqi Security Forces. The data are not perfect, and may underestimate the number of attacks,[124] but they nonetheless provide an indication of trends over time. The data presented in Figure 5.3 indicate that the daily average number of attacks carried out on all targets in Iraq rose from some 15 in June 2003 to around 70 by June 2004.

Coalition forces bore the brunt of these attacks. As illustrated in Figure 5.4, SIGACTS against coalition forces rose from around 12 per day in June 2003 to around 50 per day in June 2004.

---

[124] For instance, in periods of major unrest, there is a tendency by reporting units to combine multiple incidents into one report. Furthermore, if coalition forces are not directly targeted, then they are more likely to notice and hence report major events such as mortar or rocket attacks rather than small-arms fire.

Figure 5.3
All Significant Attacks

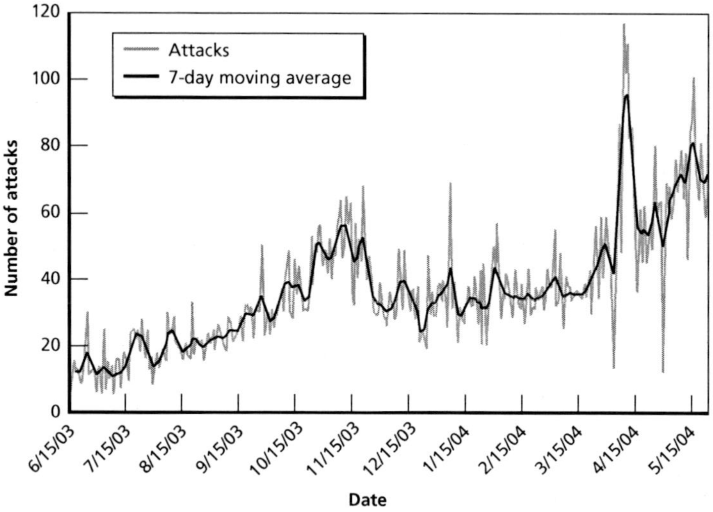

SOURCE: Charts derived from U.S. Department of Defense, CPA Daily Threat Updates (unclassified).
NOTE: Includes attacks against all types of targets (civil and military).
RAND *MG374-5.3*

Figure 5.4
Attacks on Coalition Forces

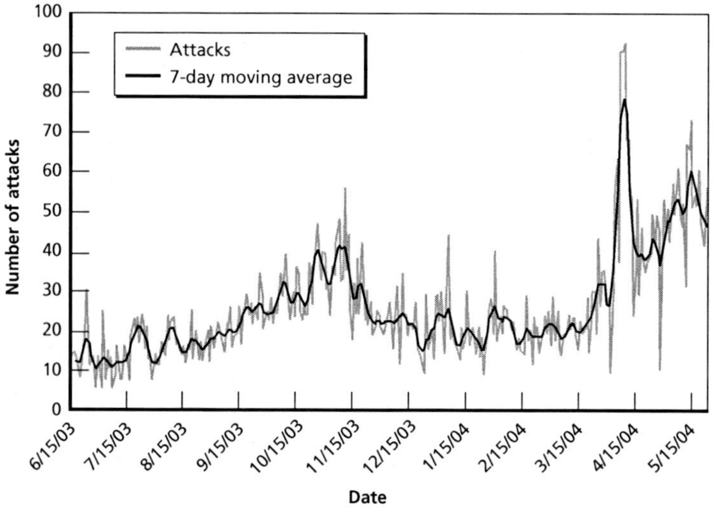

SOURCE: U.S. Department of Defense.
RAND *MG374-5.4*

Public U.S. Defense Department data do not directly link SIGACTS with resultant casualties, but the broad coalition casualty trends can be recreated from coalition forces casualty records. Between May 2003 and November 9, 2004, 904 coalition military personnel had been killed by hostile acts and 7,916 U.S. service personnel had been wounded in action (WIA). A monthly breakdown of coalition killed by hostile fire and U.S. military WIA indicates no improvement over time, with significant peaks during major upsurges in violence as in October–November 2003 and April 2004, as illustrated in Figure 5.5.[125]

Figure 5.5
Coalition Military Casualties

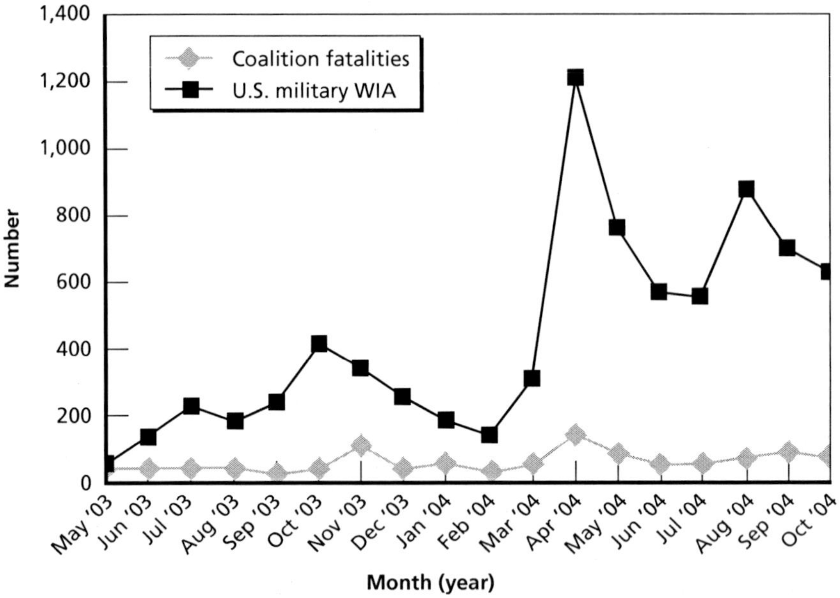

SOURCE: Iraq Coalition Casualty Count.
RAND *MG374-5.5*

---

[125] As of August 28, 2004. Iraq Coalition Casualty Count, http://icasualties.org/oif/.

Over the course of 2003–2004, insurgents and terrorists broadened their targeting to civilians and Iraqi government institutions. The trend in attacks on ISF has been noted in Figure 5.1. Figure 5.6 below uses U.S. Defense Department data, which likely under-reports attacks, to demonstrate how attacks on civilians increased from a daily average of around 2 in June 2003 to almost 30 in June 2004. Although it has been the major attacks, such as car bombings, that make the headlines, at least as important are the targeted attacks on the professionals who are working to reconstruct civil society and government institutions. Local councilors have been frequent targets,

Figure 5.6
Attacks on Iraqi Civilians and Infrastructure

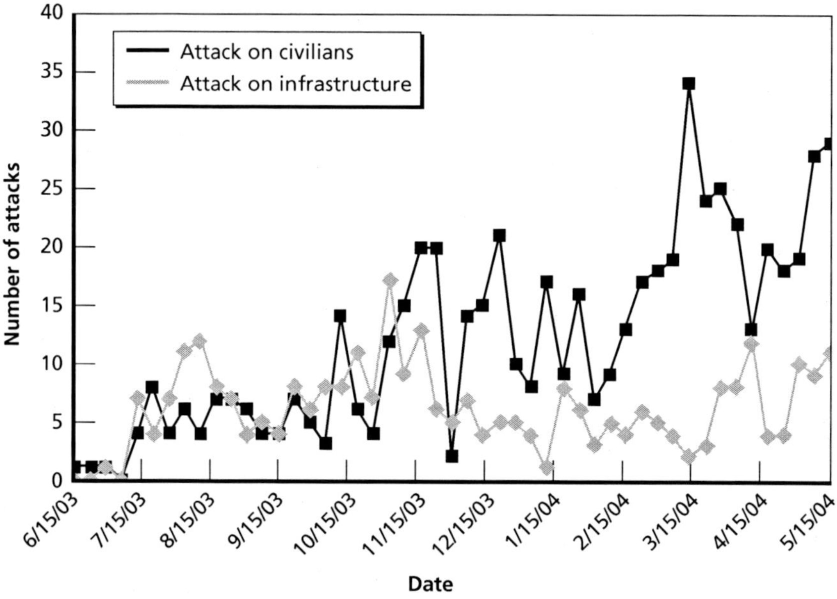

SOURCE: U.S. Department of Defense.
RAND *MG374-5.6*

and 37 education professionals have been murdered since May 2003.[126]

In addition to causing casualties, insurgent attacks on infrastructure have been designed to hamper reconstruction. These attacks rose from a negligible amount to around 11 per day in June 2004. Although many of these are criminally motivated, a coordinated campaign of attacks on road, rail, and air transportation routes, as well as on the electrical infrastructure and oil export facilities, has significantly slowed Iraqi reconstruction.

Comprehensive data on Iraqi civilian casualties are not systematically released in public by coalition forces or the Iraqi government.[127] The project Iraq Body Count, working from online media sources, has calculated that between 7,050 and 9,196 Iraqi civilians have been killed since May 1, 2004.[128] This figure includes fatalities from direct acts of violence by coalition forces, terrorists, insurgents, criminality, and "indirect effects," such as deaths due to diseases subsequent to damage to vital infrastructures.[129] The Brookings Institution's reconstruction index estimates that between 11,400 and 22,200 Iraqi civilians died from acts of war and violent crime between May 2003 and July 30, 2004.[130] A study published in *The Lancet* estimated that some 100,000 extra Iraqi civilian deaths occurred under occupation, the majority from violence, many attributable to coalition air strikes.[131]

---

[126] U.S. Department of State, *Iraq Status Report*, September 8, 2004d.

[127] The Iraqi Ministry of Health releases casualty figures after incidents, but it is not clear whether this is systematically collated over time.

[128] As of November 16, 2004. Iraq Body Count Project, www.iraqbodycount.net/bodycount.htm.

[129] These figures are not wholly reliable, since the linkages from direct violence to indirect fatalities are sometimes tenuous. The RAND terrorism database, drawing on press accounts of political violence in Iraq, which underreport casualties, provides a total of 775 civilian and ISF fatalities and 1,669 injuries from June 2003 to mid-June 2004.

[130] O'Hanlon and Lins de Albuquerque (2004).

[131] Les Roberts, Riyadh Lafta, Richard Garfield, Jamal Khudhairi, Gilbert Burnham, "Mortality Before and After the 2003 Invasion of Iraq: Cluster Sample Survey," *Lancet*, October 29, 2004.

Nationwide crime statistics do not exist in Iraq. But during 2004, the Baghdad Police Department began to collate statistics of reported and detected crimes.[132] While these figures are even more problematic than most crime statistics, they do provide a sense of the scale and of trends. According to these figures, the annualized murder rate in Baghdad rose from 3.6 per 100,000 inhabitants before the war to just over 23 in 2003 and over 24 in 2004 (see Figure 5.7). It is

Figure 5.7
Baghdad Murders

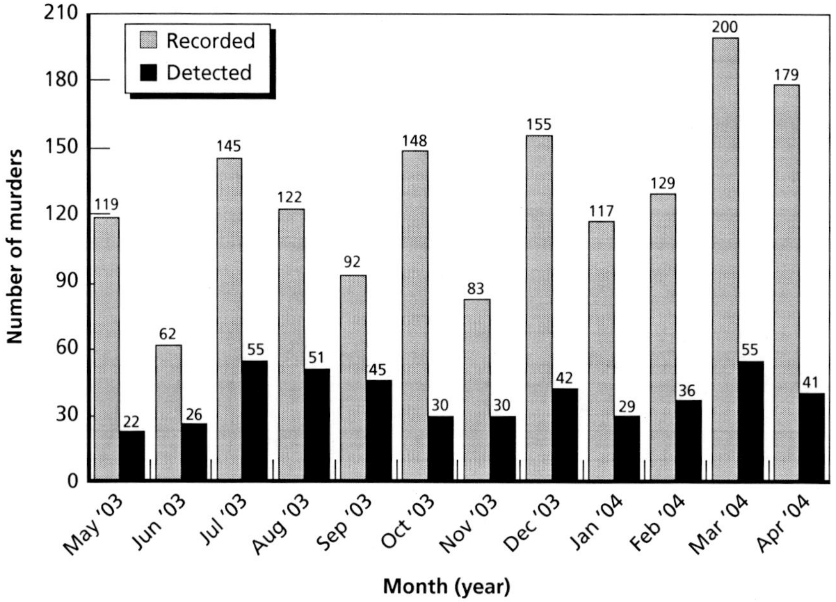

SOURCE: Baghdad Police Department.
RAND *MG374-5.7*

---

[132] CJTF-7 did seek to collect crime data from its MSCs across the country, but a comparison with the Baghdad IPS data indicated that the coalition figures underreported crime, at least in the capital.

important to note, however, that the Baghdad police statistics do not include deaths from political violence or terrorism, making any wider comparisons difficult.

Major property theft showed a similar jump after the war. Reported cases of car theft, carjacking, and armed robbery increased from a monthly average before the war of 47 to 284 in 2003 and 2004 (see Figure 5.8).[133] Anecdotal evidence also indicates an epidemic of kidnappings for ransom; however, most cases are not reported to the police, with families preferring to pay a ransom or rely

Figure 5.8
Baghdad Major Thefts (auto theft, carjacking, armed robbery)

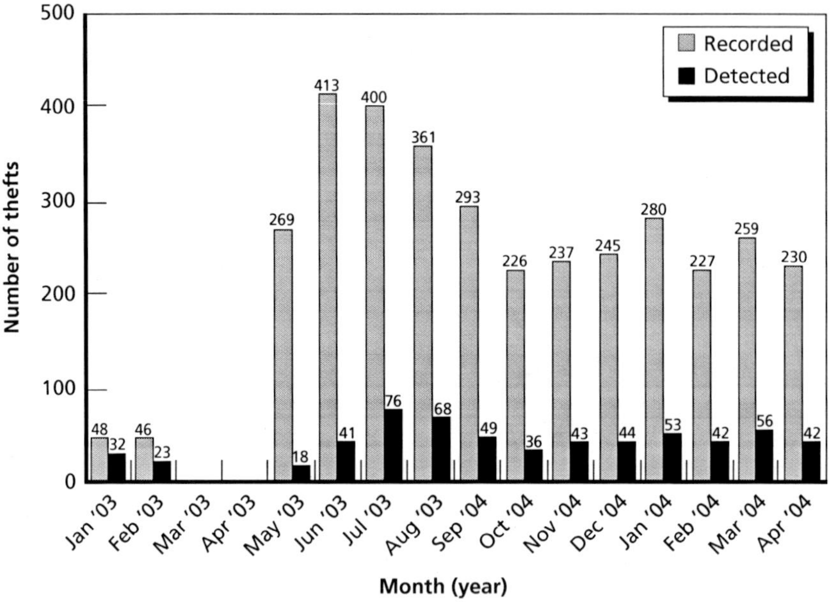

SOURCE: Baghdad Police Department.
RAND *MG374-5.8*

---

133 It is not worth distinguishing between these categories, since car jackings are often reported as auto theft or armed robbery.

on tribal or family links to mediate with the kidnappers. Overall, the Baghdad police criminal statistics staff estimate that some 100 percent of murders and almost 100 percent of major property crimes are reported, but that few assaults, kidnappings, or cases of petty crime are brought to the attention of the police.

Another aspect of crime that is of great significance to the Iraqi economy is widespread smuggling. Illegal exports of subsidized fuels, for instance, are in part responsible for domestic fuel shortages that have strained the Iraqi budget and provoked public disorder. Although it is not possible to assess the extent of smuggling, it is noticeable that the Department of Border Enforcement did start collecting the 5 percent reconstruction levy at 17 border points of entry on April 15, 2004. Somewhat to the surprise of CPA advisors, the $2.7 million collected in the first 15 days made its way to the Ministry of Finance. However, it was noticeable that the stated receipts did not vary in accord with reported changes in traffic at the border points, leading to concerns about corruption at the point of collection.[134]

Fear of Crime and Perceptions of Security

Victim surveys and polls regarding public perceptions and fears of crime are fraught with methodological difficulty; the problems with polling in post-authoritarian Iraq are evident. Nonetheless, a reasonably robust series of polls have been developed in Iraq over the past year. These provide some insight into Iraqi perceptions of security issues. Two authoritative polls were published in June 2004 by the U.S. State Department and by Oxford Research International (ORI). These polls demonstrate that security remained the main concern of Iraqi citizens, that fears of street crime[135] and terrorism have increased

[134] CPA (2004m).

[135] This has had a particular impact on the security and freedom of movement of Iraqi women, whose access to education, health care, and employment has been restricted by the rise in street crime and sexual assaults. UNCHR (2004), para. 80.

during 2004, and that the public expresses a high degree of confidence in the Iraqi Police Service to tackle law-and-order issues.[136]

The State Department poll, sampling some 2,600 residents in 10 cities in April and May 2004, indicated that respondents continued to place security and safety at the top of their priorities.[137] Indeed, the priority accorded to security had increased since January. Street crime had become a growing concern for residents in Baghdad and Mosul, while respondents in Basra expressed increasing concern at terrorist bombings.[138] The ORI poll, covering 3,000 respondents in 17 provinces, put peace and stability at the top of respondents' concerns.[139] Seventy percent of respondents put "regaining public security" as their first priority for the coming year. In line with other polls, the ORI survey found that street crime ranked above terrorism in respondent's concerns.[140]

One of the consistent factors in the polling data has been the high respect accorded by respondents to the IPS. They usually rate higher than the IAF and much higher than coalition forces, whose presence was opposed by a majority of respondents. In the State Department poll, 61 percent of Baghdad respondents expressed confidence that the IPS and army could maintain security without the coalition, and 61 percent expressed support for a family member joining the IPS.[141] In the ORI poll, when asked to express degrees of

---

[136] These trends are supported by CSIS's assessment of security trends, which relies on a combination of polling data, official reporting, and press reporting. Rick Barton and Bathsheba Croker, *Progress or Peril? Measuring Iraq's Reconstruction*, Washington, D.C.: Center for Strategic and International Studies, September 2004, pp. 18–31.

[137] U.S. Department of State, *Opinion Analysis*, M-71-04, June 17, 2004b.

[138] However, this may have been because the poll was conducted shortly after a major suicide bombing in Basra; it may represent a spike rather than a trend in the polling data.

[139] Oxford Research International, *National Survey of Iraq*, Oxford, UK, June 2004.

[140] Some 55 percent named fighting crime as the most important security issue, with 31 percent identifying terrorist bombings of civilian targets as the most important issue. However, when asked—"What makes you feel insecure?"—29 percent mentioned bombings and a lack of security, while 19 percent mentioned crime and the lack of law enforcement.

[141] Respondents in Basra were consistently more ambivalent about the presence of coalition forces, and a striking 75 percent recorded support for a family member joining the IPS.

confidence in various institutions, with 4 equaling a great deal and 1 equaling not at all, the police scored 3.02. This came just behind Iraq's religious leaders, who scored 3.4 and have consistently topped poll ratings.

Aside from opinion polls, another measure of perceptions of security is the attitudes of the contractors and NGOs that are engaged in the reconstruction of Iraq. In September 2004, it was reported that many of the remaining foreign NGOs in Iraq were making preparations to withdraw from the country.[142] This attitude is not surprising. While there is no reliable and comprehensive list of contractor casualties in Iraq since May 2003, one partial list records 185 fatalities and 15 missing as of mid-November 2004.[143] The impact of the violence is reflected in the Bush administration's July 2004 report to Congress, which noted that

> security problems have slowed reconstruction. Disruptions due to attacks and threats against drivers and vehicles have slowed the delivery of construction materials and supplies; attacks and threats have also been made against technical experts repairing, installing, and commissioning specialized equipment, particularly impacting the pace of power generation projects .... A number of firms supporting the electrical sector have either withdrawn staff from Iraq or have severely limited their movement beyond secured facilities.[144]

Judicial Effectiveness

Metrics for judicial effectiveness, such as the time from detention to trial and output of cases, were collected on an ad hoc basis by coalition military lawyers and the CPA's justice ministry advisors. However, by June 2004, the Iraqi Council of Judges had been unable to

---

[142] Agence France-Presse, "Most Foreign NGOs in Iraq Preparing to Leave: Coordinator," September 8, 2004.

[143] Iraq Coalition Casualty Count, Contractors—A Partial List, http://icasualties.org/oif/Civ.aspx.

[144] *Quarterly Report to Congress* (2004).

institute a routine data collection procedure to allow it to monitor judicial performance. In late spring of 2004, the CPA did develop a methodology for assessing systemwide effectiveness of the judicial system, but this metric was not implemented before the dissolution of the CPA.

The final assessments of CPA's judicial advisors in June 2004 indicated that the Iraqi judicial system had a lot further to go.[145] By June, the CPA had set a detention-to-trial target of one month. But it was only able to move toward achievement of this target in Baghdad by sending its judicial assessment and reconstruction team to review some 2,000 cases of criminal and security detainees, computerizing Baghdad's courts, developing a prisoner transportation plan for Baghdad, and training police investigators on interrogation techniques and criminal procedures.[146]

More fundamental problems with the Iraqi justice system were revealed in advisors' statements that even the Central Criminal Court of Iraq, established to handle the more difficult cases, was plagued by the weakness of the investigative agencies. As MoJ advisors noted, "law-enforcement agencies are too easily intimidated."[147] There remained a pressing need for specialized investigative teams made up of police and judicial officials able to resist the pressures of violence and corruption that hampered the imposition of a rule of law in Iraq.[148]

Public opinion polls to date have only partially addressed perceptions of corruption or judicial integrity. A poll conducted in August 2004 in the area of operations of the UK-led Multi-National Division (South East) provided some insights into public perceptions

---

[145] An assessment reflected in other independent, systematic assessments such as Barton and Croker (2004), p. 85.

[146] CPA (2004m).

[147] CPA (2004m).

[148] *Quarterly Report to Congress* (2004). These figures differ slightly from those collated by the MoJ in its June 2004 strategic plan report.

of the judicial system.[149] The data showed a fairly stable view since June 2004 that 60 percent of respondents would use a court of law, but that there was a high level of concern about corruption and delays in the courts. Some 30 percent of respondents expressed a preference for using a tribal or sharia court. More systematic and quantifiable indicators of the effectiveness of Iraq's judicial system are not yet available. World Bank[150] and Transparency International[151] data on corruption and rule of law are not available for Iraq for 2003 and 2004. Freedom House's 2004 data merely mention an increase concerning civil liberties for Iraq.[152]

However, qualitative reports by human rights observers provide another measure since these address the failings of judicial systems and of the rule of law. The UN High Commissioner for Human Rights, in its June 2004 report, acknowledged that the Iraqi people "have been relieved of the massive, systematic and institutionalized violations of human rights that took place under the preceding regime." It then pointed to a long list of measures that the IIG needed to take to institutionalize and expand the judicial and legal reforms and human rights measures that had been made under the CPA, as well as dealing with transitional justice issues and completing work begun to eliminate torture as a routine police practice.[153] Amnesty International echoed these recommendations, noting, for instance, the necessity of setting up a commission of legal experts,

---

[149] The security situation, however, meant that the poll included little input from al-Amara, Dhi Qar, and Basra. Multi-National Division (South East), *Iraqi Opinion Trend Analysis*, September 12, 2004.

[150] World Bank, Governance Indicators, 1996–2004, 2005.

[151] Transparency International, *Global Corruption Report 2004*, Berlin, 2004.

[152] Iraq's rating is placed at Political Rights 7 (no change), Civil Liberties 5 (increase), with an overall rating of "not free." Freedom House, *Freedom in the World 2004*, Table of Independent Countries—Comparative Measures of Freedom, 2004b.

[153] UNCHR (2004).

reforming the penal code, and amending the statute of the Special Tribunal.[154]

An additional issue in Iraq has been the behavior of coalition military and intelligence agencies. As Amnesty International put it: "there is in effect a two-tier system whereby people detained by the Coalition Forces have fewer safeguards than those held under Iraqi [the] justice system."[155] As reports on the abuse of security detainees held at Abu Ghraib prison have highlighted, there have been "serious violations of human rights and humanitarian law" by coalition personnel.[156] The administration of justice by multinational forces and intelligence agencies clearly undermined some of the progress made in reforming the Iraqi justice and penal systems.[157]

Coalition Forces and Security

Perhaps the most comprehensive effort to assess security outcomes has been that undertaken by coalition forces in Iraq for their own planning purposes. While the details and the results of the methodology are classified, the method combines qualitative and quantitative assessments of key factors in each region of Iraq, such as strength and capability of Iraqi security forces, level of insurgent or criminal threat, and capacity of local governance institutions.[158] Based on this assessment, CJTF-7 and its successor, MNF-I, have drawn up timetables for the withdrawal of coalition forces from providing the core of security at the local level. CJTF-7 had intended to withdraw from most local security operations by early 2004. But by the start of 2004, it

---

[154] Amnesty International, *Iraq: Human Rights Protection and Promotion Vital in the Transitional Period*, June 28, 2004a.

[155] Amnesty International (2004a).

[156] UNCHR (2004), p. 3.

[157] Amnesty International, *Iraq: One Year on the Human Rights Situation Remains Dire*, March 18, 2004b; *Final Report of the Independent Panel to Review DoD Detention Operations*, August 24, 2004.

[158] This method of assessment may, of course, not help us measure security for Iraqis, since ISF casualties may merely replace coalition casualties. Nonetheless, it has provided a method that mixes qualitative and quantitative approaches to assessing outputs and, to some extent, outcomes.

became evident that delays in the rollout of a robust police force would delay this transition at least until late 2004. The April 2004 uprisings and subsequent collapse of ISF in many parts of the country made it likely that this transition would be pushed back further. The fact that ISF remained unable to take more than a supporting role in the suppression of the Mahdi's army uprising in August 2004 demonstrated again the unreadiness of the Iraqi security sector to impose order without international military assistance.

Conclusions

The lessons from Iraq can be summarized by examining three stages in the security sector development process: the mobilization of inputs, the translation of inputs into outputs, and the linkage between outputs and outcomes.

Mobilizing Inputs

The inputs for developing Iraq's security sector were funds, equipment, expatriate advisors, and coalition forces. In all areas, Iraq suffered from too little, too late. The coalition undertook limited prewar planning for reconstructing Iraq's internal security sector, and especially for the police force. After the fall of Baghdad, the coalition was unprepared for the outbreak of widespread looting, political violence, and the collapse of the Iraqi security forces. The lack of prewar preparation meant that the CPA was consistently trying to overcome challenges that could have been anticipated.

During 2003 and the first quarter of 2004, funding was cobbled together from Iraqi funds and via CERP. Peacetime contracting processes, a lack of personnel, and logistical difficulties delayed the translation of funds into personnel and equipment on the ground.[159]

---

[159] According to the CPA Inspector General, of 2,117 authorized positions, the CPA had only 1,196 personnel on staff as of March 8, 2004, 56 percent of total authorized slots. CPA, *Audit Report: Management of Personnel Assigned to the Coalition Provisional Authority in Baghdad*, Report by the Inspector General of the Coalition Provisional Authority, Baghdad, 04-002, June 25, 2004l, p. 1.

These problems led to critical delays in the supply of vital equipment, such as vehicles and communications gear, that dogged the Iraqi security forces through 2004. The lack of expatriate advisors and civilian police likewise slowed the program to build capability in the police and justice systems. Funding and contracting delays, security concerns, and the unwillingness or inability of U.S. and UK agencies to deploy the right personnel in sufficient numbers all affected the program. These delays meant that coalition military units undertook the bulk of program implementation in the policing and justice sectors; this reality was formally recognized with the creation of CPATT in 2004. Although U.S. MP units and European units under British command often provided excellent support to the Iraqi police, they were understrengthed and overstretched. Most importantly, support to the IPS was not perceived as the core coalition mission until very late.

Translating Inputs into Outputs

Once inputs have been mobilized, the next step is to translate these into outputs. For the police, the outputs have been identified as police personnel, police capability, and institutional development. In light of the deteriorating security situation, the failure to attract extra coalition partners, and pressures on the U.S. military to keep down troop numbers in Iraq, there was a tendency for the coalition forces to focus on rapidly increasing the numbers of ISF. This was a feature of the police, FPS, and ICDC programs in the second half of 2003. However, by the spring of 2004, it was becoming evident to the CPA that quantity at the expense of quality was a self-defeating strategy. Nonetheless, the basic dilemma remained that producing high-quality forces and leadership took time and that there was an immediate, critical need for Iraqi "boots on the ground."

Quality in terms of personnel, capable units, and robust governance institutions can only be developed over long periods of time, with substantial foreign assistance and buy-in from the local leadership. In a situation of scarcity, the November 15 agreement forced the CPA to accelerate its efforts. While Iraqi governments since July 2004 have been committed to working with the international community to build capable security forces, it is less clear how committed they are to thoroughgoing institutional transformation.[160]

Perhaps the most important outstanding institutional questions for Iraqi governments are (1) Will the police revert to a centralized model dedicated to regime protection, or will the seeds of a decentralized, democratic model have been sown?[161] (2) What will be the future internal security role of the IAF and ING? (3) How will Iraq develop effective, coordinated, and accountable internal security intelligence structures to supplement the police?[162]

Linking Outputs to Outcomes

The relationship between the capabilities of the Iraqi internal security sector and security outcomes, such as amount of political violence, crime rates, or public confidence, is not a simple one. Even in stable, peaceful societies, the linkages between the police and justice sectors capabilities and crime rates are hotly disputed. As of the date of this writing, the fact is that multinational forces retain de facto primary responsibility for internal security in most parts of the country. In the face of multiple, overlapping insurgencies and terrorist campaigns that appear to be growing in skill and lethality,[163] it is too early to discern a noticeable impact of the Iraqi security sector on the level of political violence.

However, while organized crime remains rampant, there are some indications that ordinary crime is being brought down and that the population has some confidence in the ability of the police to rebuild law and order. Meanwhile, other measures of the rule of law

---

[160] For instance, anecdotal evidence suggests that formalized, merit-based personnel policies have to some extent succumbed to political and personal patronage approaches.

[161] Bayley's analytical model suggests that, facing a high level of collective violence and high crime, Iraq's police may evolve toward the authoritarian regime police model, perhaps along the lines of South Korea or China. Bayley (1985), pp. 222–226.

[162] Initial indications point to a disturbing lack of coordination and the development of multiple, competing agencies with arrest powers.

[163] Thomas Ricks, "U.S. Troops' Death Rate Rising in Iraq," *Washington Post*, September 9, 2004.

remain in the balance in Iraq. Corruption is only beginning to be tackled. Property rights are not protected, although some work has begun on resolving property disputes and revamping the land registry. Population identification measures such as identification cards, passports, personnel vetting systems, and border controls remain embryonic, but programs are under way to rectify these gaps.

Policy Implications

The lack of prewar planning and preparation hampered the Iraq police assistance mission; the collapse of the state institutions and the violent insurgency made the task much harder. The lessons of Iraq for U.S. security policy are familiar from previous experiences with post-conflict policing:

- Dissolving the security forces of a transitioning country can create a situation of "emerging anarchy" and contribute to political instability. This implies that (1) programs to dissolve existing security services and replace them with new ones must be thoroughly planned and gradual, and (2) intervening military forces must have the mandate and force structure to fill the security gap in the wake of major combat operations.
- There is an invariable tendency by the intervening body to concentrate on building "fielded forces"—police and military—and to invest in tangibles such as equipment and infrastructure. Less effort tends to be devoted to intangibles such as managerial capacity building and institutional development, or to the wider rule-of-law continuum—notably the justice sector and prisons.
- It takes time to mobilize the required inputs (funds, personnel, equipment), so preparation needs to start early.
- Neither the United States nor the United Kingdom finds it easy to rapidly deploy civilian policing expertise in either an executive or an advisory capacity; both countries therefore need to develop their own capabilities and to improve and use the UN

civilian police system, supported by countries with constabulary capabilities.[164]

Finally, despite a troubled start, Iraq and its foreign partners are now developing comprehensive plans and putting in place resources and staff to implement a wide-ranging and long-term reform of the Iraqi police and justice sector.[165] These plans will only succeed if the United States and its partners make a long-term civil-military commitment to sustain these programs. When the United States failed to sustain a long-term commitment with such countries as Somalia and Haiti, and the police and justice sectors quickly deteriorated. An important element of this commitment will be to reorient the policing program around measurable indicators of progress toward improving public safety for Iraqis. It will also be important to ensure that the justice sector and other rule-of-law instruments such as anti-corruption efforts are given equal priority to the build-up of "hard" elements such as police and military forces.

---

[164] Perito (2004).

[165] Anthony Cordesman, *Iraqi Force Development: An Iraqi View*, Washington, D.C.: Center for Strategic and International Studies, March 6, 2005.

CHAPTER SIX

Measuring Success

How successful have U.S. and allied efforts been in reconstructing internal security structures during nation-building operations? This chapter examines that question by looking at data from Kosovo, Afghanistan, and Iraq, and comparing the data with other cases in which the United States has helped reconstruct security during nation-building missions. These post–Cold War cases are Panama, El Salvador, Somalia, Haiti, Bosnia, and East Timor.

The data and case studies in Chapters Three, Four, and Five suggest that there is a relationship between the level of inputs, outputs, and outcomes, and these relationships may be tempered by the conditions at the onset of reconstruction. In Kosovo, for example, the large amount of financial assistance, duration of assistance, size of international military and police, and size of national police were important components in improving the rule of law and decreasing levels of violence. So was the existence of a peace agreement. However, the absence of a strong and functioning central government, effective security forces, and a viable rule of law at the beginning of reconstruction created significant challenges.

The limited data make it impossible to conduct reliable statistical correlations. While large levels of inputs and outputs will probably not guarantee effectiveness, low levels will make it difficult for outside powers to improve internal security regardless of initial conditions. For each of the cases, we gather cross-cutting data on four basic components of internal security: initial conditions, inputs, outputs, and outcomes. These elements correspond to the theoretical model we derived in Chapter Two. Initial conditions are the factors present at the onset of reconstruction. They include the existence and effectiveness of a functioning central government, security bodies, and justice system, as well as the existence of a peace settlement. Inputs refer to the amount of resources used in reconstructing internal security, such as the amount of financial assistance provided and international personnel deployed. The amounts used, not the amounts budgeted, are the most relevant numbers. In practice, however, the data available made it difficult to distinguish between sums allocated and sums expended. Outputs refer to completed work, such as the number of police and military personnel trained. Finally, outcomes refer to conditions that directly affect the public, such as crime rates or perception of the rule of law. Outcomes are not what governments and international institutions do, but represent the consequences of their efforts.

Chapter Six proceeds in two steps. First, it compiles and analyzes data on initial conditions, inputs, outputs, and outcomes to illustrate whether and how the three case studies differ from each other and the additional cases. Second, it offers a brief conclusion about improvement in each case and provides rough guidelines for future attempts at reconstructing internal security.

Initial Conditions

In assessing U.S. and allied reconstruction efforts, it is important to consider the initial conditions and the institutions with which they had to work. Reconstructing internal security can be significantly affected by at least four factors at the beginning of reconstruction: the existence of a peace agreement, the strength of the central government, the status of security forces, and the status of the rule of law.

First, the presence of a peace agreement or formal surrender affected stability in several cases because it helped convince combatants to demobilize and demilitarize. In Kosovo, for example, Yugoslav military and police forces withdrew as a condition of the military technical agreement to end the conflict. However, nearly half the cases lacked either a peace agreement or formal surrender, including Afghanistan and Iraq. The absence of an agreement in these cases increased security challenges because there was little "buy in" from opposing factions. These included warlords and regional commanders in Afghanistan, and militia and insurgents in Iraq. Second, the existence of a strong, functioning central government affected efforts to reconstruct internal security. Most of the cases, including Kosovo, Afghanistan, and Iraq, lacked a strong central government. In these countries, the United States and other allies faced a host of challenges. They had to deal with powerful militias or criminal organizations that usurped state functions and controlled territory. They also had to devote valuable resources to building the central government's capacity so that it could function. Third, the status of security forces affected success. In most cases, the security forces were in poor condition at the beginning of reconstruction, including Kosovo, Afghanistan, and Iraq. In Afghanistan, warlords and regional commanders controlled substantial territory, and Afghan police had not been through any formal training in several decades. In Iraq, the government's security apparatus evaporated following the overthrow of Saddam Hussein's regime, triggering an immediate rise in petty theft and organized crime. Fourth, the status of the rule of law was important. There was no functioning rule of law in most cases, including Kosovo, Afghanistan, and Iraq. This created a significant challenge for the United States and other allies, since rule-of-law institutions are difficult to change. They are deeply embedded in the societal fabric, are heavily influenced by cultural norms and values, and can take a long time to change.

Inputs and Outputs

Although many of the reconstruction missions involve several of the same actors, it is difficult to find consistent and comprehensive data on all but the headline aspects of police and justice reconstruction. As

Table 6.1
Conditions When Reconstruction Began

Country	Peace Agreement or Formal Surrender	Strong Central Government	Status of Security Forces	Status of Rule of Law[a]
Panama (1989)	No	Yes	Fair; near-total destruction of Panamanian Defense Forces	Good
El Salvador (1992)	Yes; 1992 Chapultepec Agreement	Yes	Good; but highly repressive	Fair
Somalia (1992)	No	No	Poor; warlords controlled much of the country	Poor; informal justice system
Haiti (1994)	Yes; 1994 Carter-Cedras Agreement	No	Fair; but repressive	Poor
Bosnia (1995)	Yes; 1995 Dayton Accord	No	Good	Poor
East Timor (1999)	Yes; 1999 independence referendum and ratification by Indonesia	No	Poor; exodus of most Indonesian police in 1999	Fair; adopted Indonesian law
Kosovo (1999)	Yes; 1999 military technical agreement	No	Poor; security forces withdrew	Poor; informal justice system
Afghanistan (2001)	No	No	Poor; warlords controlled much of the country	Poor; informal justice system
Iraq (2003)	No	No	Poor; security apparatus largely evaporated	Poor

[a] The rule of law is based on Freedom House ratings during the first year of reconstruction. A score of "good" corresponds with a Freedom House score of one or two; "fair" corresponds with a score of three, four, or five; and "poor" corresponds with a six or seven. Freedom House (2004a).

the case studies in Chapters Three, Four, and Five demonstrate, data quality and reporting have not been priorities in most missions. Therefore, the comparative quantitative overviews presented here need to be regarded as best estimates rather than detailed analyses. Furthermore, since the components of a successful internal security system are interrelated, it would be good to assess reconstruction efforts across these pillars. However, this is not always possible.

Inputs

It would be ideal to collect input data in four key areas. The first arca is international financial assistance spent on the police and justice sectors. The second includes the number of international military, police personnel, advisors, and contractors. Third is the length of time in which assistance has been given. The fourth category includes the amount and type of equipment provided by the international community. Because many of these data are not available consistently across multiple case studies, we used the data that are available. They include

- International financial assistance for reconstruction
- Duration of international security assistance
- Number of international military forces
- Number of international civilian police.

Financial Assistance. We use as a proxy the total amount of financial assistance per capita for reconstruction, since reliable data on security sector assistance were unavailable. This information is useful for two reasons. First, it captures the reality that most components of reconstruction—such as reconstructing health care, education, and energy—ultimately contribute to stability and security. Because security sector reform was an important component in all these reconstruction efforts, we assume that it constituted a significant percentage of overall assistance in all cases. Second, overall financial assistance is an indicator of the international community's interest and seriousness in reconstructing.

Figure 6.1 summarizes the amounts of assistance given to each country. There was significant variation in the financial assistance provided to Afghanistan, Kosovo, and Iraq. They ranged from a low of $30 per person in Afghanistan to a high of $526 per person in Kosovo within the first two years, with Iraq falling in between these extremes, at $225 per person. The funding provided to Kosovo was about 2.3 times greater than the Iraq mission, which, in turn, was 7.5 times as much as that provided to Afghanistan. The overall data can be broken down into three levels of support: low, moderate, and high.[1] Relative to the remaining six countries, Afghanistan was most similar to Panama and El Salvador. Each received the lowest levels of

Figure 6.1
Annual Economic Assistance Per Capita

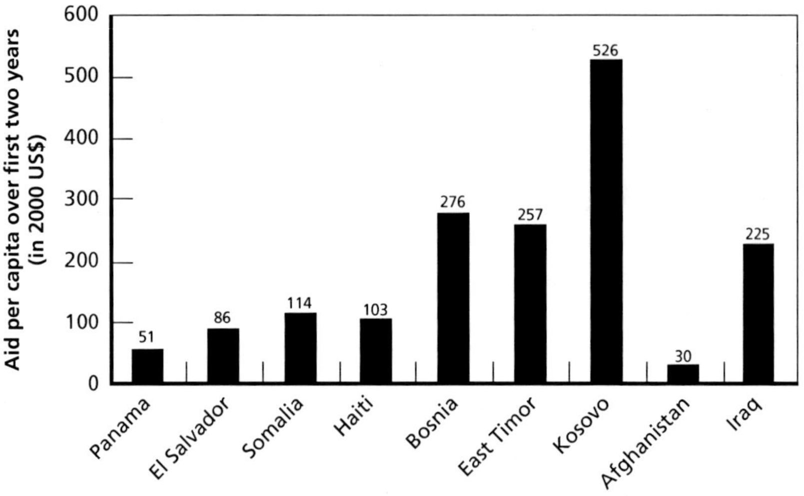

SOURCE: World Bank (2004).
RAND *MG374-6.1*

[1] Unless otherwise noted, when we rank order inputs, outputs, and outcomes, such as "low," "medium," and "high," we use natural break points in the data to differentiate levels. As such, we make no claim as to whether a characteristic is low or high, for example, on a substantive scale, but rather we suggest that the characteristic of a particular case is low or high compared with the values of other cases.

assistance (under $100 per person). Iraq received a moderate level of assistance, which was closest to the funding amounts provided to Bosnia ($276) and East Timor ($257). Kosovo received the largest amount of assistance, almost doubling that provided to Bosnia, which had the second highest amount.

Duration of Security Assistance. There is some variation in the length of time the United States and allied countries provided security assistance. As Figure 6.2 illustrates, reconstruction efforts have also been brief in Afghanistan and Iraq, but these operations are ongoing. The United States and its allies provided significant assistance for four years or fewer in all these cases. During the early post–Cold War period, the United States and its allies tended to define their objectives rather narrowly, focusing on exit strategies and departure deadlines. As experience with reconstruction efforts grew, however,

Figure 6.2
Duration of Major Security Assistance, by 2005

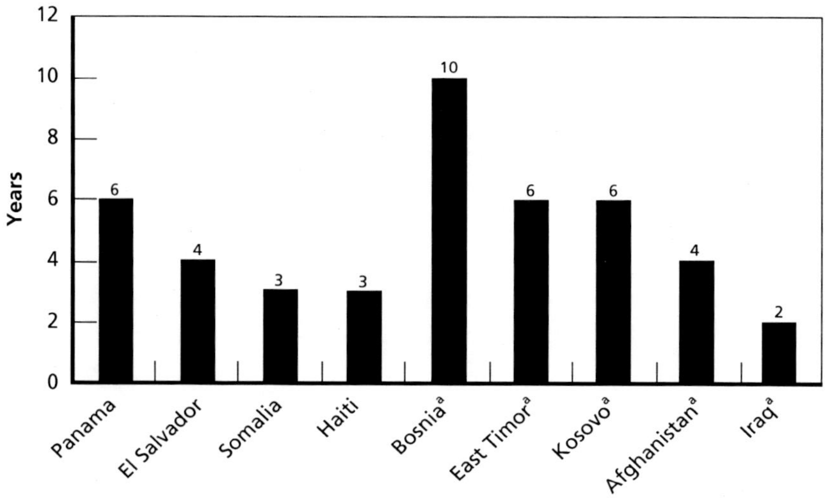

[a]Ongoing operation.
RAND *MG374-6.2*

the United States increasingly recognized that internal security reform required more time to ensure sustainability. Consequently, the United States and its allies provided assistance to Bosnia, East Timor, Kosovo, and Panama for more than five years.

International Military and Police Levels. Figures 6.3 and 6.4 summarize international military and police levels for each of the nine cases over time. External military forces and civilian police with executive authority have been used to stabilize post-conflict countries and train internal security forces. There were considerable differences in the level of international military provided to reconstruction efforts

Figure 6.3
International Military Per Capita

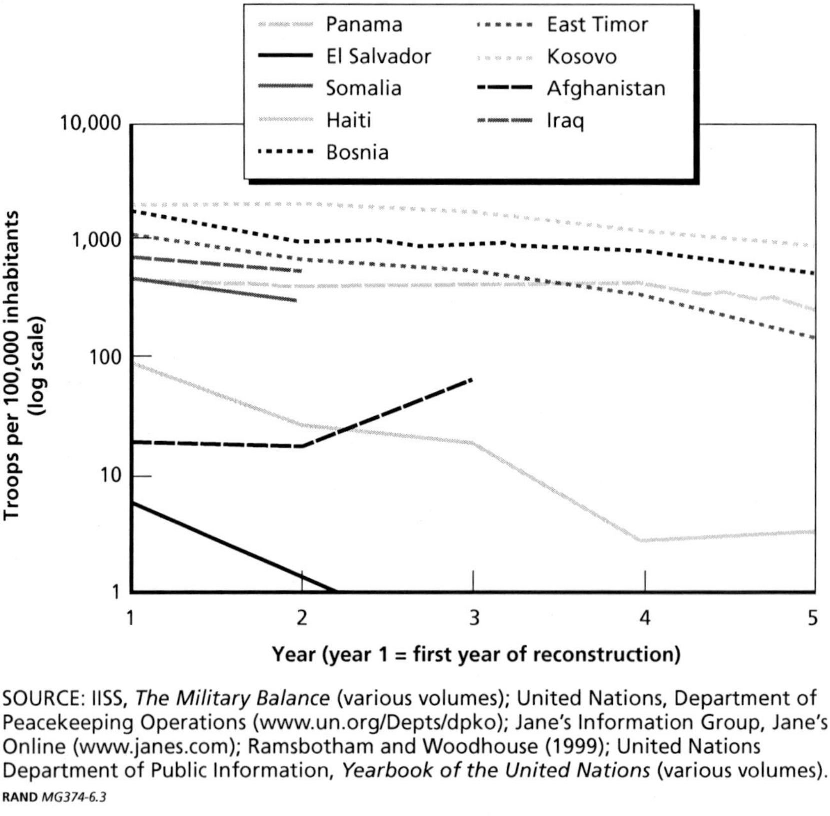

SOURCE: IISS, *The Military Balance* (various volumes); United Nations, Department of Peacekeeping Operations (www.un.org/Depts/dpko); Jane's Information Group, Jane's Online (www.janes.com); Ramsbotham and Woodhouse (1999); United Nations Department of Public Information, *Yearbook of the United Nations* (various volumes).
RAND *MG374-6.3*

in Afghanistan, Kosovo, and Iraq. In the first year of reconstruction, Kosovo (2,058 soldiers per 100,000 inhabitants) received almost three times the international military support as Iraq (709). Afghanistan received much less international military support (19) than Iraq and considerably less than Kosovo. Afghanistan's low level of international military deployment most closely resembled that given to Haiti and El Salvador. The assistance given to Iraq resembled that given to Panama and Somalia. Much higher levels of international military existed in East Timor, Bosnia, and Kosovo in the first year after major combat. The small populations of the countries may have

Figure 6.4
International Civilian Police Per Capita

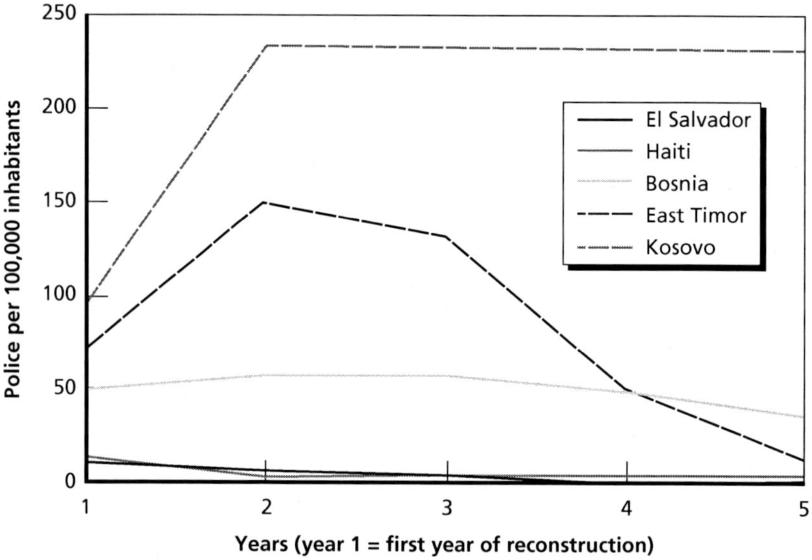

SOURCES: Perito (2002a); IISS, *The Military Balance* (various volumes); United Nations, Department of Peacekeeping Operations (www.un.org/Depts/dpko); Jane's Information Group, Jane's Online (www.janes.com); Ramsbotham and Woodhouse (1999); United Nations Department of Public Information, *Yearbook of the United Nations* (various volumes); Oakley, Dziedzic, and Goldberg (1998); Dobbins et al. (2005); United Nations (1999), p. 1.
NOTE: Panama, Somalia, Afghanistan, and Iraq had no CIVPOL.
RAND *MG374-6.4*

made it easier to deploy larger numbers of forces per capita. Longitudinally, military support reduced in all cases, except Afghanistan. It increased from 19 troops per 100,000 inhabitants during the first year of reconstruction in Afghanistan to 63 by year three.

International civilian police are a crucial component of police reform efforts. The United States and allied countries have deployed international police to help military forces restore security, build and train local police forces, and provide security for local inhabitants. Neither Afghanistan nor Iraq received any assistance in the form of international police with executive authority. This increased the burden on U.S. and coalition military forces to handle public security and police training functions, or to contract out training to private companies such as DynCorp. The United States and its allies did not deploy international civilian police forces with executive authority to Panama or Somalia.[2] This was in stark contrast to Kosovo, which, with 95 police per 100,000 inhabitants, had the greatest number of international police of all nine cases. In the first post-conflict year, the levels of civilian police in Bosnia and East Timor were somewhat comparable to Kosovo.

Figure 6.4 illustrates whether and how international police rates varied longitudinally. Like the first year, no international civilian police with executive authority were deployed to Afghanistan or Iraq. Conversely, Kosovo and East Timor experienced much more variation. Between the first and second year, international civilian police increased from 95 to 234 per 100,000 inhabitants in Kosovo and from 71 to 151 in East Timor. While the rate of international police remained stable from the second year onward in Kosovo, it dropped precipitously over this same period in East Timor. Over the first five years of reconstruction, there was relatively little change in deployment for El Salvador, Haiti, and Bosnia.

Prewar Planning. Prewar planning also varied widely among the cases. Planning is critical to outline strategic objectives and ensure

---

[2] In a few cases, such as Iraq, the United Kingdom and other European countries deployed some civilian police as advisors and trainers. However, these individuals did not carry out policing tasks.

that appropriate levels of funds, equipment, personnel, and trained and configured military and police forces are at hand. It should involve answering such questions as: What are the primary objectives of the operation, including key security and justice goals? Who is in charge? What are the key tasks, and how should they be prioritized? How can the programmatic elements best be assembled? How should progress be measured?

In Kosovo, the U.S. Department of Justice's ICITAP and OSCE began detailed planning prior to reconstruction. They developed comprehensive plans for a first-responder system and a police force, and significantly enhanced the establishment of stability in Kosovo. In Afghanistan, there was little prewar planning because of the short time horizon. Less than three months transpired between the September 11, 2001, terrorist attacks in New York and Washington and the December 5, 2001, Bonn Agreement that jump-started reconstruction. Most of this time was devoted to emergency response efforts in New York and Washington, collecting information on who was responsible and planning and executing the combat phase of the operation. There was virtually no time to plan for reconstruction. In Iraq, planning efforts were undermined by faulty assumption about postwar conditions. The United States and the United Kingdom conducted extensive planning for postwar Iraq. But most of the planning focused on humanitarian relief and was based on the assumption that the institutions of the Iraqi state, including police and armed forces, could be relied on to keep the state functioning and to maintain order after the overthrow of the regime.

Outputs

To assess how effectively international inputs have been translated into police and justice outputs, it would be useful to gather data on the following four categories. First, it would be helpful to analyze the number of indigenous personnel trained and deployed, such as police, other security forces, judges, prosecutors, and prison guards. The second category includes the amount and quality of infrastructure built or refurbished, such as police stations, courts, jails, and prisons. Third, it would be useful to gather qualitative information on police and justice sector capacity. These would include assessments of the quality of training offered to internal security personnel, the capability of the police force in various areas, the lawfulness and legitimacy of the police, and the process by which various components of the justice system are reviewed and held accountable. The fourth category includes numbers and proportions of former combatants processed through demobilization, demilitarization, and reintegration programs. For the purposes of this overview, the only reliable data available were the number of national police and, to a lesser extent, the total number of police trained.

National Police. Figure 6.5 presents data on national police.[3] First, we can compare differences in the rate of police five years after the end of major combat. This should allow sufficient time for international forces to complete most police training. The number of police personnel was higher in Iraq (335 per 100,000 inhabitants in year two) than either Kosovo (272 in year five) or Afghanistan (175 in year three). Considering all the cases, international police rates in year five spanned from a low of nearly zero in Somalia, where warlord militia replaced a national police force, to a high of 542 in Bosnia.

It is difficult to compare levels of police employees without some form of benchmark. One useful benchmark is the average investment in police employees across the cases, which in the first post-conflict year is 293 police per 100,000 inhabitants. A second metric is to compare the police level in these cases with other countries that demonstrate variation in terms of development level, geographic location, and contribution to reconstruction efforts. For comparison, we found the following rates (per 100,000 inhabitants) of police employment: Argentina (542), England and Wales (234), France (211), Germany (292), Guatemala (234), Singapore (324),

[3] The figures from Bosnia were not plotted on the graph, since its police levels were so high.

Figure 6.5
National Police Per Capita, Except Bosnia

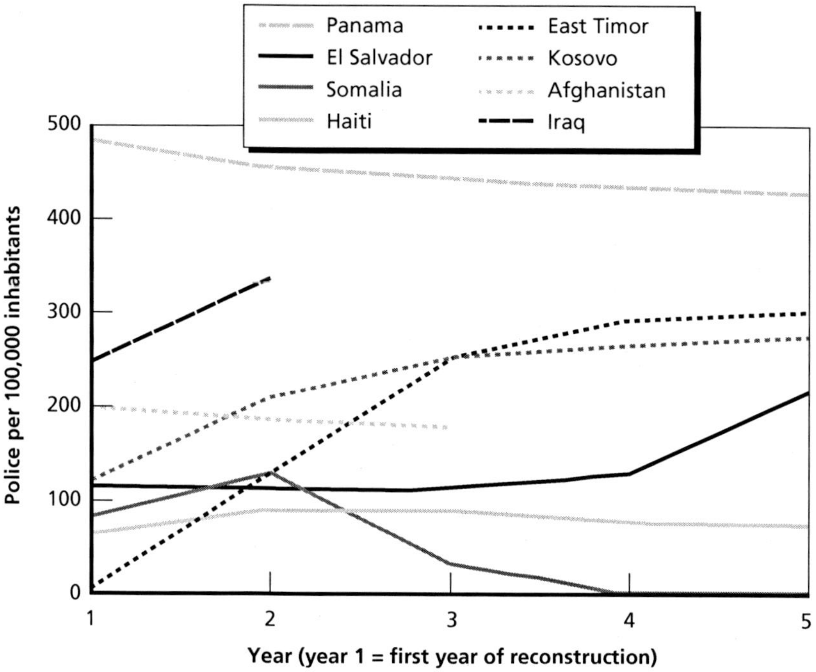

SOURCES: IISS, *The Military Balance* (various volumes); United Nations, Department of Peacekeeping Operations (www.un.org/Depts/dpko); Jane's Information Group, Jane's Online (www.janes.com); U.S. Department of State, *Country Reports on Human Rights Practices* (various volumes); Stanley and Loosle (1998), p. 130; Call (1998), p. 340; *Iraq Ministry of Interior Briefing* (2003); U.S. Department of State (2004d); UN Secretary General Reports to the Security Council: S/2001/983 (October 18, 2001); S/2002/1233 (November 6, 2002); S/2003/944 (October 6, 2003); S/2004/333 (April 29, 2004); S/2000/1196 (December 15, 2000); S/2002/62 (January 15, 2002); S/2002/1126 (October 9, 2002); S/2003/675 (June 26, 2003); S/2004/71 (January 26, 2004); S/1995/1031 (December 13, 1995), S/2000/529 (June 2, 2000); S/1995/231 (March 28, 1995); S/1995/614 (July 24, 1995); S/1996/416 (June 5, 1996). The Iraq numbers are best estimates. Beginning in November 2004, the U.S. State Department stopped reporting the total number of police on duty.
NOTE: Bosnia was excluded because the figures are significantly higher than the other cases. Bosnia had 1,333 police per 100,000 inhabitants by the end of 1996; 1,232 by the end of 1997; 1,050 by the end of 1998; 857 by the end of 1999; and 542 by the end of 2000.
RAND *MG374-6.5*

and the United States (244).[4] The average level of police in the first post-conflict year of comparison countries can be used to compare the cases and distinguish this output as low, moderate, and high. Values near the average-level benchmark and close to the midrange of the comparison countries represent a modest investment; those falling farthest below and above these levels are considered low and high outputs, respectively. At the latest reconstruction year, the police levels were low in Somalia at zero per 100,000 inhabitants, Haiti at 76, Afghanistan at 175, and El Salvador at 216 police. They were medium in East Timor at 303 and Kosovo at 272. And the police levels were high in Iraq at 335, Panama at 428, and Bosnia at 542. Afghanistan's low level of police deployment is less than that in all the reconstruction countries except Somalia and Haiti, and all comparison benchmark countries. Iraq's police rate was greater than all the reconstruction countries except Panama and Bosnia, and greater than all the comparison benchmark countries except Argentina.

Second, there are similarities and differences in the way police personnel rates changed over time. The limited availability of data makes this examination difficult. Nonetheless, the data that are available provide some useful insights. Police rates in Kosovo and Iraq, like those in East Timor and El Salvador, increased over the course of reconstruction. The police rate increased from 120 to 272 in Kosovo and from 247 to 335 in Iraq. On the contrary, Afghanistan, like Panama, Somalia, and Bosnia, experienced a decline in police levels. The decline was most severe in Somalia. The Auxiliary Security Force, which was built by the U.S. Marines and Army MPs, completely dispersed when fighting intensified between United Nations Operations in Somalia II (UNOSOM II) and Mohamed Farah Aideed's Somali National Alliance.

Police Trained. Ideally, all indigenous police working the street should be fully trained. Unfortunately, this is not always the case.

---

[4] These rates are for the year 2000, except for Argentina and the United States, which correspond to 1999. UNODC, *Seventh United Nations Survey on Crime Trends and the Operations of Criminal Justice Systems (1998–2000)*, Division on Policy Analysis and Public Affairs, 2000.

Figure 6.6 compiles the best available data on the percentage of police trained after three years. The length of police training varied across the cases from several weeks to several years, and the quality of training varied considerably as well. The data fall into three general groups, based on the percentage of at least several weeks of basic training for indigenous police. First, more than 80 percent of national police on the street in El Salvador, Haiti, East Timor, and Kosovo had received some type of U.S., European, or UN training. A second group includes Panama and Afghanistan, which had between 40 percent and 60 percent of police forces trained. The final group includes Somalia, Bosnia, and Iraq. All had fewer than 40 percent of their national police forces trained under the auspices of U.S., European, or UN trainers (note that data on Iraq did not extend past the first two years).

Figure 6.6
Percentage of Police Trained After Three Years

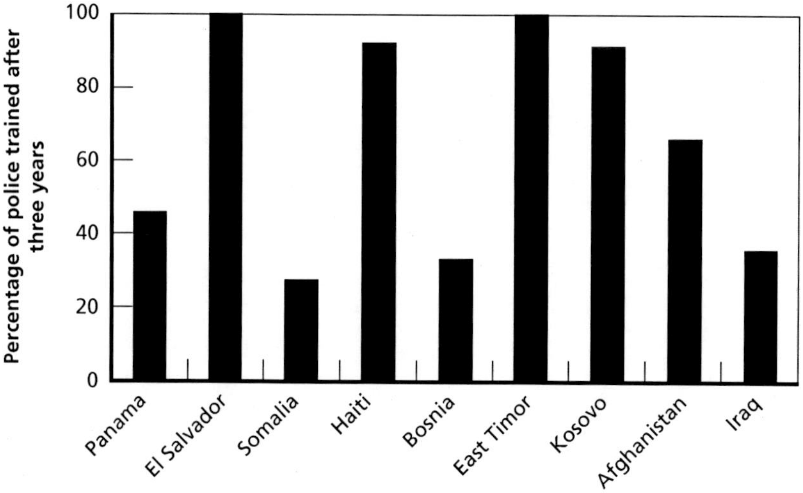

SOURCES: Call (1998), pp. 315–363; Perito (2002a); Bailey et al. (1998), pp. 215–252; United Nations, Report of the Secretary General, S/2002/1223, November 6, 2002; U.S. State Department (2004b); *Iraq Ministry of Interior Briefing* (2003); U.S. Department of State (2004d).

RAND *MG374-6.6*

This clearly shows that, of our case studies, the greatest success in transforming inputs into trained police occurred in Kosovo, whereas the least success has occurred in Iraq. It is illustrative to reconsider police levels here. Iraq had significantly higher rates of national police deployment relative to Kosovo and Afghanistan, but a significantly lower proportion of trained police. This finding suggests increasing police rates may inhibit the ability to train police employees. If we assume that an untrained officer is ineffective, if not dangerous or counterproductive, to ensuring security, the inverse relation between police rates and training needs to be seriously considered prior to initiating reconstruction efforts. Planning the correct force size so that all police officers are properly trained may improve effectiveness at both establishing security and saving scarce resources.

Outcomes

How effective were U.S. and allied efforts to reconstruct foreign police, internal security services, and the justice sector during nation-building efforts? Attempts to quantify outcomes of complex processes suffer because of the unavailability of precise statistical measures.[5] This effort is no exception. The choice of outcome metrics was determined by the availability of data and their suitability for examining the reconstructing of police forces and the justice sector. But we have compiled data on three cross-cutting outcome measures: homicide rates, deaths from terrorist and insurgent attacks, and the rule of law and civil liberties. These indicators provide a useful metric of the security environment for the indigenous population. Other useful data, which were unavailable across the cases, would be public perception of security, rule of law, and corruption of the justice system and security forces.

For homicides, we collected information on per capita rates. Since data on homicide rates were unavailable for Afghanistan,

---

[5] David H. Bayley, *Policing for the Future*, New York: Oxford University Press, 1994.

Somalia, and Iraq (except for Baghdad), we also collected information on the number of deaths caused by terrorist or insurgent attacks from the RAND-MIPT Terrorism Incident Database. Finally, we collected information on the rule of law and civil liberties from Freedom House's database, Freedom in the World.

We are less interested in comparing across cases. Such an analysis tells little about the improvement or deterioration in security and justice conditions because the countries started from different conditions when reconstruction began. It is implausible, for example, to expect Afghanistan and Somalia to establish a functioning rule of law within five years, when they began with no formal judicial system. Consequently, we are more interested in examining how these measures changed over time within each country. Did homicide rates and terrorism casualties increase or decrease? Did the justice system become more effective or less effective? In Chapters Three, Four, and Five, we discussed additional outcome measures that were associated with the specific security challenges in Kosovo, Afghanistan, and Iraq. In the Afghanistan chapter, for example, we collected information on the cultivation and production of opium poppy, the power of regional commanders, and Afghan public perceptions of security.

Homicide Rates

Homicide rates varied across the cases, as illustrated in Figure 6.7. During the first five years of reconstruction, they steadily declined in Kosovo from 13 homicides per 100,000 inhabitants to three. Not only was the substantive homicide level higher in Baghdad, but the exact opposite trend occurred in Iraq. Homicide rates increased in Baghdad from 23 to 32, or 35 percent, over the first two years. Baghdad's experience with homicide somewhat mirrored that in El Salvador, Panama, and Bosnia. In these countries, homicide rates also markedly increased after reconstruction efforts began.[6] If we consider

[6] Homicide figures have to be treated with caution. Although crime is most likely to be reported in official statistics, in some cases, such as Iraq, official police statistics exclude deaths from political violence.

Figure 6.7
Homicide Rates

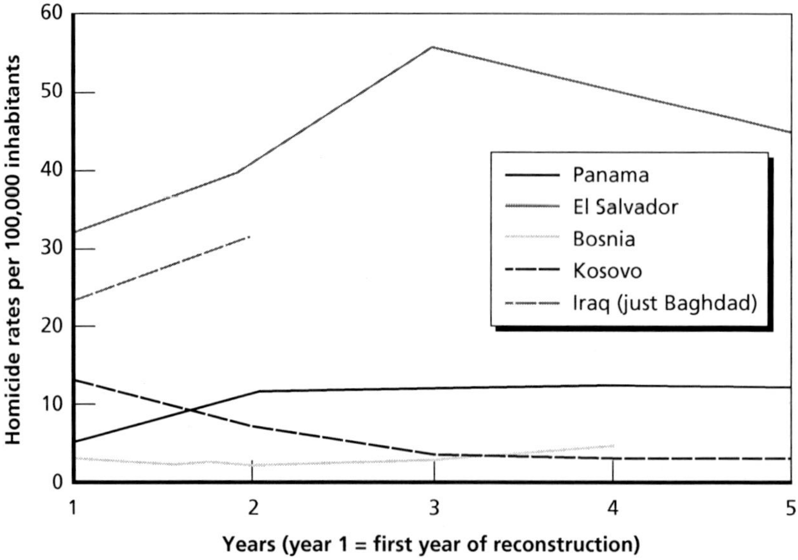

SOURCES: WHO (2002); WHO (2003); United Nations (various volumes). Iraq crime data supplied by Baghdad police, and population data supplied by Iraqi Ministry of Planning and Development Cooperation's Central Statistical Organization; Pan American Health Organization, Health Analysis and Information Systems Area, Regional Core Health Data Initiative; author's estimates.
RAND *MG374-6.7*

just the first two years, consistent with the available data for Baghdad, homicide rates increased 26 percent in El Salvador and 123 percent in Panama, but declined 24 percent in Bosnia. Bosnia increased in the third and fourth succeeding years to levels greater than it experienced in the first post-conflict year. In fact, homicide rates in El Salvador were among the highest in the world throughout the 1990s. We could find only the homicide rate for the fourth year of reconstruction in Haiti, which was 17 per 100,000 inhabitants. This information was not available for Somalia or East Timor.

To place these homicide rates in context, it is useful to compare them with those in other countries. In 1999, the homicide rate was seven per 100,000 inhabitants for Argentina and five for the United

States. In 2000, it was two in England and Wales and France, one in Germany and Singapore, and 25 in Guatemala. From this we can determine whether homicide appears to be more prevalent or less prevalent than in the comparison countries.[7] The homicide rates in all our sample countries were higher than the rates in England and Wales, France, Germany, and Singapore. The rate in Baghdad, as in El Salvador, was also higher on average than the rates in Argentina, Guatemala, and the United States. Kosovo's homicide rate was less than that in Guatemala, and in several years less than that experienced in Argentina and the United States.

Deaths from Terrorist and Insurgent Attacks

The number of deaths from terrorist and insurgent attacks—especially the change over time—is an important measure of the security environment, since it incorporates data on civilians killed. Information on the number of U.S. or coalition forces killed, which is sometimes used as a proxy, provides little information on how safe the population feels. Figure 6.8 shows data for Somalia, Afghanistan, and Iraq using a log scale. In Iraq, the number of deaths increased 272 percent from 2003 to 2004 (reconstruction years one to two). In Afghanistan, the number increased 246 percent from 2002 to 2004 (reconstruction years one to three). In Somalia, the number of deaths from terrorism or insurgency increased in 1993 (year two of reconstruction), then fell slightly in 1994 and significantly in 1995 before rising again in 1996. In all three cases, these deaths increased from end of major combat through the second post-conflict year.

Rule of Law and Civil Liberties

Outcome measures for the justice system were difficult to compile, especially for such countries as Afghanistan and Somalia, which lacked a formal justice system. Table 6.2 uses data from the Freedom

---

[7] Note that this is not a direct comparison because the exact year of a given year of reconstruction (e.g., year one) varies across cases. Nonetheless, we can use the data as a general guide for comparison.

Figure 6.8
Deaths Caused by Terrorist and Insurgent Attacks

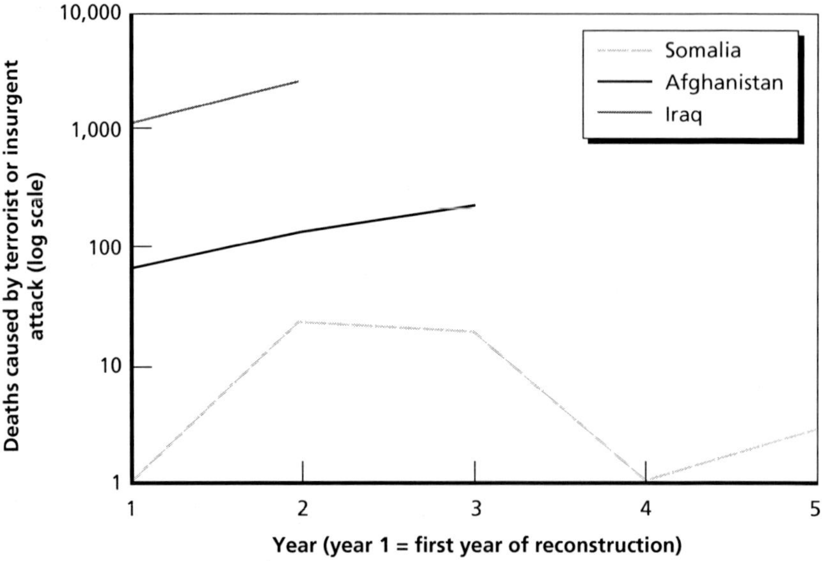

SOURCE: RAND-MIPT Terrorism Incident Database; U.S. Department of Defense, Directorate for Information Operations; Brookings Institution, Iraq Index (www.brookings.edu/iraqindex).
RAND *MG374-6.8*

in the World database. It captures data on the freedom of expression and belief within countries, as well as the rule of law. For example, is there an independent judiciary? Does the rule of law prevail in civil and criminal matters? Are police under direct civilian control? Is there protection from police terror, unjustified imprisonment, exile, or torture? Ratings range from 1, which indicates substantial civil liberties and a functioning rule of law, to 7, which indicates no civil liberties and little or no functioning rule of law. We are particularly interested in changes over time within each case.

Table 6.2 shows that Afghanistan mirrored Kosovo's slight improvement in rule of law and civil liberties in years one through three. Both began with the worst possible assessment in year one,

Table 6.2
Rule of Law and Civil Liberties

	Years[a]				
Country	**1**	**2**	**3**	**4**	**5**
Panama	2	2	3	3	3
El Salvador	3	3	3	3	3
Somalia	7	7	7	7	7
Haiti	7	5	5	5	5
Bosnia	6	6	5	5	5
East Timor	4	3	3	3	
Kosovo	7	7	6	6	5
Afghanistan	7	7	6		
Iraq	7				

[a] Year 1 = first year of reconstruction.
NOTE: Ratings range from 1, which indicates substantial civil liberties and a functioning rule of law, to a 7, which indicates no civil liberties and little or no functioning rule of law. The ratings process is based on a checklist of 15 civil liberties questions. For more information on the methodology, see Freedom House (2004a).

remained at this level in the second year, but then progressed in year three. The assessment of Kosovo's rule of law and civil liberties improved one more unit again in year five. It is unclear whether Afghanistan will continue to progress as Kosovo did, and it is too early to make definitive judgments about Iraq. Like Afghanistan and Kosovo, the assessment of rule of law and civil liberties slightly improved in Haiti, Bosnia, and East Timor. Despite reconstruction efforts, this outcome measure stayed the same in El Salvador and Somalia. This is particularly troublesome for Somalia, since it consistently was rated as having the most ineffective rule of law. Only in Panama did these qualities become worse over the course of reconstruction. Although this suggests a decline in progress, the estimate of rule of law and civil liberties in the latest year is still much less than that for Kosovo or Afghanistan.

Achieving Success

What do these measures suggest about overall efforts to reconstruct foreign police, internal security, and the justice sector? In particular, which countries experienced improvements following U.S. and allied reconstruction efforts? All societies in transition experience a rise in crime and an increase in violence as old security institutions are broken down and new ones are built. Thus, an increase in violence and crime, especially in the initial period after reconstruction begins, does not by itself demonstrate that the mission is failing. In addition, the overall objectives of a nation-building mission—such as the creation of a peaceful, democratic, and market-oriented government—can be achieved against the backdrop of some increase in criminality and violence. However, rising levels of crime and political violence after several years do provide an important indication of the competence of police and other internal security forces. The issue, therefore, is one of degree and duration.

The limited data make it impossible to provide a firm conclusion. As Figure 6.9 illustrates, however, we have adopted a rough matrix that summarizes effectiveness in two categories: the level of violence and the rule of law. The x-axis indicates the level of violence; the y-axis indicates the rule of law. This leads to four quadrants. We code the lower-left quadrant as successful, since it includes decreasing levels of violence and an improving rule of law. The lower-right quadrant is mixed because it includes increasing levels of violence but an improving rule of law. Cases in the upper-right quadrant are unsuccessful, since they have increasing levels of violence and a deteriorating rule of law. Although none of our cases falls in the upper-left quadrant, we assume that cases located there would be mixed and include decreasing levels of violence but a deteriorating rule of law. The figure is meant to be illustrative, rather than statistically rigorous. The locations of countries are rough estimates. We plotted the countries according to the percentage increase or decrease in homicide or terrorist rates over the first five years of reconstruction. Because reconstruction in Afghanistan and Iraq has not yet lasted for five years, we measured change through the most recent year.

Figure 6.9
Outcome Measures

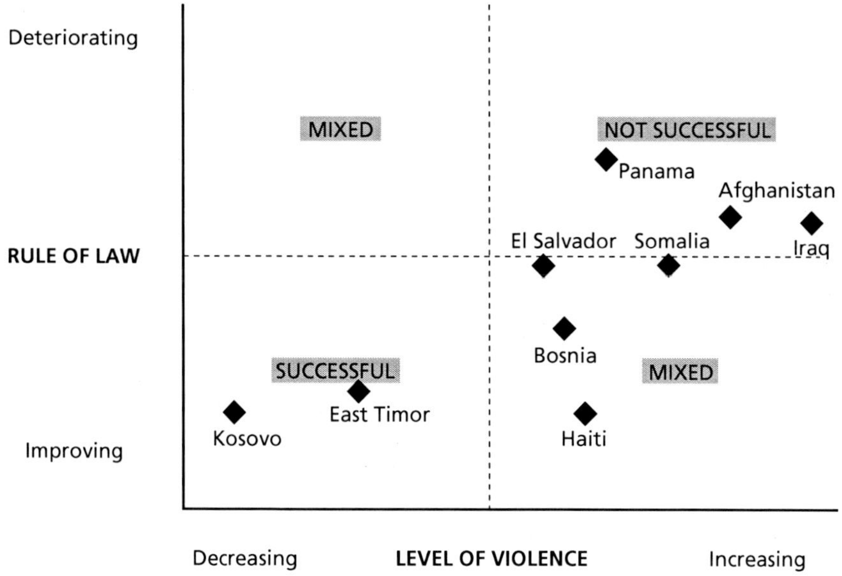

RAND *MG374-6.9*

How effective were efforts in Kosovo, Afghanistan, and Iraq in establishing stability and an effective rule of law? Based on these estimates, Kosovo was most successful and had decreasing levels of violence and an improving rule of law. Thus far, Afghanistan has had increasing levels of violence since 2002 and a slightly deteriorating rule of law. It is still too early to assess Iraq. But current data show increasing levels of violence and little change in the rule of law.

Overall, changes in the level of violence varied across the cases.[8] Changes in the rule of law varied, from improving conditions in

---

[8] The level of violence increased 134 percent in Panama, 40 percent in El Salvador, 200 percent in Somalia, 81 percent in Haiti, 59 percent in Bosnia, 246 percent in Afghanistan, and 272 percent in Iraq. It decreased 299 percent in Kosovo. For Haiti, we used data from the World Bank Governance Indicators data set on "political stability," which showed Haiti declining from 43.9 in 1996 to 24.2 in 2000. Since we could find no quantitative data on East Timor, we made a qualitative judgment. Based on a review of UN documents and inter-

Kosovo to a significant deterioration in Panama.[9] The countries denoted in the lower-left quadrant were the most successful cases, since they experienced decreasing violence and an improved rule of law. Those in the upper-right quadrant were the least successful, since they experienced increasing violence and a declining rule of law. Those in the upper-left and lower-right quadrants were mixed, since they experienced varying levels of change.

The cases can be divided into at least three categories. U.S. and allied efforts to reconstruct internal security in Kosovo and East Timor were most successful. The rule of law improved over the course of reconstruction, and the level of violence declined. Why were Kosovo and East Timor comparatively effective? The data and case studies suggest that there is a relationship between the level of inputs, outputs, and outcomes, and that these are tempered by conditions at the beginning of reconstruction. The amount of financial assistance, duration of assistance, size of international military and police, and size of national police (and the proportion that is trained) for Kosovo and East Timor were consistently high. Kosovo and East Timor had the highest level of civilian police forces, which were armed and given arrest authority. While it is important to ensure that military authorities are ready to assume public security responsibilities after major combat, it is also important to recognize the successful use of civilian police and the growing reliance of UN missions on a strong police component. In Kosovo, for example, carabinieri and gendarmerie forces were placed under civilian, not military, authority. This contrasts with recent U.S. practices in Iraq and Afghanistan.

Reconstruction efforts in Panama, Iraq, and Afghanistan have not been successful, although it is still too early to tell in Iraq and

views with UN staff in New York, we believe there was a modest decrease in violence from September 1999 to 2005. See, for example, the chapter on East Timor in Dobbins et al. (2005).

[9] The rule of law increased 40 percent in Haiti, 20 percent in Bosnia, 40 percent in Kosovo, 33 percent in East Timor, and 17 percent in Afghanistan. There was no change in Somalia and El Salvador. There was a decline of 50 percent for Panama. Because Freedom House had only one data point for Iraq (2003), we made a qualitative judgment on the level of rule of law based on the analysis in Chapter Five.

Afghanistan. Panama experienced a reduction in the perception of the rule of law and an increase in homicide rates. Unlike Kosovo and East Timor, Panama received significantly less international assistance. The level of financial assistance was the lowest of all the cases we examined, except for Afghanistan. The United States also deployed medium levels of military forces and no international civilian police to Panama. The duration of assistance in Panama (six years) was similar to Kosovo and East Timor (five years each), but the operations in these latter cases are still under way. While a proper assessment of Iraq and Afghanistan is not possible because insufficient time has elapsed, our estimates suggest that U.S.-led efforts in Iraq thus far have been ineffective.

Reconstruction efforts in the remaining cases were mixed. Bosnia and Haiti experienced increased levels of violence and instability, but the rule of law improved over the course of reconstruction. El Salvador and Somalia were slightly less effective. The perception of the rule of law and civil liberties did not change over time. Homicide became more problematic in El Salvador, and insurgency levels increased in Iraq and Somalia. The mixed outcome was partly attributable to low inputs and outputs. All these cases, except for Bosnia, received lower levels of international aid than did Kosovo and East Timor. A number of factors, such as ethnic tensions, contributed to the poor outcome in Bosnia.

Staffing and Funding Guidelines

Given the high level of inputs, outputs, and outcomes in Kosovo and East Timor, it is possible to derive rough guidelines for future reconstruction missions. First, our findings suggest annual financial assistance should be at least $250 per capita over the first two years of nation-building. While this number covers all sectors, such as political and economic reform, establishing security should be the most important initial objective of policymakers.

Second, security assistance should last for at least five years. Time is needed to train, equip, and mentor police and other security forces, as well as build and refurbish infrastructure. Justice systems can be extremely difficult and time consuming to build, especially in countries with little formal rule of law when reconstruction begins. A long duration appears to be a necessary, but not sufficient, condition for success. The United States and other donors provided assistance to Kosovo and East Timor, our two successful cases, for at least five years. But they provided assistance to Panama, the least successful case, for six years.

Third, the level of at least 1,000 soldiers per 100,000 inhabitants appears necessary for success, especially where there is a potential for severe instability. Troops are critical for defeating and deterring insurgents, patrolling borders, securing roads, and combating organized crime. In year one, there were 2,100 soldiers per 100,000 inhabitants in Kosovo and 1,100 in East Timor.

Fourth, reconstruction efforts likely require at least 150 international civilian police per 100,000 inhabitants. Police are important in conducting general law enforcement functions such as policing streets, as well as more specific functions such as conducting counter-drug operations. By year two, East Timor had an international civilian police rate of 151 and Kosovo had 234. Reaching such a ratio may be much more challenging in larger countries. It is also important to assess the security conditions to determine whether and how to adjust the suggested levels. These levels of troops and police may not always be necessary. In cases in which all sides of a war may be exhausted by fighting and have agreed to a peace settlement or formal surrender, lower ratios may suffice.

Fifth, the level of domestic police should be at least 200 police per 100,000 inhabitants after five years. East Timor had 303 and Kosovo had 272 after five years. Even further, it is necessary that these officers be trained. After the first three years, East Timor had all its officers trained, whereas Kosovo had more than 9 out of every 10 officers trained. In contrast, by 2004, 46 percent of police were trained in Panama, and 36 percent were trained in Iraq.

We have insufficient data to argue that large levels of inputs and outputs will guarantee effectiveness, defined as an improvement in the rule of law and an improvement in such security metrics as homicide rates and terrorist rates over the course of reconstruction. But we believe that low levels will make it difficult for outside powers to improve internal security.

CHAPTER SEVEN

Conclusion

In this final chapter, we draw conclusions from the case studies and derive policy recommendations to help the United States and the international community improve their performance in the delivery of post-conflict policing. The importance of building "strong" state institutions for economic and political development is now recognized by the international community.[1] Among the most crucial of such institutions are those that fulfill the core functions of a state—namely, the maintenance of internal security. Beyond the maintenance of public order, these institutions are vital if crime is to be controlled, property rights are to be protected, and resources channeled in an open and transparent manner rather than via corruption or a black market. Effective and democratic internal security institutions that underpin a rule of law, therefore, are vital for political transition toward a more democratic system that respects civil liberties and are necessary for economic growth.[2]

While the importance of these institutions for longer-term political transition and development is becoming increasingly clear, their importance for the short-term post-conflict and reconstruction phases of nation-building cannot be overstated. In nation-building

[1] By strong state institutions, we mean that the institutions possess significant capacity to make and implement policy. However, the scope of state activity that is conducive to economic and political development remains contested. Fukuyama (2004), pp. 3–15.

[2] Martin Wolf, *Why Globalization Works*, New Haven, Conn.: Yale University Press, 2004, pp. 67–75.

operations, achieving order in the immediate aftermath of intervention or regime change is the most important determinant of success. In the short term, a collapse of order can have lasting effects on the credibility and capabilities of the nation-building effort.[3] In the medium term, success in parts of the nation-building effort can become difficult if a comprehensive approach to bolstering the rule of law has not been undertaken, as was the case in Haiti and El Salvador. From a U.S. national security perspective, effective internal security institutions are also vital. The jihadist terrorism that poses a major national security threat to the United States and many of its allies cannot be countered solely by the security services of the developed nations. The internal security agencies of developing nations stand in the front line of the struggle against both domestic and international Islamist terrorism. Just as the U.S. and its allies worked to bolster the internal security capacity of allied states during the Cold War struggle against communist subversion, they will increasingly support internal security programs in states threatened by or serving as havens for jihadist movements.[4]

Despite the importance of helping to create effective and democratic internal security institutions, developed nations do not have a good record. In terms of long-term institutional development, the record from the postcolonial and Cold War era is distinctly problematic. Many of the former colonial or mandatory territories were left with powerful security sectors, notably the military; they often saw the military play a leading role in politics. During the Cold War, for example, the U.S. Department of Defense, Central Intelligence Agency, Department of State, and USAID provided assistance to police and internal security forces in such countries as Vietnam,

---

[3] The collapse of order has been acknowledged in Iraq by former CPA Administrator L. Paul Bremer. Robin Wright and Thomas E. Ricks, "Bremer Criticizes Troop Levels," *Washington Post*, October 5, 2004.

[4] There is often a conflict between the short-term policy goal of bolstering policing capacity to counter immediate security threats and building democratic policing institutions. In certain cases, the U.S. approach to the human rights records of allied internal security agencies has paralleled the approach taken during the Cold War, when reform was subordinated to effectiveness.

Korea, and El Salvador. Successive U.S. administrations were influenced by "modernization theory" in offering internal security assistance and argued that weak state institutions would create ideal conditions for communist exploitation. Many of the developing states helped by the United States and its allies during the Cold War built extremely powerful internal security apparatuses, which served to protect the regime rather than enforce the rule of law.[5]

In the post–Cold War period, the international experience with post-conflict policing has likewise been varied. In the immediate post-conflict phase, when international forces are the primary sector actor, there is a mixed record. Panama and Iraq are notorious examples of what can go wrong, while East Timor provides a better model of how it can go well. In the reconstruction phase, a great deal of experience has been garnered about how to reconstruct and reform the police and justice sectors. But the case studies show significant variation in the ability of the international community to design and implement effective programs and to achieve the desired results.

Based on the summary case studies discussed in this report, we can draw some lessons on the key challenges that have faced post-conflict policing since 1989. We analyze these lessons through the three-part model outlined in Chapter Two: the mobilization of inputs, the translation of inputs into outputs, and the linkage to security outcomes.

Mobilizing Inputs

We have argued that there is no simple, quantitatively verifiable link between the amounts of external inputs and the security outcomes in a post-conflict situation. Nonetheless, we can conclude that too little external financial and materiel assistance will make it very difficult to ensure a successful outcome. Afghanistan demonstrates this clearly. The same can be said of international military forces. Large numbers

---

[5] Latin America and the Middle East/North Africa are perhaps the most notorious examples. But Africa boasted many instances of this phenomenon.

do not necessarily guarantee success. However, small per-capita numbers make it difficult to ensure order in the immediate post-conflict phase, especially if there is widespread violence. Similarly, although the deployment of large numbers of civilian police or advisors does not guarantee a more secure outcome, a failure to do so will place a serious burden on international military forces, which end up having to train, equip, and mentor indigenous police forces.

While the absolute amount of external assistance provided is important, its timing is at least as significant. In most post-conflict situations, there is a "golden hour" of perhaps between one and three months during which the external intervention may enjoy popular support, and international legitimacy, and during which insurgents or criminals will be off-balance. If the intervention adopts a "light footprint" approach, as in Iraq and Afghanistan, then it risks squandering the opportunity. Intervening early with overwhelming "force"—to include civilian assets and financial assistance—is easier than trying to retrieve a deteriorating security situation when consent is declining and spoilers are on the offensive.

It is important therefore to mobilize large amounts of inputs early in a mission. However, the problems faced by all nation-building operations in rapidly mobilizing funds, people, and equipment are well known.[6] These problems are particularly acute in the area of policing and justice. There is no cadre of international policing experts that can be deployed from crisis to crisis as there is for humanitarian relief; no nation has a reserve of deployable police officers comparable to its reserve of deployable military forces.[7] We can highlight the "input" lessons identified by concentrating on four aspects: planning and preparation, funds and equipment, international personnel, and international military forces.

---

[6] International Policy Institute, *A Case for Change: A Review of Peace Operations*, London: King's College, 2003.

[7] James Burack, William Lewis, and Edward Marks, *Civilian Police and Multinational Peacekeeping—A Workshop Series: A Role for Democratic Policing*, National Institute of Justice, Washington D.C., October 6, 1997 (published in January 1999).

Planning and Preparation

There will always be political sensitivities that restrict the amount of planning and preparation that can precede a nation-building mission, especially in an international context. However, the price for inadequate planning, as in the case of Iraq, can be catastrophic. Once an operation begins, there is never time for policymakers to reflect on the strategic priorities or to adjust their standard templates to the peculiarities of the circumstance. This sort of analysis and integration of standard best practices, along with a knowledge of local cultures and requirements, needs to take place before an operation is initiated. Such prior planning will also make it easier to close the "security gap" by ensuring that funds, equipment, personnel, and appropriately trained and configured military forces are in hand.

Funds and Equipment

An inevitable characteristic of multilateral nation-building operations is the time required to collect pledges of financial assistance and to turn these into actual payments. However, it is also striking that even in unilateral operations run by the United States, such as Iraq, it takes a long time to mobilize funds. In Iraq, a combination of political, bureaucratic, and security factors meant that, by the fall of 2004, less than 10 percent of the funds allocated to the Ministry of Interior had been disbursed. These schedules translate into on-the-ground delays, whether in terms of employing contractors, building facilities, or providing equipment. One part of the answer is to have on hand a reserve of funds and reserves of appropriate equipment, along with framework contracts with suppliers of critical services and infrastructures. Another answer lies in modifying peacetime accounting and contracting regulations to take account of the urgent security requirements of post-conflict situations.[8]

---

[8] There will be conflicts between the need for speed and the requirements for accountability and oversight. Within the U.S. government, the Defense Department acquisition procedures were not well suited to the requirements of Iraq. USAID, and notably its Office of Transition Initiatives, did have in place flexible, rapid response mechanisms that also provided oversight and accountability.

These case studies demonstrate that corruption can also affect the delivery of funds and equipment. The role of U.S. contractors in Iraq and the United Nation's oil-for-food program show that corruption can be as much a problem for the United States, its allies, and international organizations as it is for indigenous governments. Countries with poorly functioning justice systems are also likely candidates for corruption. In Afghanistan, corruption was endemic in the justice system, partly because unqualified personnel loyal to various factions were sometimes installed as court officials. Steps need to be taken to increase transparency in awarding contracts, to monitor financial transactions, and to hold accountable those who are guilty. Accountability could include a range of measures, from prosecuting U.S. individuals or companies guilty of corruption, to withholding assistance from corrupt foreign governments or agencies.

International Personnel

Even if the political commitment is achievable for deploying police or judicial personnel, or if the funds are available to deploy contractors, there is a lag in the speed with which international personnel can be deployed. Formed constabulary units such as gendarmerie can often deploy rapidly, almost on military timescales. UN civilian police missions or bilateral police and justice advisory and training missions, however, take much longer to move into action. This was evident in cases as different as Kosovo and Iraq.

There is also the question of what international advisors do when they arrive in theater. Quite different models have been applied in different circumstances. In Kosovo and East Timor, the international civilian police took on an executive role and effectively constituted the internal security institutions while training and mentoring their successors. In Bosnia and Iraq, the international police advisors and trainers were restricted to an advisory capacity, focused on building the capacity of the host-nation institutions.

In addition, the quality of international personnel has been the subject of much debate. Reports from the Balkans threw doubt on the abilities of many of the advisors deployed, notably from developing countries. There have also been critiques of the U.S. approach of relying on contractors to mobilize, deploy, and manage personnel. Indeed, in light of the U.S. experience, the United Nations has discouraged contributing nations from using the contractor-led approach. However international personnel are mobilized, as with any aspect of an international mission, it will be important to build in quality control measures from the outset.[9]

Two measures are important in this respect. The first is the quality of oversight by the responsible government agency in the sending country and the nation-building mission. The case studies discussed here indicate that this oversight does need to be strengthened and standardized to ensure that the quality of personnel and their performance are ensured. The second measure is training and preparation for the post-conflict environment. Most law enforcement personnel deployed for international civilian police missions have experience only with domestic policing. Those from Western countries will, generally, have operated in a much more stable and secure environment than that found even in the most benign nation-building operation. To date, training and indoctrination programs for deploying personnel have been much more cursory than those for their military compatriots deploying to theater.

A more fundamental problem relates to the supply of potential international police advisors and judicial advisors. The countries with the most robust internal security institutions will be reluctant to release their best police and judicial personnel who are needed at home. This may contrast with less developed countries that have weaker institutions, which may see financial benefits from deploying personnel. Moreover, supplier organizations, such as police associations, have not prioritized the international assistance mission. In most countries, service with an international police mission does not benefit the individual in terms of career progression.[10]

---

[9] United States Institute of Peace, *American Civilian Police in UN Peace Operations: Lessons Learned and Ideas for the Future*, July 6, 2001.

[10] This is a particular challenge in countries like the United States and United Kingdom, whose police forces are often focused on local needs and are not responsive to national priorities. UK House of Commons Defence Committee, *Oral Evidence of Dr Owen Greene,*

Military Forces

International military forces have two critical roles to play in post-conflict policing: (1) imposing order and (2) supporting the internal security capacity-building and reform mission. Since 1989, the U.S. military has had a mixed record of imposing order in the immediate post-conflict phase. The reasons include an institutional reluctance to take on the policing mission, a lack of training, and, at times, the deliberate sizing of forces to preclude engaging in such missions.[11] The U.S. Department of Defense is now devoting greater effort to fielding forces able to impose order in the immediate aftermath of an intervention.

However, even if international military forces are able to fill the immediate security gap and prevent looting, crime, and an immediate outbreak of political violence, they also retain a critical medium-term responsibility to support the reconstruction and reform of internal security institutions. The U.S. military has long understood that it has a role to play here; however, it has displayed a reluctance to take too active a role in an area that it regards as being one that civilian agencies should lead.[12] In Iraq, it was a year before CJTF-7 adopted support to Iraqi security forces as part of its mission statement. Militaries that have more experience with counterinsurgency and colonial policing find this mission more of a natural fit. There are some potential indicators that a more proactive military role is envisaged by the U.S. Department of Defense.[13] In addition, as Figure 7.1

Chief Constable Paul Kernaghan, Mr Stephen Pattison and Mr Stephen Rimmer, London, HC 65-I, January 26, 2005.

[11] The contrast between Kosovo, where post-conflict stability was a criteria for the deployed force size, and Iraq, where it was not, is striking.

[12] Headquarters, Departments of the Army and Air Force, *Military Operations in Low Intensity Conflict,* Field Manual 100-20/Air Force Pamphlet 3-20, December 5, 1990; Headquarters, Department of the Army (2003); U.S. Army, Marine Corps, Navy, and Air Force (2003).

[13] Headquarters, Department of the Army, *Counterinsurgency Operations*, Field Manual-Interim 3-07.22, October 2004; U.S. Joint Forces Command, *Stability Operations Joint Operating Concept,* Norfolk, Va., September 2004.

Figure 7.1
The Military-Civilian Gap

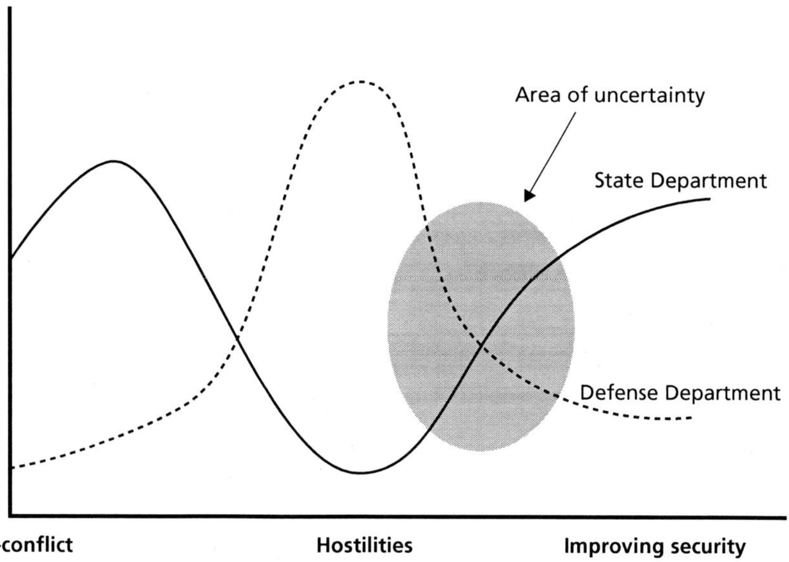

SOURCE: Office of the Coordinator for Reconstruction and Stabilization, U.S. Department of State.
RAND *MG374-7.1*

illustrates, there is a current gap in planning and operational capacity between the U.S. military and such civilian agencies as the Department of State and USAID. There is little joint civilian-military planning across these departments, limited civilian capacity to deploy with military units during stabilization operations, and little agreement about transferring from military to civilian responsibilities as the security situation stabilizes.

Translating Inputs into Outputs

Once the international inputs are available, the task for the nation-building mission is to translate these into the tangible outputs that make a direct contribution to the state's rule-of-law capacity. Because this translation is the core task of missions in theater, the quantifiable outputs, such as numbers of police personnel trained, tend to become the targets on which the mission focuses.

As with any process that seeks to translate raw materials into tangible products, the key to how much "bang for the buck" is achieved will be in the management and design of the operation. The case studies outlined here highlight a number of different models for how the program can be managed. At the macro level, a program may report to a single government such as the United States, an ad hoc coalition, or a UN mission. It is not self-evident that one model is more effective than another. It is true that the dispersed management model used in Afghanistan (the "lead nation" concept) appears to have worked poorly. At the same time, though, the theoretically unified command structure of the CPA in Iraq replicated many of the bureaucratic divisions of a typical UN-led operation. The cases indicate that the military ideal of "unity of command" is unlikely to be achieved in a post-conflict reconstruction mission. Instead, it will be important to build mechanisms to achieve "unity of effort" in designing the management structures for the international mission.

Furthermore, the effectiveness of the translation will be affected by a host of factors outside the control of the international program managers. The politics of the host nation, the level of insecurity, and the absorptive capacity of existing institutions will all affect the success of the program. The cases examined here remind us of the developmental mantra that programs must be locally owned and concentrate on building indigenous leadership and management capacity. Following this approach is the only way to ensure that reform is sustainable. But it will often be frustrating for the international interveners who will be seeking exit strategies for their forces.

It may be helpful to address lessons learned on outputs in four qualitative areas: trained personnel, infrastructure and facilities, institutional development, and results of the DDR process.

Trained Personnel

There will be a wide disparity in the quality of human capital with which a training program works. In East Timor, Somalia, and

Kosovo, there was essentially no police force on which to build. In Haiti, Bosnia, and Iraq, police and other internal security agencies did exist but, to varying degrees, were ineffective, thoroughly corrupt, and antidemocratic. The nature of the human capital will obviously determine whether the focus needs to be more on education and retraining or on training from scratch.

In the case studies presented here, there were a variety of approaches to police and judicial personnel. Examples range from working with existing personnel who were gradually retrained, to dismissing existing personnel and bringing new recruits on board. In some missions, multiple approaches were followed at the same time. In Iraq, the army and corrections service were rebuilt from the ground up, the judiciary was lightly purged, and the police service was gradually reformed at the same time as new personnel were recruited and trained. While there will be no one-size-fits-all model, a compromise will always have to be found between leaving a security gap through dismissal of existing personnel and the dangers of leaving existing personnel in positions of responsibility. This compromise will require a mixture of filling the security gap by international military or police forces and by individual review to weed out discredited personnel, especially in senior positions.[14]

On the training of security personnel—notably police—the cases illustrated here have strengthened the argument that recruit training or cursory retraining of existing personnel is not enough. As with training and education programs in developed countries, reform will only come about if training and mentoring are provided at multiple levels over extended periods of time. Field training programs, long-term mentoring, continuous professional education, and management and specialist training are key to institutionalizing reformed practices, attitudes, and new skills. It is important to impart new skills to the recipients of training, whether it be in forensics, investigative methods, firearms, or personnel management. At least as important, however, is to ensure that the ongoing training helps to

[14] The Judicial Review Committee in Iraq, which reviewed in some detail every single member of the judiciary, may be a useful method to adopt.

drive cultural change among its recipients. One way to make this impact may be to encourage officials from the host nation to observe practices in democratic states to find ways to adapt such practices to their context. This may be a better option than encouraging international advisors to import wholesale systems and procedures from their home jurisdictions.[15]

Another aspect of internal security personnel is the question of the optimum size of the police and the judiciary. The perceived optimum size of police forces in the cases studied here varied widely. We argued in Chapter Six that a marginal increase in police strength, by itself, may not have a demonstrated effect on violence or crime.[16] But completely withdrawing police generally increases crime.[17] Therefore, introducing police into communities with no police produces an "absolute benefit." This is the case in many post-conflict situations. The various nation-building missions discussed here used rough rule-of-thumb measures to set the target strengths of the forces they were building. In the debate on numbers, crucially important is the substantial body of evidence that "what" the police do affects crime. For instance, the evidence supporting general crime prevention strategies such as random patrols is poor, whereas the evidence demonstrating the utility of focused crime prevention strategies such as directed patrol is much stronger.[18] This evidence implies that concen-

---

[15] Deborah G. Wilson and William F. Walsh, "Reflections on the Transfer of Knowledge to Support Democratic Policing in Hungary and Romania," in National Institute of Justice and Bureau of International Narcotics and Law Enforcement Affairs, *Policing in Emerging Democracies: Workshop Papers and Highlights*, Washington D.C., December 14–15, 1995 (published in October 1997).

[16] National Research Council, *Fairness and Effectiveness in Policing: The Evidence*, Washington, D.C.: National Academies Press, 2004.

[17] On the effect of police strikes and service suspension, see Tuija Makinen and Hannu Takala, "The 1976 Police Strike in Finland," *Scandinavian Studies in Criminology*, Vol. 7, 1980, pp. 87–106, and Gerald Clark, "What Happens When the Police Go on Strike," *New York Times Magazine*, November 16, 1969, pp. 45, 176–185, 187, 194–195.

[18] On the ineffectiveness of preventive patrol, see George L. Kelling, Tony Pate, Duane Dieckman, and Charles E. Brown, *The Kansas City Preventive Patrol Experiment: A Summary Report*, Washington, D.C.: Police Foundation, 1974. On the effectiveness of directed patrol, see Lawrence W. Sherman, James W. Shaw, and Dennis P. Rogan, *The Kansas City Gun*

tration on numbers at the expense of quality or reformed practices is a mistake.

Infrastructure and Facilities

The reconstruction of infrastructure and facilities for internal security institutions should be a more straightforward task than achieving cultural change in the police force or judiciary. Here too, Western technocratic models of policing will come into conflict with local practices.[19] An important guide will be to provide infrastructure and facilities through a development lens. Where police aid missions are managed by Western personnel with little development experience, the tendency is to import state-of-the-art solutions, whether in terms of prison design, communications equipment, or weaponry. These may be inappropriate for the local context and may be unsustainable by the local budgetary and technological base. The provision of bicycles rather than squad cars to police in parts of Haiti, for instance, proved appropriate to local needs.

Institutional Development and Reform

It is difficult to measure progress in institutional development and reform. But without a robust institutional development and reform program, it is unlikely that the rule of law will prevail—regardless of how many security forces are fielded, trained, and equipped. Institutional development includes the building of institutional capacity for internal security organizations to undertake security tasks. It is about increasing *effectiveness* and can include programs such as establishing specialist policing entities (e.g., special investigative units, public order units, intelligence); building command, control, and coordina-

---

Experiment, Washington, D.C.: National Institute of Justice, 1995, and Edmund F. McGarrell, Steven Chermak, Alexander Weiss, and Jeremy M. Wilson, "Reducing Firearms Violence Through Directed Police Patrol," *Criminology and Public Policy*, Vol. 1, No. 1, 2001, pp. 119–148.

[19] In Iraq, for instance, the desire of CPA police advisors to ensure that new patrol cars were distributed to police personnel undertaking mobile patrols were stymied by the Iraqi practice of providing the best vehicles to senior officers as a perk of the job and signifier of status.

tion capabilities; or improving management, personnel, and financial processes.

At the same time, because we have a normative goal of helping to build internal security institutions that will support the transition to democracy, institutional reform will be required. The precepts of this "democratic policing" have been extensively surveyed. U.S. and allied policymakers in all the programs outlined in this study sought to instill at least some of these precepts in their programs.[20]

In most post-conflict cases, there may be a tendency to prioritize development over reform. This may be a sound objective, but unless the policing institutions can ensure basic public order, the prospects for the emergence of democratic policing institutions—indeed for a democratic state—are minimal. Nonetheless, it will be important from the outset to try to mainstream reforms in conjunction with the development program. From the case studies discussed here, we can identify five key aspects to institutional development and reform: the nature and structure of internal security institutions, ministry development, national security policy capacity, societal governance institutions, and sustainability. In the case studies examined above, these were addressed to varying extents and in varying ways.

The *nature and structure* of the internal security institutions will be crucial not just to the effectiveness and accountability of the internal security sector but also to the long-term political trajectory of the country. There is no universal template for an effective and democratic internal security sector. For instance, the United States has a very decentralized policing structure, and France has a centralized structure. Both countries enjoy effective and democratic policing. Instead, solutions will have to be sought that deliver the desired effects in the particular political and institutional context. However, structural questions that need to be tackled include the degree of centralization over the police force, the presence or absence of a "third force" (a paramilitary force that is functionally and organizationally distinct from the police and military), the role of the military in

---

[20] Bayley (2001).

internal security, and the degree of independence awarded to the judiciary. Dealing with these "macro issues" will lead to the next step of addressing issues such as the structure of the police force and the nature of police-community relations.

One vital issue, to which too little systematic attention has yet been paid, is the nature and role of domestic intelligence agencies. Nation-building operations have often shied away from this domain because of the association of such institutions with human rights abuses, or, as in Iraq and Afghanistan, they have left the task to agencies with a relatively narrow operational mandate, such as the U.S. Central Intelligence Agency. The creation of effective and accountable intelligence agencies is too important to be ignored or left to Western intelligence agencies.

Institutional development in the *security ministries* in a post-conflict state needs to be tackled in the wider context of public administration reform, since the aim should be to civilianize such ministries and to embed them into the civil service by adopting similar practices. However, international programs to build security forces often move faster and with more resources than public administration reform programs, which tend to attract less-intense attention and to proceed over much longer timescales. This process risks a mismatch between the capabilities of the front-line forces and their civilian governance institutions. Put simply, if a state emerges from a period of post-conflict reconstruction with a powerful military, police force, or intelligence agency—but weak civilian oversight and management at the ministry level—it will be hard to reimpose this civilian control.

Above the level of the individual ministries, an important part of the institutional development agenda is to enable the central government to develop and implement broad *national security policy*. In Afghanistan and Iraq, this was done by helping the host country build a national security council structure. At their best, these structures can help the center of government take a strategic view of its priorities, coordinate policy, and make rational resource allocations over the longer term.[21]

Outside the central government, a vital part of institutional development and reform is the strengthening of *local and civic society governance mechanisms*. The devolution of authority over internal security forces will always face the risk of undermining common national standards and of a local community using the local police or judiciary for parochial purposes. Nonetheless, a degree of devolution will be important to ensure accountability to the local community. This has the advantage both of making the security "producers" (police, judges) more responsive to the needs of their "consumers" (local citizens) and of increasing popular ownership of the internal security outcomes. The intention is to help generate the local demand for reform that will ultimately drive reform much more than externally imposed solutions.[22]

Sustainability is the final element of institutional development. In the immediate post-conflict phase, external involvement is likely to be significant. However, reforms will be successful only if they are sustainable. At one level this requires that they be fiscally sustainable. There is no point in using international aid to build a massive police force and buy expensive equipment if the host state has to slash the budget and police numbers within a couple of years when the aid dries up. At another level, the key will be to encourage the development of local demand for reform. Measures such as civic education and transparency programs may help citizens come to expect effective, honest, and impartial service from the internal security sector. If the political process allows citizens to articulate these expectations,

---

[21] Sierra Leone's recent national security strategy does this.

[22] This does not imply, however, a blind replication of the Western concept of community-oriented policing. This concept will have to be adapted to the local environment to ensure that democratic policing is promoted and not subverted. Clifford Shearing, "Toward Democratic Policing: Rethinking Strategies of Transformation," in National Institute of Justice and Bureau of International Narcotics and Law Enforcement Affairs, *Policing in Emerging Democracies: Workshop Papers and Highlights*, Washington, D.C., December 14–15, 1995 (published in October 1997).

there is a greater likelihood that the reform program will be sustainable in the longer term.

Disarmament, Demobilization, and Reintegration Process

A formal DDR process may not be necessary in every post-conflict case, and there is a danger in applying a standardized DDR template. Nonetheless, DDR programs for former fighters, whether belonging to the former regime or to opposition forces, are an important contributor to security in the short and long term. Political calculations will affect the shape and fate of DDR programs. But the design, resourcing, and degree of local ownership of such programs will dramatically affect their success or failure. The Kosovo Protection Corps has had some success in integrating former fighters; whereas in Iraq, the transition and reintegration program was started late, was not adequately resourced, and has been allowed to atrophy since the transition of authority.

Our case studies indicate a number of general lessons on DDR. First, the DDR of insurgent groups into a democratic political process is critical to ensure a lasting peace. As Iraq and Afghanistan demonstrate, without some form of DDR, there can be no lasting peace. Second, demobilizing police and other security forces into a country with high unemployment can increase crime. Third, a significant amount of DDR resources need to go into the "R"—finding jobs for ex-combatants and reintegrating them into society. El Salvador demonstrates the importance of the latter two points. Delays in reintegrating former Farabundo Martí National Liberation Front (FMLN) and government combatants into society, and a lack of funding for the land program, left thousands of former fighters unemployed. Poor economic conditions and high unemployment in the immediate post-conflict period made it particularly difficult to find jobs. Consequently, crime rates soared. The homicide rate one year after the United Nations departed El Salvador was one of the highest in the world.

Outcomes and Implications

What are the implications for the U.S. government that should inform its approaches to policing in post-conflict situations? Not surprisingly, the policy implications we have drawn match in many ways those provided in David Bayley's thorough literature review on the topic.[23] Afghanistan and Iraq have reinforced well-worn lessons, even if they have provided new models for the management and implementation of post-conflict policing programs. Although the international community learned a great deal about post-conflict policing during the 1990s, the United States and its allies applied few of the lessons to Afghanistan or Iraq. As summarized in Table 5.8, we believe it is important to highlight the following implications for U.S. action on post-conflict security.

Give as Much Attention to Planning Post-Conflict Policing as to Planning Combat Operations

There are three key factors that would improve performance here. First, as Bayley points out, "international CIVPOL operations need to develop the sort of intelligence capacity considered standard in military operations."[24] In many of the cases studied here, the international police mission was hampered by a remarkably limited knowledge base about the host country's internal security system. This limitation stems from the failure both to collect and disseminate the right information and to involve knowledgeable individuals from the host nation. Even the State Department "Future of Iraq" project, which has sometimes been regarded as an example of prewar planning that was ignored, did not seriously address internal security institutions.

Second, institutional mechanisms for planning must be improved. Unlike the combat phase of most interventions, the post-

---

[23] The policy implications we have drawn overlap in many ways with those provided in David Bayley's thorough literature review on the topic, published in 2001. Bayley (2001).

[24] Bayley (2001), p. 58.

Table 7.1
Summary of Recommendations for U.S. Action

Recommendation	Detail
Give as much attention to planning post-conflict internal security as to planning combat operations	• Gather systematic, actionable intelligence on internal security systems prior to an intervention • Improve institutional planning mechanisms within the U.S. government • Ensure pre-intervention mobilization of post-conflict police and justice resources
Negotiate a peace treaty or formal surrender	• In cases of civil war, devote sufficient resources to negotiating a peace treaty among warring parties • In cases of interstate war, secure a formal surrender from defeated parties where possible
Fill the security gap quickly with U.S. (and allied) military and constabulary forces	• Amend U.S. joint doctrine, training, and posture • Develop shared (combined) international military doctrine and practices on post-conflict policing • Boost U.S. and international deployable constabulary forces
Develop comprehensive doctrine for post-conflict internal security reconstruction	• Develop shared international doctrine informed by best practices • Lay out options to ensure unity of command and effort via a new U.S. presidential directive on stability operations • Codify holistic approaches to rule-of-law sector • Integrate internal security reconstruction and reform programs with the wider conflict management agenda
Build mechanisms to ensure faster mobilization of personnel, funds, and equipment	• Improve U.S. government capabilities to rapidly mobilize, deliver, and manage police and justice resources • Encourage the development of international initiatives such as the UN civilian police system and the European Union's policing and justice programs
Focus on outcome measures to shape programs	• Develop and use outcome-based metrics to define program success and managerial performance

conflict phase, including policing, usually receives little attention. This is in part a result of the weakness of the institutions in the United States and other governments charged with policing reform; they simply do not have the corporate capacity to undertake detailed pre-intervention planning.[25] It is also a failure of political will at the national and international levels, since it is the task of the political leadership to make the public case for the lengthy preparation, extensive resourcing, and long-term commitment that is required for post-conflict policing missions.

Third, the early mobilization of policing resources must be ensured to take advantage of the golden hour. By having in place plans, staffs, funds, personnel, and equipment before any intervention, the international community will be much better placed to avoid the debilitating deployment lag that has affected all previous operations. The philosophy needs to be one of policing "shock and awe" rather than that of "too little, too late." Key aspects include planning a coercive posture against potential insurgents, criminals, and warlords; agreeing on unified direction from legitimate civil authority; developing integrated multiagency and multinational unity of purpose; and developing a sophisticated media operation.[26]

Negotiate a Peace Treaty or Formal Surrender

Peace treaties and formal surrenders are highly correlated with peaceful environments. Peace treaties are usually indicators of relatively low levels of hostility because, at the moment of signing, they represent the parties' will to end the violent phase of their conflict. They also facilitate international involvement in the form of loans and foreign aid. Formal surrenders can also increase the likelihood of stability. The destructive defeat of a regime undermines its credibility and demonstrates that it can no longer deliver vital needs to the population. This lesson was ignored in Iraq and Afghanistan, where the United States and its allies did not secure either a peace treaty or formal surrender. The broader lesson is to direct sufficient diplomatic and military resources toward negotiating peace treaties among war-

---

[25] Work under way in Washington (State Department's Coordinator for Reconstruction and Stabilization) and in London (the interdepartmental Post Conflict Reconstruction Unit) should help address this issue.

[26] U.S. Joint Forces Command (2004), p. 31.

ring parties in cases of civil war, and formal surrenders from defeated powers in cases of interstate war.

Fill the Security Gap Quickly with U.S. (and Allied) Military and Constabulary Forces

The U.S. military has sought to avoid being tasked with filling the security gap that invariably emerges after an intervention. The painful experience of Iraq may have forced a change in attitudes, but more far-reaching changes are required than simply the creation of extra military police or civil affairs units.[27] The key will be to ensure that U.S. defense joint doctrine, training, and force structures incorporate the post-conflict policing and security sector reform roles. More broadly, it will be important that all allied forces engaged in an intervention operate according to a common[28] policing and security sector reform doctrine.[29]

However, filling the security gap with international military forces will always be a second-best solution in the absence of sufficient, deployable international policing assets. Constabulary forces, such as the Italian carabinieri, are a more appropriate instrument and their use needs to be encouraged. They may however never be available in sufficient numbers for large-scale operations, meaning that the U.S. needs to consider how it can develop its own constabulary force to bolster the efforts being made by its allies.[30]

---

[27] According to Secretary of Defense Donald Rumsfeld's FY 2006 budget testimony before the House Armed Services Committee, "the Army is retraining relatively under-used artillerymen to form 18 provisional military police companies." See armedservices.house.gov/testimony/109thcongress/RumsfeldBudgetTestimony2-16-05.pdf (accessed June 2005).

[28] "Combined," in U.S. Department of Defense terminology.

[29] In Iraq, for instance, the Ukrainian, Polish, and Spanish units appeared to be even more reluctant than U.S. Army units to engage in security sector reform.

[30] Perito (2004).

Develop Comprehensive Doctrine for Post-Conflict Internal Security Reconstruction

To ensure that civil-military planning and implementation for post-conflict policing proceeds more smoothly, the United States needs to develop, adopt, and share with its allies a common doctrinal approach to reconstruction of the internal security sector in post-conflict environments. Although the concept of doctrine may seem overly militaristic, police forces use doctrine in all but name. Civilian agencies such as the U.S. Departments of State and Justice should distil lessons learned and good practices into a shared doctrine. The benefit of a shared interagency and international doctrine is that it would provide a common frame of reference for planners and managers of post-conflict policing operations. They can focus on optimizing the program for the particular environment they encounter, rather than spending time arguing over first principles—as so often happens.

This doctrine should lay out command and control of nation-building missions. Ideally, the doctrine should flow from a new iteration of the Clinton administration's Presidential Decision Directive 56 on "Managing Complex Contingency Operations." After coming into office, the Bush administration developed National Security Policy Directive XX. It was broader in scope than PDD-56 and provided guidance on warning, advanced planning, prevention, and response options for what it called "complex contingency operations." With regard to interagency strategy and planning, NSPD-XX called for the establishment of an National Security Council–chaired Contingency Planning Policy Coordination Committee at the Assistant Secretary level to lead the development of interagency contingency plans for emerging crises. It focused on U.S. objectives, a desired end state, policy options, interagency responsibilities, resource issues, and strategies for various aspects of the operation. Unfortunately, NSPD-XX was never signed by the President. This created confusion about agency roles and responsibilities, which complicated efforts to respond to the crises in Afghanistan and Iraq.

At least two documents would be helpful to rectify these problems. One is a presidential directive on the civilian component of nation-building operations. Critical questions include: What is the lead civilian agency for nation-building operations? What are the primary objectives? What are the key tasks, how should they be prioritized, and which agencies are in charge of which tasks? The doctrine also needs to take a holistic approach to the internal security sector. It should treat the internal security sector as a whole, as part of the broader security sector. It should therefore include the criminal justice and intelligence institutions. This will help avoid the often repeated mistakes in which these institutions are developed—or not developed—independently of the police.

The second document is a U.S. Defense Department directive on the military component of nation-building operations, what the department refers to as "stability operations." The directive should set policy for the Defense Department, be signed by the Secretary of Defense, and assign roles and responsibilities for the military component of stability operations. It should assign the U.S. Army as the lead agency for stability operations, since this branch of the military plays the most significant military role in rebuilding countries after major combat.

In developing this policy and doctrine, the United States and its allies need to be realistic about the limits of our knowledge about how to successfully transfer strong state institutions to developing countries. U.S. Cold War–era foreign internal defense programs have been criticized for adopting a positivist and technocratic approach.[31] Today's programs, often implemented by Western policing, justice, and intelligence professionals, are not that different in their conceptual basis.[32] To ensure that reconstruction and reform programs are of lasting value, it will be important for internal security specialists and development specialists to work together with regional experts to structure programs that are adapted to the context.

---

[31] Rosenau (2003).

[32] For instance, in Iraq, the preexisting traffic police appear to have done a fair job of regulating traffic, although low-level corruption was built into the system. In its efforts to drive through anticorruption measures, the CPA sought to impose a zero-tolerance approach to corruption, which may have unnecessarily undermined the effectiveness of the traffic police. William Langewiesche, "Welcome to the Green Zone: The American Bubble in Baghdad," *The Atlantic Monthly*, November 2004.

Furthermore, this doctrine should be informed by the broader agenda of conflict mitigation and management. A significant body of research has demonstrated the complex dynamics of internal conflict and highlighted how state security institutions can sometimes contribute to, or at least allow the escalation of, internal conflict. Development actors such as USAID have established conflict assessment methodologies that seek to understand the roots, motives, means, opportunities, and triggers for internal conflict.[33] The United Kingdom's DFID has adopted similar approaches to understanding how external assistance can be used to drive change and prevent or manage conflicts.[34] These methodologies are implicitly mirrored by some of the military campaign plans drawn up by intervening international forces, which often address the symptoms of conflict (e.g., physically neutralizing terrorists and criminals), the means (e.g., disarmament programs), and the motives (e.g., by providing social services to disadvantaged communities).

This broader perspective on conflict prevention and management needs to inform the design and implementation of internal security reform. The focus of such reform programs is often on tangible, institutional results ranging from the production of trained police personnel to the building of ministry capacity. However, building quality enforcement institutions is only one element of an approach to conflict prevention and management. These institutions concentrate largely on reducing the opportunity for conflict to escalate. Broader conflict prevention and management programs need to address the political or economic roots of conflicts as well as the organizational and logistical means by which discontent can be translated into organized violence. Although initiatives in some of these areas may seem outside the remit of a security sector reform

---

33 USAID, *Conflict Prevention and Foreign Assistance*, January 7, 2002.

34 Alex Duncan, "Strategic Conflict Assessment and Political Analysis: What Are the Synergies?" paper prepared for workshop on sharing approaches to understanding drivers of change and political analysis, Organisation for Economic Co-operation and Development, Paris, June 1–2, 2004.

program, let alone an internal security reform program, they need to be treated as integral rather than as "nice to have" add-ons.[35]

Build Mechanisms to Ensure Faster Mobilization of Personnel, Funds, and Equipment

Preplanning, common doctrine, and joint exercises will all help to accelerate the usually slow deployment of personnel, funds, and equipment for post-conflict policing operations. In addition, the U.S. government needs to build mechanisms that enable it to deploy such resources much faster. Initiatives such as the State Department's Coordinator for Stabilization and Reconstruction should provide means through which to improve capabilities. Funding and equipment are relatively easy to stockpile. But the United States needs to do much better at identifying and mobilizing internal security professionals into post-conflict situations. The problems that are faced have been extensively diagnosed. For example, the federal government controls only specialized policing agencies, whose personnel are not suited to supervise general policing reforms. In addition, state and local law enforcement and justice institutions cannot spare personnel. Innovative solutions will have to be found to fill this capability gap.

Internationally, the United States needs to encourage similar initiatives. The UN civilian police system requires strengthening so that potential contributors to international policing missions are assisted to prepare, train, and make available personnel. Significant multilateral proposals such as that for a European gendarmerie and for a European Human Security Force need to be encouraged and supported.[36]

---

[35] One approach to designing such programs is to focus on altering public attitudes, such as through media campaigns and supporting media capacity building. Another approach might be to manage conflicts either through official institutions such as alternative dispute resolution mechanisms or through civil society institutions that may rely on traditional methods of conflict resolution. The latter may not always be an ideal solution. In Iraq, this approach would have involved empowering tribal leaders and legitimizing the violent enforcement of blood feuds.

[36] Signature of Declaration of Intent for a European Gendarmerie Force, September 17, 2004; *A Human Security Doctrine for Europe*, The Barcelona Report of the Study Group on Europe's Security Capabilities, September 15, 2004.

Focus on Outcome Measures to Shape Programs

Policing assistance programs have fallen into the trap of many domestic governmental reform programs, namely: "[P]rogram evaluations that emphasize outputs rather than outcomes as a measure of success inhibit organizational creativity."[37] The tools we have to assess internal security outcomes remain limited. However, by building such assessments into current and future assistance programs and encouraging host nations to undertake such assessments, we will be better placed to optimize assistance programs.[38] Another advantage of using outcome-based measures to evaluate performance will be that they should encourage experimentation by local managers, whether international or local, rather than an adherence to largely meaningless output targets. In addition to the outcome measures outlined here—such as homicide rates, levels of political violence, and public opinion polls of security and the justice system—more tactical outcome measures may also be appropriate. In Somalia, for example, the U.S. military collected such indicators as the death rate per day due to starvation, new patients with gunshot wounds in hospitals, and the street price of an AK-47.[39] All outcome measures, however, should be tied to the overall mission objectives. In the case of internal security, the two primary objectives are establishing stability and a rule of law.

---

[37] Bayley (2001), p. 24.

[38] For instance, public opinion polling can be adjusted to address perceptions of corruption or judicial integrity. International advisors can assist in the development of systemwide criminal justice metrics systems as they undertake routine projects such as the installation of IT systems.

[39] Headquarters, United States Marine Corps, *Small Wars*, 2005.

Bibliography

Afghan Government Inter-Ministerial Reintegration Team, *Disarmament, Demobilization, and Reintegration (DDR) in Afghanistan*, working draft, Kabul, April 2004.

Afghan Ministry of Defense, *Afghan National Army Public Investment Programme*, Kabul, 2004a.

———, *Securing Afghanistan's Future: Accomplishments and the Strategic Path Forward, National Army*, Kabul, January 2004b.

Afghan Presidential Office of National Security, *Afghanistan National Threat Assessment*, Kabul, 2004.

Afghanistan Non-Governmental Organization Security Office, *ANSO Security Situation Summary*, various weekly reports, September 2004.

Afghanistan Stabilization and Reconstruction: A Status Report, Hearing Before the Committee on Foreign Relations, United States Senate, 108-460, January 27, 2004.

Agence France-Presse, "Most Foreign NGOs in Iraq Preparing to Leave: Coordinator," September 8, 2004.

al-Marashi, Ibrahim, "Iraq's Security and Intelligence Network: A Guide and Analysis," *Middle East Review of International Affairs*, Vol. 6, No. 3, September 2002.

America's Watch, *El Salvador's Decade of Terror: Human Rights Since the Assassination of Archbishop Romero*, New Haven, Conn.: Yale University Press, 1991.

Amnesty International, *Afghanistan: Crumbling Prison System Desperately in Need of Repair*, New York, 2003.

———, *Iraq: Human Rights Protection and Promotion Vital in the Transitional Period*, New York, June 28, 2004a.

———, *Iraq: One Year on the Human Rights Situation Remains Dire*, New York, March 18, 2004b.

Anonymous, *Imperial Hubris: Why the West Is Losing the War on Terror*, Washington, D.C.: Brassey's, 2004.

The Asia Foundation, *Voter Education Planning Survey: Afghanistan 2004 National Elections,* Kabul, 2004.

Asian Development Bank and World Bank, *Afghanistan: Preliminary Needs Assessment for Recovery and Reconstruction*, Kabul, January 2002.

Ayubi, Nazih, *Over-Stating the Arab State: Politics and Society in the Middle East,* London: I. B. Tauris, 1996.

Bailey, Michael, Robert Maguire, J. O'Neil, and G. Pouliot, "Haiti: Military-Police Partnership for Public Security," in Oakley, Dziedzic, and Goldberg (1998).

Barton, Rick, and Bathsheba Croker, *Progress or Peril? Measuring Iraq's Reconstruction*, Washington, D.C.: Center for Strategic and International Studies, September 2004.

Bayley, David H., *Patterns of Policing: A Comparative International Analysis*, New Brunswick, N.J.: Rutgers University Press, 1985.

———, *Policing for the Future,* New York: Oxford University Press, 1994.

———, "The Contemporary Practices of Policing: A Comparative View," in James Burack, William Lewis, and Edward Marks, eds., *Civilian Police and Multinational Peacekeeping—A Workshop Series: A Role for Democratic Policing*, Washington, D.C.: National Institute of Justice, October 6, 1997 (published in January 1999).

———, *Democratizing the Police Abroad: What to Do and How to Do It*, Washington, D.C.: National Institute of Justice, June 2001.

BBC News Online, "Bomb Kills Oil-for-Food Auditor," July 3, 2004.

Beblawi, Hazem, and Giacomo Luciani, eds., *The Rentier State*, New York: Croom Helm, 1987.

Bensahel, Nora, "Humanitarian Relief and Nation Building in Somalia," in Robert J. Art and Patrick M. Cronin, eds., *The United States and*

Coercive Diplomacy, Washington, D.C.: United States Institute of Peace Press, 2003.

Berman, Eric, *Managing Arms in Peace Processes: Mozambique*, Geneva: United Nations Publications, 1996.

Bhatia, Michael, Kevin Lanigan, and Philip Wilkinson, *Minimal Investments, Minimal Results: The Failure of Security Policy in Afghanistan*, Kabul: Afghanistan Research and Evaluation Unit, June 2004.

Biddle, Stephen, *Afghanistan and the Future of Warfare: Implications for Army and Defense Policy*, Carlisle, Pa.: Strategic Studies Institute, U.S. Army War College, November 2002.

Blaxland, Joan, *Information-Era Maneuver: The Australian-Led Mission to East Timor*, Duntroon, Australia: Land Warfare Studies Centre, June 2002.

Bradsher, Henry S., *Afghanistan and the Soviet Union*, Durham, N.C.: Duke University Press, 1985.

Brands, H. W., *The Devil We Know: Americans and the Cold War*, New York: Oxford University Press, 1993.

Brookings Institution, Iraq Index, www.brookings.edu/iraqindex.

Bryden, Alan, and Heiner Hänggi, eds., *Reform and Reconstruction of the Security Sector*, Münster, Germany: Lit Verlag, 2004.

Burack, James, William Lewis, and Edward Marks, *Civilian Police and Multinational Peacekeeping—A Workshop Series: A Role for Democratic Policing*, Washington, D.C.: National Institute of Justice, October 6, 1997 (published in January 1999).

Call, Charles T., "Institutional Learning Within ICITAP," in Oakley, Dziedzic, and Goldberg (1998).

Chesterman, Simon, "Walking Softly in Afghanistan: The Future of UN State-Building," *Survival*, Vol. 44, No. 3, Autumn 2002.

———, *You, the People: The United Nations, Transitional Administration, and State-Building*, New York: Oxford University Press, 2004.

Ciavarella, Carla, *Reform of the Penitentiary System in Afghanistan,* Kabul: United Nations Office on Drugs and Crime, 2004.

Civilian Police Advisory Training Team (CPATT), status update, August 2004.

Clark, Gerald, "What Happens When the Police Go on Strike," *New York Times Magazine*, November 16, 1969.

Cloud, David S., and Carlotta Gall, "U.S. Memo Faults Afghan Leader on Heroin Fight," *New York Times*, May 22, 2005.

Collier, David, "The Comparative Method: Two Decades of Change," in Dankwart A. Rustow and Kenneth Paul Erickson, eds., *Comparative Political Dynamics: Global Research Perspectives*, New York: HarperCollins, 1991.

Cordesman, Anthony H., *The Iraq War: Strategy, Tactics, and Military Lessons*, Washington, D.C.: Center for Strategic and International Studies, 2003.

———, *Inexcusable Failure: Progress in Training the Iraqi Army and Security Forces as of Mid-July 2004*, Washington, D.C.: Center for Strategic and International Studies, July 20, 2004a.

———, *The Critical Role of Iraqi Military, Security, and Police Forces*, Washington, D.C.: Center for Strategic and International Studies, September 27, 2004b.

———, *Iraqi Force Development: An Iraqi View*, Washington, D.C.: Center for Strategic and International Studies, March 6, 2005.

Coalition Provisional Authority (CPA), "Armed Forces and Militia Transition and Reintegration," fact sheet, undated, www.cpa-iraq.org/transcripts/20040607_MNFI_factsheet.html (as of May 2005).

———, "Dissolution of Entities," CPA Order 2, May 23, 2003a.

———, *Iraq Police: An Assessment of the Present and Recommendations for the Future*, Baghdad, May 30, 2003b.

———, "Creation of the Department of Border Enforcement," CPA Order 26, August 24, 2003c.

———, "Establishment of the Iraqi Civil Defense Corps," CPA Order 28, September 3, 2003d.

———, "Re-Establishment of the Council of Judges," CPA Order 35, September 15, 2003e.

———, "Commission on Public Integrity to Combat Government Corruption," press release, January 31, 2004a. Online at www.iraqcoalition.org/pressreleases/20040131_IGC_integrity_PR.html (as of May 2005).

———, "Iraqi Inspectors General," CPA Order 57, February 10, 2004b.

———, "Law of Administration for the State of Iraq for the Transitional Period," March 8, 2004c.

———, "Ministry of Defense," CPA Order 67, March 21, 2004d.

———, "Ministerial Committee on National Security," CPA Order 68, April 4, 2004e.

———, "Local Governmental Powers," CPA Order 71, April 6, 2004f.

———, "The Central Criminal Court of Iraq (Amended)," CPA Order 13, April 22, 2004g.

———, "Board of Supreme Audit," CPA Order 77, April 25, 2004h.

———, "Transfer of the Iraqi Civil Defense Corps to the Iraqi Ministry of Defense," CPA Order 4, April 25, 2004i.

———, "Armed Forces and Militia Agreement Announced," press release, June 5, 2004j.

———, "Establishment of the Judicial Review Committee," CPA Order 15, June 23, 2004k.

———, *Audit Report: Management of Personnel Assigned to the Coalition Provisional Authority in Baghdad*, Report by the Inspector General of the Coalition Provisional Authority, Baghdad, 04-002, June 25, 2004l.

———, *Strategic Plan*, Baghdad, June 25, 2004m.

———, *An Historic Review of CPA Accomplishments*, Baghdad, June 28, 2004n.

———, *MoI Finance Files*, Baghdad, September 2004o.

"Country Risk Assessment: Afghanistan," *Jane's Intelligence Review*, Vol. 16, No. 5, May 2004.

Daalder, Ivo H., and Michael E. O'Hanlon, *Winning Ugly: NATO's War to Save Kosovo*, Washington, D.C.: Brookings Institution Press, 2001.

Davis, Anthony, "Kabul's Security Dilemma," *Jane's Defence Weekly*, Vol. 37, No. 24, June 12, 2002.

———, "Afghan Security Deteriorates as Taliban Regroup," *Jane's Intelligence Review*, Vol. 15, No. 5, May 2003.

DFI Financial Reporting Matrix, June 26, 2004, www.cpa-iraq.org/budget/DFI_intro1.html (as of May 2005).

Dobbins, James, Seth G. Jones, Keith Crane, Andrew Rathmell, Brett Steele, Richard Teltschik, and Anga Timilsina, *The UN's Role in Nation-Building: From the Congo to Iraq*, Santa Monica, Calif.: RAND Corporation, MG-304-RC, 2005.

Dobbins, James, John G. McGinn, Keith Crane, Seth G. Jones, Rollie Lal, Andrew Rathmell, Rachel Swanger, and Anga Timilsina, *America's Role in Nation-Building: From Germany to Iraq*, Santa Monica, Calif.: RAND Corporation, MR-1753-RC, 2003.

Dodge, Toby, *Inventing Iraq: The Failure of Nation-Building and a History Denied,* New York: Columbia University Press, 2003.

Donnan, Shawn, "Evidence Grows Over Jakarta Hand in Violence," *Financial Times*, November 25, 1999.

Dow Jones International News, "Tiny Iraq NATO Mission Sticks to Training, Not Fighting," August 26, 2004.

Dubois, Thomas R., "The Weinberger Doctrine and the Liberation of Kuwait," *Parameters*, Vol. 21, No. 4, Winter 1991–1992.

Duncan, Alex, "Strategic Conflict Assessment and Political Analysis: What Are the Synergies?" paper prepared for workshop on sharing approaches to understanding drivers of change and political analysis, Organisation for Economic Co-operation and Development, Paris, June 1–2, 2004.

Eck, John E., and Edward R. Maguire, "Have Changes in Policing Reduced Violent Crime? An Assessment of the Evidence," in Alfred Blumstein and Joel Wallman, eds., *The Crime Drop in America*, New York: Cambridge University Press, 2000.

Economist Intelligence Unit, www.eiu.com.

Edelstein, David M., "Occupational Hazards: Why Military Occupations Succeed or Fail," *International Security*, Vol. 29, No. 1, Summer 2004.

Einhorn, Jessica, "The World Bank's Mission Creep," *Foreign Affairs*, Vol. 80, No. 5, 2001.

Etzioni, Amitai, "A Self-Restrained Approach to Nation-Building by Foreign Powers," *International Affairs*, Vol. 80, No. 1, 2004.

European Commission, *Iraq Assistance Programme*, Brussels, COM(2004) 667, March 4, 2004.

Fallows, James, "Blind into Baghdad," *The Atlantic Monthly*, January/February 2004.

Ferguson, Chris, "Police Reform, Peacekeeping and SSR: The Need for Closer Synthesis," *Journal of Security Sector Management*, Vol. 2, No. 3, September 2004. Online at www.jofssm.org/issues/jofssm_0203_ferguson.doc (accessed June 2005).

Final Report of the Independent Panel to Review DoD Detention Operations, August 24, 2004.

Freedom House, *Freedom in the World 2003: The Annual Survey of Political Rights and Civil Liberties*, New York, 2003.

———, *Freedom in the World 2004: The Annual Survey of Political Rights and Civil Liberties*, 2004, New York, 2004a.

———, *Freedom in the World 2004*, Table of Independent Countries—Comparative Measures of Freedom, 2004b, from www.freedomhouse.org/research/freeworld/2004/table2004.pdf (as of May 2005).

Fukuyama, Francis, *State-Building: Governance and World Order in the 21st Century*, Ithaca, N.Y.: Cornell University Press, 2004.

Gaddis, John Lewis, *Strategies of Containment: A Critical Reappraisal of Postwar American National Security Policy*, New York: Oxford University Press, 1982.

Gall, Carlotta, "21 Killed in Afghanistan Attacks Directed at Provincial Governor," *New York Times*, August 15, 2004.

Ganzglass, Martin R., "The Restoration of the Somali Justice System," in Walter Clarke and Jeffrey Herbst, eds., *Learning From Somalia: The Lessons of Armed Humanitarian Intervention*, Boulder, Colo.: Westview Press, 1997.

German Federal Ministry of the Interior, *Assistance in Rebuilding the Police Force in Afghanistan*, Berlin: Federal Foreign Office and Federal Ministry of the Interior, March 2004.

Giddens, Anthony, *The Nation-State and Violence: Volume Two of a Contemporary Critique of Historical Materialism*, Berkeley, Calif.: University of California Press, 1997.

"Global Posture: Testimony as Prepared for Delivery by Secretary of Defense Donald H. Rumsfeld, Senate Armed Services Committee,"

Washington, D.C., September 23, 2004 at www.defenselink.mil/speeches/2004/sp20040923-secdef0783.html (as of May 2005).

Gompert, David C., Olga Oliker, and Anga Timilsina, *Clean, Lean and Able: A Strategy for Defense Development*, Santa Monica, Calif.: RAND Corporation, OP-101-RC, 2004.

Gormley, William T., and David L. Weimer, *Organizational Report Cards*, Cambridge, Mass.: Harvard University Press, 1999.

Government of Afghanistan, *Justice Public Investment Programme*, Kabul, February 2004a.

———, *Berlin Conference Security Paper*, Kabul, March 2004b.

Hagen, William H., "The Balkans' Lethal Nationalisms," *Foreign Affairs*, Vol. 78, No. 4, July/August 1999.

Hartmann, Michael E., *International Judges and Prosecutors in Kosovo: A New Model for Post-Conflict Peacekeeping*, Special Report 112, Washington, D.C.: U.S. Institute of Peace, 2003.

Hatry, Harry P., *Performance Measurement: Getting Results*, Washington, D.C.: Urban Institute Press, 1999.

Headquarters, Department of the Army, *Stability Operations and Support Operations*, FM 3-07, February 2003.

———, *Counterinsurgency Operations*, FM-I 3-07.22, October 2004.

Headquarters, Departments of the Army and Air Force, *Military Operations in Low Intensity Conflict,* Field Manual 100-20/Air Force Pamphlet 3-20, December 5, 1990.

Headquarters, United States Marine Corps, *Small Wars*, 2005.

Hersh, Seymour M., "The Other War: Why Bush's Afghanistan Problem Won't Go Away," *The New Yorker,* April 12, 2004.

Higgins, Andrew, "As It Wields Power Abroad, U.S. Outsources Law and Order Work," *Wall Street Journal*, February 2, 2004.

Hill, Luke, "NATO to Quit Bosnia, Debates U.S. Proposals," *Jane's Defence Weekly*, Vol. 40, No. 23, December 10, 2003.

Hoffman, Bruce, *Inside Terrorism*, New York: Columbia University Press, 1998.

Human Rights Watch, *All Our Hopes Are Crushed: Violence and Repression in Western Afghanistan*, New York, 2002.

———, *Claims in Conflict: Reversing Ethnic Cleansing in Northern Iraq*, New York, August 2004.

A Human Security Doctrine for Europe, The Barcelona Report of the Study Group on Europe's Security Capabilities, September 15, 2004.

Huntington, Samuel P., *The Clash of Civilizations and the Remaking of World Order*, New York: Simon & Schuster, 1996.

International Legal Assistance Consortium (ILAC), "Lawyers Call for International Role in Iraq," undated.

International Advisory and Monitoring Board, *Development Fund for Iraq Statement of Cash Receipts and Payments for the Period from 22 May 2003 to 31 December 2003 (with Independent Auditors' Report)*, June 29, 2004. Online at www.iamb.info/auditrep/r052203a.pdf (as of June 2005).

International Bar Association, "IBA's Human Rights Institute Successfully Completes First Major Training Course for Iraq's Judges, Prosecutors and Lawyers," press release, March 8, 2004.

International Crisis Group (ICG), *Kosovo Report Card*, Washington, D.C., August 28, 2000.

———, *Courting Disaster: The Misrule of Law in Bosnia and Herzegovina*, Sarajevo and Brussels, Balkans Report No. 127, March 2002.

International Institute for Strategic Studies (IISS), *The Military Balance*, London: Oxford University Press, various volumes.

International Policy Institute, *A Case for Change: A Review of Peace Operations*, London: King's College London, 2003.

International Republic Institute, Afghanistan Election Day Survey, Washington, D.C., October 9, 2004.

Iraq Body Count Project, www.iraqbodycount.net/bodycount.htm.

Iraq Coalition Casualty Count, http://icasualties.org/oif/.

Iraqi Ministry of Defense, submissions to Second Donor Committee meeting, Qatar, May 25–26, 2004, at www.uniraq.org/donors/nonUN120.asp (as of June 2005).

Iraqi Ministry of Finance, *2004 Budget*, Baghdad, October 2003.

Iraqi Ministry of Interior, submissions to Second Donor Committee meeting, Qatar, May 25–26, 2004, at www.uniraq.org/donors/nonUN120.asp (as of June 2005).

Iraqi Ministry of Justice, submissions to Second Donor Committee meeting, Qatar, May 25–26, 2004, at www.uniraq.org/donors/nonUN120.asp (as of June 2005).

———, *Revisions to 2004 Budget, Ministerial Allocations*, Baghdad, April 10, 2004.

Jalali, Ali A., "Afghanistan: The Anatomy of an Ongoing Conflict," *Parameters*, Vol. 31, No. 1, Spring 2001.

Jane's Information Group, Jane's Sentinel Security Assessments, Serbia and Montenegro, Kosovo Special Profile, online, April 21, 2004a.

———, *Security and Foreign Forces: Afghanistan*, Coulsdon, UK, 2004b.

Jane's Intelligence Review, Vol. 15, No. 5, May 2003.

Judah, Tim, "The Taliban Papers," *Survival*, Vol. 44, No. 1, Spring 2002.

Kaufmann, Daniel, Aart Kraay, and Massimo Mastruzzi, *Governance Matters III: Governance Indicators for 1996–2002*, Washington, D.C.: World Bank, 2003.

Kelling, George L., Tony Pate, Duane Dieckman, and Charles E. Brown, *The Kansas City Preventive Patrol Experiment: A Summary Report*, Washington, D.C.: Police Foundation, 1974.

Killick, John, *The United States and European Reconstruction, 1945–1960*, Edinburgh, UK: Keele University Press, 1997.

King, Jeremy, A. Walter Dorn, and Matthew Hodes, *An Unprecedented Experiment: Security Sector Reform in Bosnia and Herzegovina*, London: Saferworld, September 2002.

Langewiesche, William, "Welcome to the Green Zone: The American Bubble in Baghdad," *The Atlantic Monthly*, November 2004.

Law of Administration for the State of Iraq for the Transitional Period, Chapter 3, Article 27D, March 8, 2004.

Linn, Brian McAllister, *The U.S. Army and Counterinsurgency in the Philippine War, 1899–1902*, Chapel Hill, N.C.: University of North Carolina Press, 1989.

Luciani, Giacomo, "Allocation vs. Production States: A Theoretical Framework," in Beblawi and Luciani (1987).

Makinen, Tuija, and Hannu Takala, "The 1976 Police Strike in Finland," *Scandinavian Studies in Criminology*, Vol. 7, 1980.

Mani, Rama, *Ending Impunity and Building Justice in Afghanistan*, Kabul: Afghanistan Research and Evaluation Unit, 2003.

Manuel, Anja, and P. W. Singer, "A New Model Afghan Army," *Foreign Affairs*, Vol. 81, No. 4, July/August 2002.

McCormick, David H., "From Peacekeeping to Peacebuilding: Restructuring military and police institutions in El Salvador," in Michael W. Doyle, Ian Johnstone, and Robert C. Orr, eds., *Keeping the Peace: Multidimensional UN Operations in Cambodia and El Salvador*, New York: Cambridge University Press, 1997.

McGarrell, Edmund F., Steven Chermak, Alexander Weiss, and Jeremy M. Wilson, "Reducing Firearms Violence Through Directed Police Patrol," *Criminology and Public Policy*, Vol. 1, No. 1, 2001.

Miller, T. Christian, "Post-Invasion Chaos Blamed for Drug Surge," *Los Angeles Times*, October 4, 2004.

Miller, Laurel, and Robert Perito, *Establishing the Rule of Law in Afghanistan*, Special Report 117, Washington, D.C.: United States Institute of Peace, 2004.

Multi-National Division (South East), *Iraqi Opinion Trend Analysis* (IOTA), September 12, 2004.

Montgomery, John D., and Dennis A. Rondinelli, eds., *Beyond Reconstruction in Afghanistan: Lessons from Development Experience*, New York: Palgrave Macmillan, 2004.

Murray, Williamson, and Major General Robert H. Scales, Jr., *The Iraq War: A Military History*, Cambridge, Mass.: Belknap Press of Harvard University Press, 2003.

Nardulli, Bruce R., Walter L. Perry, Bruce Pirnie, John Gordon IV, and John G. McGinn, *Disjointed War: Military Operations in Kosovo, 1999*, Santa Monica, Calif.: RAND Corporation, MR-1406-A, 2002.

National Academies Press, *Evidence*, Washington, D.C., 2004.

National Commission on Terrorist Attacks Upon the United States, *The 9/11 Commission Report: Final Report of the National Commission on Terrorist Attacks Upon the United States*, New York: W. W. Norton, 2004.

National Research Council, *Fairness and Effectiveness in Policing: The National Threat Assessment*, Washington, D.C.: National Academies Press, 2004.

New York Lawyers' Committee on Human Rights, *El Salvador's Negotiated Revolution: Prospects for Legal Reform*, New York, 1993.

Norchi, Charles H., "Toward the Rule of Law in Afghanistan: The Constitutive Process," in Montgomery and Rondinelli (2004).

North Atlantic Treaty Organization (NATO), "NATO's Role in Relation to the Conflict in Kosovo," July 15, 1999, www.nato.int/kosovo/history.htm (as of May 2005).

Oakley, Robert B., Michael J. Dziedzic, and Eliot M. Goldberg, eds., *Policing the New World Disorder: Peace Operations and Public Security*, Washington, D.C.: National Defense University Press, 1998.

O'Hanlon, Michael E., and Adriana Lins de Albuquerque, *Iraq Index: Tracking Variables of Reconstruction and Security in Post-Saddam Iraq*, Washington, D.C.: Brookings Institution, updated September 10, 2004a.

———, *Afghanistan Index: Tracking Variables of Reconstruction and Security in Post-Taliban Afghanistan*, Washington, D.C.: Brookings Institution, November 15, 2004b.

Olson, Mancur, *The Logic of Collective Actions: Public Goods and the Theory of Groups*, Cambridge, Mass.: Harvard University Press, 1971.

Organisation for Economic Co-operation and Development (OECD), Development Assistance Committee, Network on Conflict, Peace and Development Co-operation, *Security System Reform: Policy and Good Practice*, October 1, 2003.

Organisation for Security and Co-operation in Europe (OSCE), "Kosovo Police Service School," *Mission in Kosovo Factsheets, Police Education*, Pristina, February 3, 2003.

———, "Kosovo: Review of the Criminal Justice System: The Administration of Justice in the Municipal Courts," *OSCE Mission in Kosovo,*

Department of Human Rights and Rule of Law, Legal System Monitoring Section, Pristina, March 2004a.

———, "New Class of Cadets to Graduate from OSCE Kosovo Police School," May 28, 2004b.

Oxford Research International, *National Survey of Iraq*, Oxford, UK, June 2004.

Pan American Health Organization, *Regional Core Health Data Initiative, 1995–2000*, Washington, D.C., 2005.

Paris, Roland, *At War's End: Building Peace After Civil Conflict*, New York: Cambridge University Press, 2004.

Perito, Robert M., *The American Experience with Police in Peace Operations*, The Academic Series, Clementsport, Nova Scotia, Canada: The Canadian Peace Keeping Press, Pearson Peacekeeping Centre, 2002a.

———, *Policing the Police in Bosnia: A Further Reform Agenda*, Sarajevo and Brussels: International Crisis Group, Balkans Report No. 130, May 2002b.

———, *Where Is the Lone Ranger When We Need Him? America's Search for a Postconflict Stability Force*, Washington, D.C.: United States Institute of Peace, 2004.

Powell, Colin L., "U.S. Forces: Challenges Ahead," *Foreign Affairs*, Vol. 72, No. 5, Winter 1992–93.

President's Commission on Law Enforcement and Administration of Justice, *Task Force Report: The Police*, Washington, D.C., 1967.

PRS Group, *International Country Risk Guide*, Vol. 24, No. 9, September 2003. Online at www.prsgroup.com/icrg/icrg.html (as of May 2005).

Quarterly Report to Congress, 2207 report, October 2004.

Quinlivan, James T., "Force Requirements in Stability Operations," *Parameters*, Vol. 25, No. 4, Winter 1995–96.

Ragin, Charles C., "Comparative Sociology and the Comparative Method," *International Journal of Comparative Sociology*, Vol. 22, Nos. 1–2, March–June 1981.

Ramet, Sabrina, *KFOR's Record in Kosovo*, Meeting Report 219, Washington, D.C.: Woodrow Wilson International Center for Scholars, November 17, 2000.

Ramsbotham, Oliver, and Tom Woodhouse, *Encyclopedia of International Peacekeeping Operations*, Santa Barbara, Calif.: ABC-CLIO, 1999.

RAND-MIPT [National Memorial Institute for the Prevention of Terrorism] Terrorism Incident Database, www.tkb.org.

Rashid, Ahmed, *Taliban: Militant Islam, Oil and Fundamentalism in Central Asia*, New Haven, Conn.: Yale University Press, 2000.

———, "Pakistan and the Taliban," in William Maley, ed., *Fundamentalism Reborn? Afghanistan and the Taliban*, New York: New York University Press, 2001.

Rathmell, Andrew, "Iraqi Intelligence and Security Services," *International Defense Review*, May 1991.

———, "Syria's Intelligence Services: Origins and Development," *Journal of Conflict Studies*, Vol. 16, No. 2, Fall 1996.

Report to Congress Pursuant to Section 1506 of the Emergency Wartime Supplemental Appropriations Act, 2003 (Public Law 108-11), *Update Report on United States Strategy for Relief and Reconstruction in Iraq*, October 14, 2003.

Republic of Iraq, *Budget Revenues and Expenses*, July–December 2003.

Ricks, Thomas, "U.S. Troops' Death Rate Rising in Iraq," *Washington Post*, September 9, 2004.

Roberts, Les, Riyadh Lafta, Richard Garfield, Jamal Khudhairi, and Gilbert Burnham, "Mortality Before and After the 2003 Invasion of Iraq: Cluster Sample Survey," *Lancet*, October 29, 2004.

Rosenau, William, "The Eisenhower Administration, U.S. Foreign Internal Security Assistance, and the Struggle for the Developing World, 1954–1961," *Low Intensity Conflict and Law Enforcement*, Vol. 10, No. 3, Autumn 2001.

———, "The Kennedy Administration, U.S. Foreign Internal Security Assistance and the Challenge of 'Subterranean War,' 1961–63," *Small Wars and Insurgencies*, Vol. 14, No. 3, Autumn 2003.

Roy, Olivier, *Islam and Resistance in Afghanistan*, 2nd edition, New York: Cambridge University Press, 1990.

Rubin, Barnett R., *The Fragmentation of Afghanistan: State Formation and Collapse in the International System*, 2nd edition, New Haven, Conn.: Yale University Press, 2002.

———, "Identifying Options and Entry Points for Disarmament, Demobilization, and Reintegration in Afghanistan," working paper, Center on International Cooperation, New York University, March 2003.

———, "(Re)Building Afghanistan," *Current History*, Vol. 103, No. 672, April 2004a.

———, *Road to Ruin: Afghanistan's Booming Opium Industry*, New York: Center on International Cooperation, October 2004b.

Rubin, Barnett R., and Andrea Armstrong, "Regional Issues in the Reconstruction of Afghanistan," *World Policy Journal*, Vol. 20, No. 1, Spring 2003.

Ryan, Alan, *Primary Responsibilities and Primary Risks: Australian Defence Force Participation in the International Force East Timor*, Duntroon, Australia: Land Warfare Studies Centre, 2000.

———, "The Strong Lead-Nation Model in an Ad Hoc Coalition of the Willing: Operation Stabilise in East Timor," *International Peacekeeping*, Vol. 9, No. 1, Spring 2002.

Schultz, Richard, *In the Aftermath of War: U.S. Support for Reconstruction and Nation-Building in Panama Following Just Cause*, Montgomery, Ala.: Air University Press, 1993.

Sedra, Mark, *Challenging the Warlord Culture: Security Sector Reform in Post-Taliban Afghanistan*, Bonn, Germany: Bonn International Center for Conversion, 2002.

Shearing, Clifford, "Toward Democratic Policing: Rethinking Strategies of Transformation," in National Institute of Justice and Bureau of International Narcotics and Law Enforcement Affairs, *Policing in Emerging Democracies: Workshop Papers and Highlights*, Washington, D.C., December 14–15, 1995 (published in October 1997).

Sherman, Lawrence W., James W. Shaw, and Dennis P. Rogan, *The Kansas City Gun Experiment*, Washington, D.C.: National Institute of Justice, 1995.

Signature of Declaration of Intent for a European Gendarmerie Force, September 17, 2004. Online at www.europa-web.de/europa/03euinf/10counc/egfdecl.htm (as of May 2005).

Singer, P. W., *Corporate Warriors: The Rise of the Privatized Military Industry*, Ithaca, N.Y.: Cornell University Press, 2003.

Skocpol, Theda, and Margaret Somers, "The Uses of Comparative History in Macrosocial Inquiry," *Comparative Studies in Society and History*, Vol. 22, No. 2, 1980.

Smith, Christopher, "The International Trade in Small Arms," *Jane's Intelligence Review*, Vol. 7, No. 9, 1995.

Solana, Javier, "NATO's Success in Kosovo," *Foreign Affairs*, Vol. 78, No. 6, November/December 1999.

Stanley, William, and Robert Loosle, "El Salvador: The Civilian Police Component of Peace Operations," in Oakley, Dziedzic, and Goldberg (1998).

Starr, S. Frederick, *U.S. Afghanistan Policy: It's Working*, Washington, D.C.: Johns Hopkins University, Central Asia–Caucasus Institute, 2004.

Statistical Office of Kosovo, *Living Standard Measurement Survey, 2000*, September 2003.

Steele, Jonathan, "Nation Building in East Timor," *World Policy Journal*, Vol. 19, No. 2, Summer 2002.

Stockholm International Peace Research Institute (SIPRI), *SIPRI Yearbook 1991: World Armaments and Disarmament*, New York: Oxford University Press, 1991.

Strohmeyer, Hansjorg, "Collapse and Reconstruction of a Judicial System: The United Nations Missions in Kosovo and East Timor," *American Journal of International Law*, Vol. 95, No. 46, 2001.

Tanham, George K., *War Without Guns: American Civilians in Rural Vietnam,* New York: Praeger, 1966.

Tapper, Richard, "Anthropologists, Historians, and Tribespeople on Tribe and State Formation in the Middle East," in Philip S. Khoury and Joseph Kostiner, eds., *Tribes and State Formation in the Middle East*, Berkeley, Calif.: University of California Press, 1990.

Tilly, Charles T., *The Formation of National States in Western Europe,* Princeton, N.J.: Princeton University Press, 1975.

———, "Means and Ends of Comparison in Macrosociology," in Lars Mjoset et al., *Comparative Social Research: Methodological Issues in Comparative Social Science,* Vol. 16, Greenwich, Conn.: JAI Press, 1997.

Transparency International, *Global Corruption Report 2004*, Berlin, 2004. Available online at www.globalcorruptionreport.org.

Tripp, Charles, *A History of Iraq,* 2nd edition, Cambridge, UK: Cambridge University Press, 2002.

UK Cabinet Office, *Iraq: Its Infrastructure of Concealment, Deception and Intimidation*, February 3, 2003.

UK Department for International Development, *Understanding and Supporting Security Sector Reform*, London, undated.

UK House of Commons Defence Committee, *Oral Evidence of Dr Owen Greene, Chief Constable Paul Kernaghan, Mr Stephen Pattison and Mr Stephen Rimmer*, HC 65-I, January 26, 2005.

United Nations, *Demographic Yearbook*, New York: United Nations, various volumes.

———, UN Secretary General Reports to the Security Council: S/2001/983 (October 18, 2001); S/2002/1233 (November 6, 2002); S/2003/944 (October 6, 2003); S/2004/333 (April 29, 2004); S/2000/1196 (December 15, 2000); S/2002/62 (January 15, 2002); S/2002/1126 (October 9, 2002); S/2003/675 (June 26, 2003); S/2004/71 (January 26, 2004); S/1995/1031 (December 13, 1995), S/2000/529 (June 2, 2000); S/1995/231 (March 28, 1995); S/1995/614 (July 24, 1995); S/1996/416 (June 5, 1996); S/2000/538 (June 6, 00); S/2000/1196 (December 15, 2000); S/2002/62 (January 15, 2002); S/2002/1126 (October 9, 2002); S2003/996 (October 15, 2003); S/2000/538 (June 6, 2000); S/2000/1196 (December 15, 2000); S/2003/113 (January 29, 2003); S/2000/538 (June 6, 2000); S/2001/926 (October 2, 2001); S/2002/62 (January 15, 2002); S2003/996 (October 15, 2003); A/58/742-S/2004/230 (2004); S/2002/1223 (November 6, 2002). All reports can be accessed at www.un.org/documents/repsc.htm (as of May 2005).

———, *Report of the Secretary-General on the United Nations Observer Mission in El Salvador*, S/1994/561, May 11, 1994a.

———, Report Issued on 28 July 1994 by the Joint Group for the Investigation of Politically Motivated Illegal Armed Groups, S/1994/989, October 22, 1994b.

———, *Report of the Security Council Mission to Jakarta and Dili*, S/1999/976, September 14, 1999a.

———, *Report of the Secretary-General on the Situation in East Timor*, S/1999/1024, October 4, 1999b.

———, Authority of the Transitional Administration in East Timor, UNTAET/REG/1991/1, November 27, 1999c.

———, *Report of the Secretary-General on the Mission in Bosnia-Herzegovina*, S/1999/1260, December 17, 1999d.

———, The Agreement on Provisional Arrangements in Afghanistan Pending the Re-Establishment of Permanent Government Institutions (The Bonn Agreement), December 5, 2001. Online at www.uno.de/frieden/afghanistan/talks/agreement.htm (as of June 2003).

———, *Report of the Secretary-General on the Situation in Afghanistan and Its Implications for International Peace and Security*, A/56/875-S/2002/278, 2002a.

———, *Report of the Secretary-General on the United Nations Transitional Administration in East Timor*, S/2002/80, January 17, 2002b.

———, *Civil and Political Rights, Including the Questions of Independence of the Judiciary, Administration of Justice, Impunity*, E/CN.4/2004/51, February 27, 2004a.

———, *Report of the Secretary-General on the United Nations Mission of Support in East Timor*, S/2004/333, April 29, 2004b.

United Nations Security Council (UNSC), *Report of the Secretary-General on the United Nations Interim Administration Mission in Kosovo*, S/2004/348, April 30, 2004.

United Nations Security Council Resolutions 1272, S/RES/1272, October 25, 1999; 1483, S/RES/1483, May 22, 2003; and 1500, S/RES/1500, August 14, 2003.

United Nations Commission on Human Rights (UNCHR), "Report of the United Nations High Commissioner for Human Rights and Follow-Up to the World Conference on Human Rights: The Present Situation of Human Rights in Iraq," June 9, 2004 (CPA submission).

United Nations Department of Peacekeeping Operations, www.un.org/Depts/dpko.

United Nations Department of Public Information, *The Blue Helmets: A Review of United Nations Peace-keeping,* 3rd edition, New York, 1996.

———, *Yearbook of the United Nations*, New York, various years.

United Nations Development Programme (UNDP), *Human Development Report 2001: Making New Technologies Work for Human Development*, New York, 2001.

———, *The Way Ahead: East Timor Development Report*, 2002, Dili, East Timor, 2002.

———, *Rebuilding the Justice Sector of Afghanistan*, Kabul: United Nations Development Program, January 2003,

United Nations High Commissioner for Refugees, *OHR Mission Implementation Plan 2004*, Sarajevo: February 2004.

United Nations Office on Drugs and Crime (UNODC), *Seventh United Nations Survey on Crime Trends and the Operations of Criminal Justice Systems (1998–2000)*, Division on Policy Analysis and Public Affairs, 2000. Available online at www.unodc.org/unodc/en/crime_cicp_survey_seventh.html (as of June 2005).

———, *Afghanistan: Opium Survey 2003*, 2003a.

———, *The Opium Economy in Afghanistan: An International Problem*, 2nd edition, Vienna, 2003b.

———, *Afghanistan: Opium Survey 2004*, Vienna, 2004a.

———, *Afghanistan: Counter Narcotics Law Enforcement*, January 2004b.

———, *Programme of the Government of Afghanistan in Co-operation with the Office on Drugs and Crime,* Progress Report, Kabul, June 2004c.

———, *World Drug Report*, New York, 2004d.

United Nations Mission in Kosovo (UNMIK), Pillar I, Police, www.unmikonline.org/justice/police.htm (as of May 2005).

———, *Annual Report,* Police Commissioners Office, 2000.

———, "Civilian Police—Mandate & Tasks," 2001a, www.unmikonline.org/civpol/mandate.htm (as of May 2005).

———, "UNMIK at a Glance," 2001b, www.unmikonline.org/intro.htm (as of May 2005).

———, "Police Report for 2002, A Year of Transition," in *United Nations Civilian Police: UNMIK,* Pristine, Kosovo: Commissioner's Press Office, 2002.

———, "Pillar 1: Police and Justice, Presentation Paper," July 2003, www.unmikonline.org/justice/documents/pillarI_report_jul03.pdf (as of May 2005).

———, "SRSG's Remarks on the Entry into Force of the Provisional Criminal Code and the Provisional Criminal Procedure Code," press release, UNMIK/PR/1163, April 6, 2004. Online at www.unmikonline.org/press/2004/pressr/pr1163.pdf (as of June 2005).

———, "PDSRSG Swears in Two Court Presidents and Six Other Kosovo Judges," press release, May 11, 2004.

United States Agency for International Development (USAID), *Conflict Prevention and Foreign Assistance*, January 7, 2002.

United States Agency for International Development (USAID), United States Office Pristina (USOP), and Organisation for Security and Co-operation in Europe (OSCE), *Judicial Assessment Mission II*, December 21, 2001.

U.S. Army, Marine Corps, Navy, and Air Force, *Peace Ops: Multi-Service Tactics, Techniques, and Procedures for Conducting Peace Operations*, FM 3-07.31, October 2003.

U.S. Census Bureau, International Data Base, www.census.gov.

United States Department of Defense (DoD), *Directorate for Information Operations.*

———, *Working Papers: Iraq Status*, June 29, 2004.

U.S. Department of Justice, "Project Overviews: East Timor," ICITAP, April 4, 2004a, www.usdoj.gov/criminal/icitap/eTimor.html (as of June 2005).

———, "Project Overviews: Kosovo," ICITAP, April 4, 2004b, www.usdoj.gov/criminal/icitap/kosovo.html (as of June 2005).

U.S. Department of State, *Country Reports on Human Rights Practices*, various volumes.

———, *Background Note: El Salvador*, 2004a.

———, *Opinion Analysis*, M-71-04, June 17, 2004b.

———, *Capitol Hill Monthly Update, Afghanistan*, June–October 2004c.

———, *Iraq Status Report*, September 8, 2004d.

———, *Iraq Status Report*, November 3, 2004e.

———, *Working Papers—Iraq Status, Addendum: Security Forces Update*, August 13, 2004d.

U.S. General Accounting Office (GAO), *Rebuilding Iraq: Fiscal Year 2003 Contract Award Procedures and Management Challenges*, GAO-04-605, June 2004a.

———, *Rebuilding Iraq: Resource, Security, Governance, Essential Services, and Oversight Issues*, GAO-04-902R, June 2004b.

United States Government Printing Office (GPO), *Legislation on Foreign Relations Through 2000,* 2001.

United States Institute of Peace, *American Civilian Police in UN Peace Operations: Lessons Learned and Ideas for the Future*, Washington, D.C., July 6, 2001.

United States Mission to Afghanistan, *Afghanistan Development Update*, Kabul, 2004.

U.S. Joint Forces Command, *Stability Operations Joint Operating Concept*, Norfolk, Va., September 2004.

U.S. War Department, *Strength of the Army*, December 1, 1945.

———, *Strength of the Army*, December 1, 1946.

Van Evera, Stephen, *Guide to Methods for Students of Political Science,* Ithaca, N.Y.: Cornell University Press, 1997.

Vera Institute of Justice, *Measuring Progress Toward Safety and Justice: A Global Guide to the Design of Performance Indicators Across the Justice Sector*, New York, November 2003.

Walters, John P., "Afghans' Drug War: U.S. Plans to Assail Several Fronts," *Washington Times*, November 26, 2004.

Weber, Max, "Politics as a Vocation," in H. H. Gerth and C. Wright Mills, eds., *From Max Weber: Essays in Sociology*, New York: Oxford University Press, 1958.

Weinberger, Caspar W., *Fighting for Peace: Seven Critical Years in the Pentagon*, New York: Warner Books, 1990.

The White House, "Managing Complex Contingency Operations," PDD-56, 1997.

———, "Strengthening Criminal Justice Systems in Support of Peace Operations and Other Complex Contingencies," PDD-71, 2000.

———, *Rebuilding Afghanistan*, 2004.

Wilson, Deborah G., and William F. Walsh, "Reflections on the Transfer of Knowledge to Support Democratic Policing in Hungary and Romania," in National Institute of Justice and Bureau of International Narcotics and Law Enforcement Affairs, *Policing in Emerging Democracies: Workshop Papers and Highlights*, Washington, D.C., December 14–15, 1995 (published in October 1997).

Wolf, Martin, *Why Globalization Works,* New Haven, Conn.: Yale University Press, 2004.

Woodward, Bob, *Bush at War,* New York: Simon & Schuster, 2002.

World Bank, *El Salvador: Meeting the Challenge of Globalization,* Washington, D.C., 1996.

———, *Bosnia and Herzegovina: 1996–1998 Lessons and Accomplishments,* Washington, D.C., 1999.

———, *Reforming Public Institutions and Strengthening Governance*, 2000.

———, Aggregate Governance Indicators Dataset, 1996–2002, 2003.

———, World Bank Development Indicators Database, 2004.

———, Governance Indicators, 1996–2004, 2005, www.worldbank.org/wbi/governance/govdata2002 (as of May 2005).

World Health Organization (WHO), Mortality Data Base, 2002.

———, *World Report on Health and Violence*, Geneva, 2003.

Wright, Robin, and Thomas E. Ricks, "Bremer Criticizes Troop Levels," *Washington Post,* October 5, 2004.

Ziemke, Earl F., *The U.S. Army in the Occupation of Germany, 1944–1946*, Washington, D.C.: Center of Military History, 1975.

Zisk, Kimberly Marten, *Enforcing the Peace: Learning from the Imperial Past,* New York: Columbia University Press, 2004.

Index